DIGITAL COMMUNITY
DIGITAL CITIZEN

Dedication: To Terri

DIGITAL COMMUNITY
DIGITAL CITIZEN

JASON B. OHLER

CORWIN
A SAGE Company

For information:

Corwin
A SAGE Company
2455 Teller Road
Thousand Oaks, California 91320
(800) 233-9936
Fax: (800) 417-2466
www.corwin.com

SAGE Pvt. Ltd.
B 1/I 1 Mohan Cooperative
    Industrial Area
Mathura Road, New Delhi 110 044
India

SAGE Ltd.
1 Oliver's Yard
55 City Road
London EC1Y 1SP
United Kingdom

SAGE Asia-Pacific Pte. Ltd.
33 Pekin Street #02-01
Far East Square
Singapore 048763

Printed in the United States of America

Library of Congress Cataloging-in-Publication Data

Ohler, Jason.
Digital community, digital citizen/Jason B. Ohler.
    p. cm.
Includes bibliographical references and index.
ISBN 978-1-4129-7144-7 (pbk. : alk. paper)
    1. Computer-assisted instruction—United States. 2. Information technology—Management—United States. 3. Internet in education—United States. 4. Educational innovations—United States. I. Title.

LB1028.5.O4 2010
371.33'44678—dc22   2010026905

This book is printed on acid-free paper.

10 11 12 13 14 10 9 8 7 6 5 4 3 2 1

Acquisitions Editor:	Debra Stollenwerk
Associate Editor:	Desirée A. Bartlett
Editorial Assistant:	Kimberly Greenberg
Production Editor:	Veronica Stapleton
Copy Editor:	Adam Dunham
Typesetter:	C&M Digitals (P) Ltd.
Proofreader:	Cheryl Rivard
Indexer:	Sheila Bodell
Front Cover Designer:	Larry Addington
Back Cover Designer:	Karine Hovsepian

Contents

Acknowledgments

In terms of inspiration, there are simply too many people to mention—but I'll try anyway. Thanks to everyone with whom I shared the educational technology revolution over the past 30 years, including the thousands of educators, colleagues, teachers, students, political leaders, businesspeople, community members, and fellow pioneers. We cultivated a vision of what personal computers could do for education before they really arrived, and then we went to work once they got here. Thanks to the many anthropologists in my life, most notably Brett Dillingham and Wally Olson, who helped me cultivate a perspective for understanding the culture of online community that has been invaluable over the years. To Clay Good, whose scientific mind keeps me on track. To John Fehringer, whose artistic mind helps me navigate the world beyond words. To Budzo Manor, a community of the highest order, whose members (Clay, Claire, Brett, Kristy, and Terri) have been exploring and practicing citizenship with gusto, compassion, and imagination for decades. To the faculty of the Media Psychology PhD program at Fielding Graduate University, who contribute greatly to my understanding of the world of media psychology. To the faculty, staff, and students of the University of Alaska, who taught me much and welcomed me and my ideas. To Amanda, whose wisdom beyond her years and heartfelt guidance convinced me to retire from my day job, making this book and other wondrous opportunities possible. To Brinton; Mariah, Gabe, and Addie; Wilder and Landry; and to Deklan and Sullivan, who are a continual and joyous reminder of why the issues addressed in this book are eternally important. To my extended family, Bethany, Torrey, and Micah, who are always just one step away. A special thanks to Mom and Dad, whose concern for an ethical world instilled in me not only a sense of right and wrong but also a respect for the heart and soul of the human condition. And to my brothers, Rick and Mike, for carrying on the tradition.

In terms of preparing this book, a very special thanks to Dr. Jean-Pierre Isbouts for helping me understand the history of citizenship. Thanks, as always, to Dr. Eric McLuhan and his Job-like patience with me as I do my best to understand his ideas and those of his father. Thanks to Nancy Willard, executive director of the Center for Safe and Responsible Internet Use, who was an invaluable help to me in understanding the world of cybersafety. And thanks also to the many people who contribute to her discussion group, from whom I have learned a great deal.

PUBLISHER'S ACKNOWLEDGEMENTS

Corwin gratefully acknowledges the following individuals for their guidance and editorial insight.

Roxie R. Ahlbrecht, Math Teacher Leader
Robert Frost Elementary
Sioux Falls Public Schools 49–5
Sioux Falls, SD

Kathy Ferrell, Instructional Coach
Excelsior Springs Middle School
Excelsior Springs, MO

Jill Gildea, Superintendent
Fremont School District 79
Mundelein, IL

Lori L. Grossman, Manager
Academic Training
New Teacher Induction, Certification, and Mentoring
Professional Development Services
Houston Independent School District
Houston, TX

Dr. Karen L. Tichy, EdD
Associate Superintendent for Instruction and Special Education
Archdiocese of Saint Louis, Catholic Education Office
St. Louis, MO

Richard Yee, Principal
Suisun Elementary School
Suisun City, CA

About the Author

Jason B. Ohler, PhD, is a professor emeritus, speaker, writer, teacher, researcher, and lifelong digital humanist who is well known for the passion, insight, and humor he brings to his presentations and writings. He has worked both online and in classrooms for over a quarter century helping students develop the new literacies they need to be successful in the Digital Age. He is a passionate promoter of "Art, the Next R" and of combining innovation, creativity, and digital know-how to help reinvent teaching and learning. He is also an enthusiastic champion of the need for students to learn how to use technology wisely and safely, with awareness and compassion, so they can become informed and productive citizens in a global digital society.

Jason is author of numerous articles, books, and teacher resources and continues to work directly with teachers, administrators, and students. Combining 25 years of experience in the educational technology field with an eye for the future, he connects with people where they are and helps them see their importance in the future development of living, learning, and working in the Digital Age. Although he is called a futurist, he considers himself a nowist, working nationally and internationally to help educators and the public use today's tools to create living environments that we are proud to call home.

"The goal," according to Jason, "is to use technology effectively, creatively, and wisely . . . to bring together technology, community, and learning in ways that work. And while we are at it, to have fun."

Introduction

Remembering My High School Library

Some of my high school experiences during the late 1960s are burned so indelibly into my psyche that I can easily relive them decades later—a kind of HDTV TiVo of the mind. One experience in particular is very clear and present as I write this book around the theme of citizenship: sitting in my high school library.

Two librarians were in charge of my high school library—Miss Phelps* and Mrs. Hoover. Perpetually hovering around age 65, they both had a kind of unapproachable, mythological status, due in no small part to the fact that their hair was always lacquered into standard issue old lady hairdos that resembled pottery projects gone awry. As students walked into the library, Miss Phelps and Mrs. Hoover would stand in position behind a polished oak counter, nodding and smiling with just enough nuance to let everyone know that they would use whatever means necessary to maintain order. Today, we would call them ninja librarians, I am sure.

To them, the library was an extension of the military, and as good soldiers they ran a tight platoon. Each book was upright, standing at attention, its spine reading from top to bottom. The card catalog was an imposing series of wooden cabinets they had arranged in a ring in the center of the room. Whenever they lectured us about entering the fortress of information that was the Dewey decimal system, their message was clear: Finding information was only for the brave.

Above all, I remember the library being filled with an excruciating silence that amplified the slightest sounds into gushers of distraction. The sound of a dress rustling or a fly trapped inside a porcelain light fixture filled the

---

*Miss Phelps was the sister of another Miss Phelps whom I hope I immortalized in an earlier book of mine called *Then What? Everyone's Guide to Living, Learning and Having Fun in the Digital Age* (Brinton Books, 2002).

room utterly, absorbing everyone's complete yet silent focus. I distinctly remember the sounds of Miss Phelps and Mrs. Hoover licking their index fingers to help them turn the pages of whatever they were reading while they stared, from behind their oak turrets, at the enemies of quiet in their midst.

Yet despite their most intimidating efforts, there were always a few naïve freshmen who could not resist taunting authority simply to see what would happen. You didn't have to do much to elicit a reaction. Just coughing in a suspicious manner could cause lockdown. Whenever someone directly challenged their authority, Miss Phelps and Mrs. Hoover would pierce them with the words that never failed to immobilize, "Young man, if you persist in talking, I will have to call your parents and tell them that you are simply not a good citizen." Recall that this was the 1960s, when threatening to call someone's parents actually meant something.

It was incredible how those words could reduce the most hardened juvenile delinquents to stammering idiots. I remember only one time when a student actually countered, arguing that it didn't say in any dictionary anywhere that a library had to be quiet. Ah, said Mrs. Hoover on that one occasion, but if there were an entry in the dictionary for *school library*, it most certainly would. And, she continued, it would most certainly go on to say that those who invaded the sacred silence of a school library were not only selfish, rude, un-American hooligans with no sense of responsibility but they were also bad citizens, pure and simple.

ISSUES OF DIGITAL CITIZENSHIP

For many of us, the concept of traditional citizenship is still closely linked to the kind of good behavior Miss Phelps and Mrs. Hoover pledged to protect and defend. Simply put, citizenship represents doing what is right and responsible within a given social context, such as being silent and afraid in a high school library.

Yet as we fast-forward to 2010, we wonder whether our notion of citizenship accurately reflects our needs. After all, a new perspective of citizenship has entered the public narrative that feels so different that we have given it its own name: *digital citizenship*. This term arises from the need to reconsider who we are in light of the globally connected infosphere in which we find ourselves. That is, given that citizenship seems to be directly related to behavior and social organization, and given that the Digital Age facilitates new kinds of both, we need to update our perspectives about citizenship to provide a more complete picture of who we are.

I frequently talk to teachers informally to gain an "in the trenches" perspective about the educational issues that arise in popular media. I have had the pleasure of engaging many teachers in discussions about digital citizenship over the years and have learned one thing above all others: It tends to inspire more of a sense of fear than opportunity.

The fear—about which I will have more to say later in the book—is quite understandable. After all, while the rest of the world pontificates about what education ought to do, classroom teachers are left to figure out what they can do. Most teachers respond to my inquiry about digital citizenship by citing the aspects of the Digital Age that worry them. The issue they most frequently identify only slightly updates something Miss Phelps and Mrs. Hoover might say: students illegally downloading material and disrespecting copyright laws in an online environment. While they identify other issues as important to the discussion of digital citizenship, such as cyberbullying and accessing inappropriate material on the web, copyright is the issue that is often mentioned first as creating the most anxiety.

The issue of using downloaded materials has emerged as a flagship digital citizenship issue for many educators largely because it serves as a metaphor for our confusion about balancing our rights, responsibilities, personal boundaries, and pursuit of the social good in the hyper-connected, disembodied ether of the digital domain. A few short years ago, it was too difficult to include an image created by someone else in a school report. Now it is too easy. The qualities of ease and opportunity, as well as the absence of immediately perceivable impacts, breathe momentum into copyright as such an important issue.

> **FYI**
>
> ### Changing Times
>
> Since the time I wrote this about a year ago, cyberbullying and sexting have surpassed copyright as the new flagship issue, shifting our priority from respect to safety.

And where there is momentum and the possibility of legal entanglement, concerns run high, beginning with the school board and cascading downward, to administrators and eventually to classrooms, where teachers and students receive the brunt of our collective anxiety. Most teachers want to do "the right thing," they just honestly don't know what that is. And given there is very little agreement in the legal community about this issue, teachers are often left to fend for themselves.

The other issues teachers cite, such as cyberbullying, sexting, and posting and accessing inappropriate material on the web, share many of the qualities of the copyright conundrum. The ease and opportunity of acting and reacting in the infosphere amplifies what we do, spreading our impacts far and wide with very little effort. At the same time, these impacts are produced without many of the mitigating effects that are present when interacting in public. The result is that one needs to see with the mind's eye in order to imagine the impacts on the receiving end of an e-mail,

YouTube post, or file download in order to interact effectively in the online global community.

But our concerns should be set within the larger arena of hope and opportunity. After all, the web gives us many wonderful things. The real challenge for each of us is to balance the connections and the disconnections offered in digital community and to develop a personal ethical core that can guide us in areas of experience that are in many ways unfamiliar. Because digital community is global, distributed, and in many cases asynchronous, older notions of "right and wrong" need to be revisited, expanded, and refreshed. Doing so requires not just developing an understanding of moral action but also of more abstract notions of ethics that frame interaction within the context of a digital, global, multicultural community.

The bottom line is that children now have to begin to think more abstractly at younger ages, challenging previously held notions about neurological and emotional development. Wisdom, once seen as the domain of the elderly, is now becoming a survival skill for kids who spend a good deal of their day in the infosphere. Clearly, it is the role of schools to help them cultivate the skills and perspectives they need to participate in the infosphere safely and responsibly, as well as boldly and with a sense of hope and adventure about the future.

CITIZENSHIP IS A TIME FOR REIMAGINATION

Currently, digital citizenship is being defined largely in terms of the issues that seem to confuse and confound our sense of what's right. There is a serious problem with this approach: We miss an opportunity to reinvent ourselves.

After all, citizenship has always been about so much more than doing the right thing when faced with morally ambiguous circumstances. It is an all-encompassing consideration of who we are and wish to be, individually and as a society.

Historically, the issue of citizenship comes under active discussion whenever society is shifting so dramatically that it is trying to redefine itself. Shifts in citizenship accompany large-scale transformational events, such as revolutions or historic elections. So it was following the American, French, and Russian revolutions. So it is whenever new political administrations significantly shift direction away from their predecessors. What eventually emerges is not just a redefinition of what it means to be virtuous but also a recasting of what society feels is truly important and how individuals need to view the new, emerging social order in terms of rights, duties, and participation. In the process, changes in citizenship redefine who is included in the new dream and who is excluded, politically and culturally. So it will be with the digital revolution and the new kind of citizenship that emerges.

Above all, redefining citizenship should redefine our hopes and aspirations, both in terms of who we want to be as well as who we don't want to be. As the term *digital citizenship* gains momentum in public discussion, we need to seize upon this opening to ask ourselves not just how we want our kids to behave but also what we want our education systems to accomplish. Until recently, asking, What do we really want for our schools? has had as much reality as asking, How many angels fit on the head of a pin? But our technology is so powerful, connective, adaptable, scalable, and promising, that this is now a very real question. We have the tools to create any kind of society, and thus educational system, that we want. The question is, *What do we want?* At the heart of our answer to that question is how we define citizenship during a time of unprecedented opportunity and how we approach developing it within the context of a school community.

WHO IS THIS BOOK FOR?

This book is for anyone with an interest in the future of K–12 education in a digitally deluged world. This includes parents with school-age children, taxpayers who want to support schools intelligently, businesses that are concerned about the future of their labor pool, community members who want what is best for their neighborhoods, and policy makers seeking to understand the challenges of a new era of education. Above all, it is for students, teachers, and administrators who compose the immediate school community population and are on the front line of trying to negotiate a path with the future of technology and learning that is socially, educationally, and ethically sound.

The perspective employed in this book reflects the many hats I have worn during my professional life as a teacher education instructor, online teacher, researcher, writer, speaker, and educational technology developer. I have spent most of my years developing new approaches to teaching and learning, onsite and at a distance, using emerging technologies and the new kinds of social learning they empower. In addition, I have spent many wonderful hours working directly with teachers and K–12 students on a number of technology and media development projects. Thus, the reader will find everything from policy perspectives to professional development exercises, all aimed at helping anyone who is interested in understanding the realities of digital citizenship within the modern educational environment.

THIS BOOK IS IN THREE PARTS

I have approached the issue of digital citizenship from three perspectives, each of which constitutes a section in this book.

Part I, The Call to Digital Citizenship, addresses how digital citizenship fits into the historical evolution of citizenship as well as the evolution of community. It focuses on the three kinds of communities and citizenship referenced in the International Society for Technology in Education's (ISTE) refreshed standards—local, global, and digital—and how each plays a role in helping to define what it means to be a citizen in the Digital Age. This includes addressing the role that schools and teachers can play in exploring, understanding, and promoting digital citizenship within their profession as well as their classrooms. Also addressed in Section I is the notion of *citizen as learner* and how communicating, learning, and being a community member changes in the Digital Age. Of specific importance is how to manage learning in the digital domain so that we can help students become lifelong learners who develop perceptions, perspectives, and habits of mind that will allow them to navigate the Digital Age creatively and critically—*creatically*, as I like to call it.

Part II is titled Seeing Technology. A theme throughout this book is that in order to become more effective digital citizens, we must first be able to see more clearly the technology we take for granted and the invisible mediascapes in which we are immersed. Cultivating this ability will allow us to evaluate the impacts of our technological lifestyles so that we can reimagine and rebuild our communities and our sense of citizenship.

Part II considers Seeing Technology in a few different ways. It focuses on trying to understand what often results when we don't try to see technology clearly—fear. Understanding what bothers and even scares us about technology will help us understand the emotional barriers we face when pursuing innovation in our schools, communities, work places, and personal lives. Part II presents tools and activities designed to help teachers and students become "de-tech-tives" so that they can see and evaluate the tEcosystem—the technological ecosystem we have come to depend on that is largely invisible to us. The goal is leadership. That is, if we can see and evaluate technology, then we have a better chance of helping students become informed citizens and effective leaders.

Part III is titled Character Education in the Digital Age and the Case of the Ideal School Board. I imagine an "ideal" school board whose members are willing to take on the many issues of digital citizenship—from digital literacy to cyberbullying—by placing their efforts within the context of character education. Part III begins with considerations of "Party-Cipation"—that is, the party that participation inspires—and then addresses the role that moral education and ethical perspective building can play in the challenges that face digital citizenship in education. It also explores a series of "inputs" to inform the school board's work, such as brain research, moral development in children, and discovering one's "ethical core." All of this is intended to help our ideal school board understand how teachers and kids think, grow, and interact in the infosphere. Our school board then looks at how character education might be employed as a means to infuse digital citizenship throughout a school community. Finally, our ideal school board considers the nature of digital literacy and its implications for citizenship as well as how to reconceive the school district's IT department so that digital citizenship can be pursued effectively within a realistic context.

It is my greatest hope that readers walk away from reading this book humming this mantra about living in the Digital Age: Technology connects us and disconnects us. It is up to us to understand how this happens so that we can become the best human beings we are capable of becoming. Technology amplifies. Let it amplify our greatest hopes for ourselves, our communities, and our planet.

AN INVITATION TO READERS TO PARTICIPATE IN THE DIGITAL CITIZENSHIP RESOURCES WIKI (JASONOHLER.COM/DC)

I wrote this book knowing that the subject of digital citizenship was in its infancy and that research and resources in this area would continue to grow quickly and in abundance. That is why I created the Digital Citizenship Resources Wiki. Through it I invite readers to participate in developing a knowledge base related to the

FYI

You can follow Jason on twitter at jasonohler.

many areas of digital citizenship addressed in this book by adding links to resources they have either created or simply find useful. The Digital Citizenship Resources Wiki is already up and running and provides links to many of the resources referenced in this book. But it needs your participation in order to be truly responsive to our collective needs in this area. To participate, go to jasonohler.com/dc. I welcome your involvement.

Preamble

Our Choice for Our Children:
Two Lives or One?

We have a fundamental question to address with regard to educating our Digital Age children. How we answer this question will determine how we plan for and implement education in the broadest sense for many years to come. In its simplest form, the question is, *Should we consider students to have two lives or one?*

Allow me to restate this question with a bit more detail: Should we consider students to have two separate lives—a relatively digitally unplugged life at school and a digitally saturated life away from school—or should we consider them to have one life that integrates their lives as students and digital citizens?

The "two lives" perspective contends that our students should live a traditional educational life at school, much like their parents did, and a second, digital life outside school. It says that the technology that kids use is too expensive, problematic, or distracting to integrate into teaching and learning. It says that issues concerning the personal, social, and environmental impacts of living a digital, technological lifestyle are tangential to a school curriculum. Above all, it says that kids will have to figure out how to navigate the digital world beyond school on their own and puzzle through issues of cybersafety, technological responsibility, and digital citizenship without the help of the educational system.

On the other hand, the one life perspective says it is time to help students blend their two lives into an integrated, meaningful approach to living in the digital age. It says that if schools don't make it their primary mission to help students understand not only how to use technology but also when and why, then we have no right to expect our children to grow up to be the citizens we want them to be and that the world needs them to be. It says that if we don't help our digital kids balance personal empowerment with a sense of community responsibility, then future generations will inherit a world that does not represent anyone's dream of what is best for humanity. It says that if we don't understand that schools are exactly the place for kids to learn how to use technology not only effectively and creatively but also responsibly and wisely, then heaven help us all.

Part I

The Call
To Digital
Citizenship

1 Becoming Digital

The Road to Digital Citizenship

A SHORT HISTORY OF EDUCATIONAL TECHNOLOGY

Pardon me while I sound like some of the elders in my family who used to tell me they trudged 10 miles, barefoot, uphill, through two feet of snow, dead, just to get to school. But unless you are old enough to belong to AARP (for those outside the United States who might not understand the reference, this equates to retirement age), your current digital lifestyle will seem like something that has always been here—you are just waiting for it to get cheaper, faster, and cooler. In order to put the concept of *digital citizenship* in historical perspective, let's consider the long, slow digital climb to the wonder machines we take for granted today. Then we will consider the concept of community and citizenship as they apply to the digital lifestyle that seems so invisible to us now.

It is no wonder that the public has little historical appreciation for the dark days of computing—our past has disappeared all around us. While antique chairs, cars, and even toasters can be restored to become useful, aesthetic memorabilia, that's not the case with passé digital technology. Old computers with hulking, fuzzy CRT monitors are simply useless, environmentally hazardous, and, above all, uncool. Thus, while some retro technologies survive to serve as historical mile markers in our midst, old computers are tucked out of sight and out of mind—in a landfill near you. The result is that when it comes to living our digital lifestyle, we know only now.

But the reality is that the revolution that has resulted in the sleek, powerful laptop computers that fit neatly in our thin briefcases started out a few short decades ago as mainframe machines that were so slow, noisy, awkward, heavy, and weak that it took geeky programmers with no illusions of having a social life to love them. When I began in educational technology in the early 1980s, the mainframe computer that was the center of my digital life was the size of two refrigerators and did far less than my iPhone does today. Yet despite their limitations, mainframes started many things that are still with us. E-mail began on mainframes, as did some other forms of social media, like computer conferencing and public discussion groups, still known as listservs. Although access to the Internet was reserved at that time for scientists and the military, many of us still managed to gather electronically by connecting our home computers to mainframes using modems and the phone system at speeds so slow you could hear each letter land on the screen with an audible *thunk*.

FYI

When Slow Was Slow

My first modem transmitted at 150 bps (bits per second). An average broadband connection today transmits at 3 mega bps. Thus in 1980, I transmitted at five one-millionths of the speed that I do today. To translate this into more comprehensible terms, if broadband speed is akin to driving a car at 50 mph, then 150 baud translates into driving .0025 miles per hour. At that rate, it would take your car 400 hours, or a little over 16 days, to go one mile.

What was noticeably absent in those days was software. The world of distributed productivity that we take for granted today, in which literally anyone with the time and inclination can create programs and other resources to share with the greater learning community, did not exist. We used a very small amount of software that had been created largely by programmers and engineers to do programming and engineering kinds of things. And as I like to remind younger readers, in the early days of computing there was nothing to click on. Everything was typed in at a blinking cursor and often inspired cryptic error messages that seemed to say, "Hey, dummy, get an engineering degree, or take a pottery class."

Most of us in education who were not programmers in the early 1980s were attracted to computers not for what they did at the time but for what we knew they would eventually do. The Apple IIe, which was one of the first personal computers to be both useful and lovable, was one of the first machines to show up in classrooms, circa the early 1980s. When Apple IIes arrived, there was very little software available for them. They booted up in the BASIC programming language and sat there, blinking at you, waiting for you to get in touch with the programmer within. One can't help but muse how different the computer revolution would have been had early computers booted up in a word processor or a painting program rather than a programming language.

TRY THIS

UNDERSTANDING YOUR OWN PERSONAL COMPUTER HISTORY

Ask your colleagues, friends, or students to investigate the following stats about their first computer, or for dramatic effect, the first computer owned by their parents: size, weight, RAM, and CPU speed. Teachers should ask students to compare and contrast the information they collect, and create a historical timeline based on what they discover.

Even though there was very little public software for educators, and no Internet to use to swap homemade programs, most of us hung in there because we knew everything would change—it was just a matter of time.

Our wait was rewarded when the program AppleWorks for the Apple IIe was released circa 1984. It combined a spreadsheet, database, and word processing program into one easy-to-use, low-cost integrated software package. This software constellation persists today as Microsoft Office, the most popular software tool set in history. AppleWorks was so useful to so many teachers that administrators bought it in bulk. The result was that suddenly the Apple IIe was not just for tinkerers and geeky hobbyists; it was for everyone. We watched with amazement as the incipient desktop computer market took off, as though millions of potential users had been just waiting on the sidelines, praying that computers would actually be able to do something useful one day. The result was that software began to proliferate, and new machines began to appear that could be used broadly in education, business, and science, as well as in our personal lives. When the IBM PC and Macintosh became generally available during the early to mid-1980s, our digital path seemed set. We had no idea where it would take us, but we were sure we were headed into a future of intellectual and creative overdrive that would rival the Renaissance.

Because I was a teacher when the first desktop computers arrived, the computer revolution was, for my colleagues and myself, an educational technology revolution.

Although educational technology existed as an area of study at universities, it was concerned largely with programming, as well as creating and studying the use of media-based instructional materials. With the arrival of individual desktop computers and useful software, everything changed. Suddenly, consumers had the chance to be creators. Technology that had once belonged only to engineers, developers, corporations, and the military was in the hands of teachers and the general public to create, tinker, play, work—and later as networks were developed—communicate, and socialize. And because kids were much more comfortable doing many of these things, they gained a new status in the classroom as expert, helper, and in some cases troublemaker by virtue of their willingness to experiment with the new machines in their midst. The pressure was on for classrooms to adjust to new relationships between students and teachers and to recast educational strategies that would put students at the center of their learning experience.

It was during the mid-1980s that the educational world in North America and elsewhere began the slow, often grudging integration of digital technology into the educational experience. As small cadres of enthusiasts experimented with the new technology in classrooms, they often encountered suspicion, cultural inertia, and the lack of a budget line item for something completely new called "hardware and software." However, while many in the mid-1980s were saying educational technology was just a fad, by the mid-1990s no one was. During the 1990s, budgets began to reflect the need for hardware, software, and professional development devoted to understanding and using emerging technology.

A few short years later, we were forced to reconcile ourselves to yet another new, expensive reality: the need to upgrade our technology every few years. Standard operating procedure included bracing ourselves for the next big thing that was just around the corner that we would simply have to have if we were to responsibly prepare students for the real world. While upgrading may seem like the status quo today, it was a brand-new concept in the 1990s. Prior to the digital technology revolution, "the stuff" that organizations purchased had a life cycle of many years. School buses seemed to last forever, as did audiovisual equipment and typewriters. Desks, chairs, and even textbooks and encyclopedias were on a very slow replacement cycle. In contrast, by the late 1990s, computers and software were expected to have a half-life of three years or less. To members of the cell phone generation, who feel compelled to replace their bulky, uncool cell phones every year, three years seems like a lifetime.

TRY THIS

TRACKING YOUR COMPUTER PAST

How many computers have you had in your life? What did you do with your old ones? How many pieces of software have you learned that you no longer use? I have used 24 word processors in my lifetime, but today I basically use just a few. This is also an interesting activity to do focusing on cell phones given that, as of this writing, web lore reports that over 400,000 cell phones are decommissioned every day.

As I write this book 28 short years after entering the educational technology revolution, I look back with disbelief at the light-years we have come. The slow-witted text entry machines of the 1980s have become point and click, lighting-fast tools for artists, scientists, economists, writers, teachers, Mom and Dad, and, most important, kids. And there is no letup in sight. The massive interconnectedness of the web has created a workforce of many millions who are idling close by, ready to jump in to create the next big thing. Those of us who don't actually crank out the code to create the new programs nonetheless have our role to play by manning the blogs, wikis, and other engines of social media to let the rest of the world know what's on the horizon. My apologies to Newton, but we have created a perpetual motion machine.

The Digital Indigenous

We make a lot of the fact that today's kids have no sense of amazement about the steady stream of innovation that has become a way of life. They are, according to Marc Prensky (2001), "digital natives" because they grew up during digital times. As the digital indigenous, they take their environment for granted.

But if they are digital natives, then my friends and I were electromechanical natives when we were growing up during the 1960s. We no more noticed the appliances in our lives than today's kids notice the digital gadgets in theirs. The common denominator between our generations is what Marshall McLuhan (McLuhan & Powers, 1989) referred to as *the figure-ground phenomenon*. Ground is the environment that we don't see yet which massages us totally, providing the unconscious social context for our actions. In contrast, figure is what we notice, the spike that transcends the constant, invisible noise of the environment. I will use *figure-ground* as a lens through which to view the issue of digital citizenship throughout this book.

For us, ground is largely the tEcosystem, the secondary ecosystem that we have created that consists of digital technology, connectivity, and the communication

---

FYI

Fogies Evolve Quickly

The technological generation gap is forever—and it's shrinking. In a <u>New York Times</u> article titled "The Children of Cyberspace: Old Fogies by Their 20s," author Brad Stone (2010) notes that technological generations are now measured in terms of 10 years: "The ever-accelerating pace of technological change may be minting a series of mini-generation gaps, with each group of children uniquely influenced by the tech tools available in their formative stages of development" (para. 5). From upstart native to old fogy in no time at all.

they facilitate. As with our primary ecosystem, we rarely notice it unless something goes awry with it. In the meantime, it completely controls us while being entirely off our radar.

In contrast, figure is the visible change—the moving ad on the webpage that keeps diverting our attention from what we are trying to read; the sensationalist media story that absorbs us despite our better judgment; and occasionally, the solid, thought-provoking piece of content that makes its way to the surface in the mediasphere. If we notice it, then it is figure. Sometimes, we even notice the technology we routinely take for granted, such as when it breaks, is missing, or presents us with those annoying upgrade glitches. But usually, it forms the ground of our daily existence by being everywhere and invisible at the same time.

While we focus on figure, we must, due to our limited perceptual capacity as human beings, ignore other potential figures, as well as the ground in which they appear. With all due respect to brain plasticity, hyperlinking, and our evolving capacity to multitask, we are still primarily serial-processing human beings when we want to investigate, reflect upon, and make decisions about an issue of importance. While we may think laterally, tangentially, and creatively as we do so, we need focus in order to analyze, draw conclusions, and communicate our findings.

Focus, once one of our most powerful talents in addressing issues of our day, is becoming a dying art. In a world of information overload, depth has been sacrificed for breadth, understanding for knowing. If there is one requirement for being a committed, effective digital citizen, it is the ability to see technology as figure against the greater ground of life and to be able to focus on what we see so that we can understand its impacts on ourselves, our communities, and the environment.

> **FYI**
>
> ### Multitasking May Be a Myth
>
> According to John Medina (2010), brain researcher and author of Brain Rules, there is substantial proof that we do not retain information nearly as well when we multitask as when we focus on a specific task.
> Continuous partial attention (Stone, 2009) is just that: partial.

That is why citizenship, an ancient social invention cultivated over millennia, has come to the fore as we begin to pull back from the screen and wonder what kind of people we want our kids to grow up to become. As we consider technology as figure, and see clearly its pervasiveness and power, we realize there is very little we can effectively legislate in a free society that will prevent technology from running amok or us from misusing its power. We will need to keep that from happening ourselves, as individuals and communities, as we make personal and collective decisions about how to use our technology individually and with each other.

Thus, it is part of our job to help students not only use technology but also to question it. Doing so does not come naturally. Our kids, like kids of any generation, will ignore what they grow up with unless we bring it to their attention. Therefore, the first place we start in the cultivation of digital citizenship is helping students to see the technology in their lives—to make technology figure rather than ground. After all, they can't question what they don't see.

In fact, if we as educators and adults are interested in continuing the mentor-mentee relationship that has existed for millennia between the old and the young, then this is a key component of our new job description: to help students see and evaluate the technology in their lives. Any consideration of digital citizenship is useless without this ability. This doesn't require mentors to be more technically competent than their mentees, just more vigilant about placing technology in a broader social context. A mantra to guide us might be:

> Students will study the personal, social, and environmental impacts of every technology and media application they use in school.

We don't want students to know just how to use technology but also when and why. We want them to be not only good workers but also good neighbors, informed voters, and involved citizens. After all, once they graduate, they may be living next door to us, if not physically then certainly digitally. We would do well to ask ourselves just what kind of neighbors we would like them to be.

A SHORT HISTORY OF ISTE STANDARDS

It was amidst the confusion, panic, and excitement of the educational technology revolution that in 1998 the International Society for Technology in Education (ISTE) developed national standards for students for the use of technology in teaching and learning, with teacher standards following in 2000, and administrator standards in 2002. These standards appeared not a moment too soon. Those of us trying to convince a skeptical public of the inevitability of digital technology in education were seen as everything from devoted utopians to big budget fringe fanatics. The ISTE standards were important because finally we could point to a nationally recognized professional group for support, recognition, and the articulation of standards that were specifically developed to address the presence of computers in classrooms.

The development of the ISTE standards were also important for historical reasons. It marked the beginning of one of the first public processes devoted to chronicling a professional understanding of what digital technology meant to education and, by implication, society at large. During the

1990s, the reality was that most of us were feeling our way in a field that was evolving so quickly in so many directions that trends were hard to discern. It wasn't until the diffusion of the Internet by the mid-1990s that the national conversation about how to use digital technology for teaching and learning began in earnest via e-mail, bulletin boards, and listservs. Millions of digital explorers were comparing notes and rethinking education in light of all the new possibilities implicit in the new technology. Simultaneously, they were helping define the digital information and communication technology industry, a vast, new human enterprise that would become part of everybody's professional and personal lives. ISTE's first standards were an attempt to make sense of these developments as they applied to the educational arena.

TRY THIS

EXPLORE THE STANDARDS IN YOUR SCHOOL DISTRICT

Whether you are a teacher, taxpayer, or simply a concerned citizen, you should know how your school views technology. Do the schools in your community have technology standards for faculty, students, or administrators? Are they based on local, state, or ISTE standards? My experience tells me that schools with active educational technology committees that talk about standards and innovative applications of technology on an ongoing basis are often the most imaginative and vibrant. Whenever possible, include community stakeholders on the committee to keep your efforts grounded in the reality of life beyond school.

ISTE standards are also historically important because we will be able to look back at their evolution as a kind of rolling time capsule that reflected how we viewed technology in education at particular points in history. We might expect very little change over time. After all, standards should reflect timeless human concerns that transcend the details of our invention. Yet ISTE updated their standards in 2008. Called "the refreshed standards," they reflect significant changes in our understanding of the evolving digital world. For this reason, the evolution from Version 1 to 2 bears our consideration.

Before discussing the changes, let's present both sets of standards.

2000 ISTE National Educational Technology Standards (NETS) for Teachers (Standards Version 1)

I. **Technology Operations and Concepts.** Teachers demonstrate a sound understanding of technology operations and concepts.

II. **Planning and Designing Learning Environments and Experiences.** Teachers plan and design effective learning environments and experiences supported by technology.

III. **Teaching, Learning, and the Curriculum.** Teachers implement curriculum plans that include methods and strategies for applying technology to maximize student learning.

IV. **Assessment and Evaluation.** Teachers apply technology to facilitate a variety of effective assessment and evaluation strategies.

V. **Productivity and Professional Practice.** Teachers use technology to enhance their productivity and professional practice.

VI. **Social, Ethical, Legal, and Human Issues.** Teachers understand the social, ethical, legal, and human issues surrounding the use of technology in PK–12 schools and apply those principles in practice.

From the 2000 ISTE National Educational Technology Standards for Teachers. Used with permission by ISTE. Available at www.iste.org/Content/NavigationMenu/NETS/ForTeachers/2000Standards/NETS_for_Teachers_2000.htm.

Compare and contrast these with the ISTE NETS refreshed standards (Standards Version 2) that replaced them in 2008:

1. **Facilitate and Inspire Student Learning and Creativity.** Teachers use their knowledge of subject matter, teaching and learning, and technology to facilitate experiences that advance student learning, creativity, and innovation in both face-to-face and virtual environments.

2. **Design and Develop Digital-Age Learning Experiences and Assessments.** Teachers design, develop, and evaluate authentic learning experiences and assessments incorporating contemporary tools and resources to maximize content learning in context and to develop the knowledge, skills, and attitudes identified in the NETS•S (NETS Standards for Students).

3. **Model Digital-Age Work and Learning.** Teachers exhibit knowledge, skills, and work processes representative of an innovative professional in a global and digital society.

4. **Promote and Model Digital Citizenship and Responsibility.** Teachers understand local and global societal issues and responsibilities in an evolving digital culture and exhibit legal and ethical behavior in their professional practices.

5. **Engage in Professional Growth and Leadership.** Teachers continuously improve their professional practice, model lifelong learning, and exhibit leadership in their school and professional community by promoting and demonstrating the effective use of digital tools and resources.

From the refreshed (2008) ISTE National Educational Technology Standards for Teachers. Used with permission by ISTE. Available at www.iste.org/Content/NavigationMenu/NETS/ForTeachers/2008Standards/NETS_for_Teachers_2008.htm.

Each standard set has a distinctly different tone. The first set stresses technology operations and integration. The subtext is that technology is to be used effectively "within the box" to support whatever best practices in education are in use at the time. In contrast, the new standards make clear that technology is changing educational practice in deep ways, and that out-of-the-box thinking has become part of the new paradigm.

We can discern the changes reflected in the refreshed standards in greater detail by considering six words that appear in the ISTE standards for the first time. These are addressed below.

Creativity and innovation. Two words that make their appearance in the new standards are *creativity* and *innovation*. They define Standard 1 for not only teachers but also for students (see sidebar).

FYI

Creativity Is Important for Students Too

Refreshed Standard 1 for students (2007) reads,
"**1. Creativity and Innovation.** Students demonstrate creative thinking, construct knowledge, and develop innovative products and processes using technology. Students:

- apply existing knowledge to generate new ideas, products, or processes.
- create original works as a means of personal or group expression.
- use models and simulations to explore complex systems and issues.
- identify trends and forecast possibilities."

From the refreshed (2007) ISTE National Educational Technology Standards for Students. Used with permission by ISTE. Available at www.iste.org/Content/NavigationMenu/NETS/ForStudents/NETS_for_Students.htm.

Note: They can also be found in the standards for administrators, but they're more subdued (www.iste.org/Content/NavigationMenu/NETS/ForAdministrators/2009Standards/NETS_for_Administrators_2009.htm).

Their prominence in the refreshed standards says three things:

1. **We must move beyond technology integration toward idea generation.** We are formally recognizing the fact that our new technologies

need to be used beyond mere curriculum integration or as a means to simply update the status quo with new tools. Instead, we need to use them to generate, explore, and use new ideas that challenge and redefine the status quo.

2. **We must shift away from operations and toward perspective.** Learning how to use digital technology is no longer the primary challenge. After all, with enough tenacity and sense of adventure, just about anyone can be a reasonably good technology user these days. The real challenge now lies in understanding how to place our new tools in a larger educational, social perspective in innovative, creative ways.

3. **We must meet new challenges with new ideas and new thinking.** The world has always been a complex place, but we were not really aware of it until recent advances in interconnectivity. The same interconnectivity that fuels our awareness forces us to share problems and opportunities within a global village with very diverse demographics. Thus, we need new ideas and new ways of thinking in order to meet new global challenges that make sense to an international, multicultural citizenry. To do this, we need to be creative and innovative in our thinking as we use the digital tools at our command.

Digital, citizenship, culture, and global. Four other important words that appear for the first time in the main headings of the ISTE standards are *digital, citizenship, culture and global*. Although they may be implied in the first set of ISTE standards, it is worth considering what their deliberate inclusion in the new standards signifies.

The word *digital* seems to replace references to "technology" found in the first set of standards. This signifies a move away from a machine focus and toward a focus on content and communication. That is, our interest has shifted from "the gear" to what we are doing with the gear. The machines themselves are analog constructs—things that take up space. The content and communication they facilitate is digital.

The appearance of the words *citizenship, culture,* and *global* are best considered with a side-by-side comparison of old and new standards that address technological impact: Standard VI from the original set and Standard 4 from the refreshed standards.

The older standard reads, "**VI. Social, ethical, legal, and human issues.** *Teachers understand the social, ethical, legal, and human issues surrounding the use of technology in PK–12 schools and apply those principles in practice.*" This suggests that as new technology appears, it is up to teachers to field the many social issues that are implied by its presence and come up with practical ways to address them in the course of their professional practice. The refreshed standard related to this area reads, "**4. Promote and Model Digital Citizenship and Responsibility.** *Teachers understand local and global societal issues and responsibilities in an evolving digital culture and exhibit legal and ethical behavior in their professional practices.*" Here the notion of responsibility is now expanded from local to global spheres. This standard further acknowledges the power and responsibility that this expansion implies.

More important, this standard expands our sense of responsibility even beyond global culture to *digital culture.* One way to view the term *digital culture* is simply as a way to describe the age in which we live, the way *industrial age culture* might describe the previous two centuries. In fact, the term *digital culture* does work well as a comprehensive description of what it means to be living at this point in history.

But I think the implications in the term *digital culture* are much broader and deeper than this. We need to recognize that we are all part of a digital culture that exists within its right. That is, we need to explicitly recognize the fact that an alternative realm of existence is now in play, the digital realm, which has enough substance and ethos to be considered its own culture. It is the emergence of this new culture that drives the demand for digital citizenship.

The following important points emerge from the presence of the words *digital, citizenship, culture,* and *global*:

1. **We must engage students in the issues and opportunities of their local community.** While we may spend a good deal of time in cyberspace, the focus of our immediate lives is still our local community, including family, school, and community.

2. **We must help students engage in a global community.** The very real impact of digital community is that we are all connected to an international world of work, play, and common social enterprise. This has always been true to some extent, in that the common objects in our homes are often crafted by people we will never meet, from lands we may never visit. But now, through the use of international networks and social media, we can pursue global community much more easily, deliberately, and purposefully. Thus, we need to prepare students to understand and flourish in a world that is far more multicultural, pluralistic, and interconnected than it was just a decade ago.

3. **We must engage students in the issues and opportunities of digital culture and digital community.** Implied here is that there are communities in VR (virtual reality) that impact and at times transcend those in RL (real life), and that these communities have

reality and significance. Authors of the book *Digital Citizenship* (Mossberger, Tolbert, & McNeal, 2008) define digital citizens simply as "those who use the internet regularly and effectively—that is on a daily basis" (p. 1). This covers most people in most developed countries. Even those who use the Internet sparingly are still immersed in the secondary effects of digital culture by virtue of the digital, networked infrastructure that supports most of what they do.

4. **We must help students participate as a citizen of local, global, and digital communities simultaneously.** The original ISTE standards were developed during comparatively unnetworked times. Issues of ethics, social perspectives, and community participation were fairly immediate in nature, temporally and spatially. Now they occur within at least three community domains: local, global, and digital. Education must participate in all three. In addition, it must address how to participate in all three simultaneously, managing the concerns of each in one integrated approach to living.

It is the focus in ISTE Refreshed Standard 4 on culture and the many realms of communities that is truly new. Communities are the inevitable result of the networks that started linking people together in the 1980s via primitive e-mail and listserv connectivity. The "ancient human" (Dertouzos, 2001) in each of us who tasted immediate, distributed communication in the early days of computer-mediated communication helped to drive bandwidth development and push social software creation to degrees of great sophistication. While Facebook might have been difficult to predict 20 years ago, in retrospect it is not the least bit difficult to understand where it came from. It is in the context of the evolving nature of connected community that we consider the evolving nature of citizenship.

TRY THIS

BRAINSTORMING ISTE STANDARDS VERSION 3.0

The future goes on for a long time, change is inevitable, and technological evolution is unimaginable. Given that, what might the next iteration of technology standards look like? Of course you can never consider something like this in isolation. You will also need to ask the following questions: What will the overall approach to educating our children look like? How much of education will happen at what we now call a school? What will the average personal information device be capable of? What will the power of the Internet be? What will we value as a society? More about peering into the future in Part II of the book.

2 Perspectives on Citizenship and Community

LISTENING TO THE ANCIENT HUMAN

It is my belief that our flagrant disregard for the past in the digital era has many drawbacks. Among them is that we tend to see everything as new, when in fact much of who we are, even in this day and age, is still quite old in that it connects rather effortlessly to the ethos of centuries of previous generations. On the one hand, e-mail, wikis, and YouTube can be seen as very new forms of communication—after all, all those wireless bits flying through the air landing on someone's screen a half a world away certainly is different. But on the other hand, we can also see them as simply our latest efforts to expand and improve individual and group communication using the tools at hand, a desire that dates back to our earliest ancestors. Both perspectives would be accurate and important in the formation of a complete picture of who we are today.

A very practical drawback of ignoring our ancient connections is that every new idea and gadget that comes along feels like a threat to our stability. I frequently see educators, business professionals, and everyday citizens who are punch-drunk from the constant assault of innovation largely because they don't see that much of what drives technological invention is the need to satisfy the ancient human in each of us (Dertouzos, 2001). And the ancient human has been longing for community and citizenship for some time.

Thus, allow me to help simplify some complex issues of digital community and citizenship and place them in some historical perspective before proceeding to more practical issues in the chapters that follow. I will use Mel Brooks as inspiration. Just as he attempted to tell the history of the world in a few hours of movie (Brooks, 1981), so will I attempt to provide a history of the salient points of this topic in just a few pages of text. The goal is to extract from this discussion those elements of citizenship and community that influence our current discussion of digital citizenship.

AN EXTREMELY SHORT HISTORY OF CITIZENSHIP

The word *citizenship* derives from the Latin *civitas,* which means "state." It also means "membership in that state"—in other words, what we would call citizenship. Most of the world relies on a legal concept of citizenship that has not been revisited in many years, namely, that while citizenship may be social in its expression, it is first and foremost a function of our association with the geographic communities in which we live. The laws, culture, and politics of those communities in turn determine our rights, privileges, and obligations as citizens.

However, there are two important points to consider. First, while communities may have existed for millennia, citizenship has not. Most historians depict what most of us would recognize as citizenship to be something that has emerged only after eons of much philosophizing, bloodshed, and trial and error. That is, citizenship may feel quite natural, but it does not occur naturally, from a political or an anthropological perspective. It behooves us to understand why this is so in order to grasp the issues involved with digital citizenship.

Second, while the current geographically based definition of citizenship might work for local community, as well as broader political entities like state and country, it doesn't work well for global or digital citizenship. In fact, the mere existence of the terms *global citizenship* and *digital citizenship* implies that traditional concepts of geography and place are not as important as they used to be to our understanding of citizenship. Thus, as we study the historical rise of citizenship, we want to understand what is old and new about emerging concepts of citizenship. Our children will need to understand both.

It Begins in Sparta

Our journey toward citizenship starts in Sparta, which was one of the first Greek "city-states," i.e., a community of villages bound by the unique social, economic, and political interests of their particular region, anchored to a core city. What made the Greek *polis* unique was that it was not governed by a king, but by a representative body of the state's citizenry (Hansen, 2006). Yet citizenship in Western culture couldn't have had a more auspicious beginning. According to citizenship scholar Derek Heater (2004), around 700 BCE those Spartans who called themselves citizens actually belonged to an elite group of warriors who were specifically trained to control the slave class. Spartan citizens ate together, trained together, shared economic opportunity together, and subjugated everyone else to tyrannical rule together. Among themselves, they were citizens. To those around them, they were a militaristic brotherhood of despots. Thus, the first chronicled example of citizenship was an Orwellian Animal Farm (Orwell, 1946), in which some people were far more equal than others.

Two important points can be gleaned from Sparta's attempt at citizenship. First, as with all experiments in social evolution, it was far from perfect. Such was the case with the new social order that emerged from the American Revolution, which at first extended universal citizenship only to white males. Second, regardless of the imperfections of the Spartan experiment, the ideal of citizenship remained to urge us forward. Within the elite class in Sparta, we can see concepts of citizenship emerge as we might recognize them today, including an emphasis on justice, representative government, civic involvement, and the development of community institutions needed to support citizenship in a public sense. Once the idea of developing a society built on civic virtue and representative government was attempted, there was no going back.

The first book in Western culture's literary pantheon devoted to exploring the concept of community and citizenship was Plato's *The Republic*. Written in 380 BCE, it is a staple of most Western civilization curricula because so much of it feels so familiar. In it, Plato lays out the philosophical and practical foundations for representative government, an approach to social organization that constituted a truly unique and extraordinary break from millennia of autocratic rule. He also described in detail the roles that citizens needed to play in helping to build an ideal society. Above all, citizens needed to be virtuous and engaged in their community. According to Plato, these behaviors were best cultivated through education.

Yet *The Republic* still falls short by modern standards of citizenship. While representative government was key to *The Republic,* it was skewed toward representation of the wealthy. This was reflected in the political makeup of Plato's city, Athens, where women, day workers, peasants, slaves, and foreign expatriates did not have the political rights enjoyed by true citizens of the mercantile and ruling classes (Hansen, 2006). While Plato called for state-run schools to help educate citizens in the ways of virtue, schooling was reserved for only the elite classes.

In order to honor my promise to be brief like Mel Brooks, I fast-forward past Aristotle (my apologies, historians) to the Roman Empire, which spanned a millennium, from roughly 500 BCE to 500 CE, and provided us language, customs, intellectual perspectives, and forms of social organization that exist today. In many ways, we in the West are the products of Greek and Roman times.

Given the Empire's longevity, and the fact that its many leaders were everything from pragmatically benevolent to sadistically tyrannical, it is difficult to characterize anything as being consistently Roman throughout all its days. But there are some general aspects of citizenship that are associated with Rome that highlight its most noteworthy accomplishments in this area. Briefly, Roman culture developed a more flexible approach to citizenship that offered different kinds of citizenship status. In the Empire, two levels of citizenship applied. The *honestiores* (senators, knights, soldiers, and veterans with honorable records) were exempt from certain punishments, such as crucifixion, and usually were at risk of only banishment or forfeiture of property. The *humiliores* (day workers, peasants, and slaves) could be punished with an array of horrible penalties, including dispatch to mines or the galleys, crucifixion, and serving as feed for wild beasts (Adkins & Adkins, 1998).

However, under the right conditions, the unthinkable could happen: Slaves could actually become citizens. Equally unique was Rome's experimentation with expanding citizenship to include favored cities outside Italy. When Roman citizens traveled to these locations, they were covered by Roman law (Adkins & Adkins, 1998). This is in contrast to the beliefs of the Greek philosophers Plato and Aristotle, who felt communities and the exercise of citizenship could be practically enforced only in small communities. The revolutionary idea embodied in Rome's concept of citizenship was that citizenship resided in the person rather than in the place. This perspective offered the first hint of citizenship that exceeded a local sphere of influence. In these efforts, we sense a bit of dabbling in universal rights, and we can feel civilization inching toward what most of us would call citizenship today. But there is still a long way to go.

Before leaving the Greek and Roman era, there is one development that transpired during this period that is worth mentioning: the concept of the cosmopolite or "world citizen" that emerged from the school of philosophy called stoicism. While stoicism is usually associated with a lack of emotion and showing a stiff upper lip during times of crisis, it was also a philosophy that championed the idea that there was a higher order of citizenship that belonged to anyone anywhere who possessed reason and a concern for all of humanity. It promoted the idea that each human being "dwells . . . in two communities—the local community of our birth, and the community of human argument and aspiration" (Nussbaum, 1997, in Cosmopolitanism, 2010). The name given to such people were *kosmopolites* or literally, "citizens of the world." Cosmopolitanism is an idea that is very alive today, surfacing in discussions of global citizenship, global education, and projects that stress a global perspective—that is, a perspective that exceeds the political boundaries and concerns usually associated with citizenship.

The reader may recall from their world history class the following two defining developments in Western civilization. First, in about 284 CE, the Roman Empire split into two parts, the Western Roman Empire, headquartered in Rome, and the Eastern Empire, headquartered in Constantinople. Then around 500 CE, the Western portion of the Empire disintegrated, a development often referred to as "the fall of the Roman Empire." Why the fall occurred is still debated, but certainly it had to do with the cumulative effects of challenges from Christianity, the crushing weight of the Empire's own bureaucracy and excesses, and invaders from outside its borders.

According to historian Dr. Jean-Pierre Isbouts (2010), the tipping point was brought about by the flight of bullion to the East to pay for luxury products (like silk and spices) that the upper classes in the West had become addicted to, so that there remained no hard cash to pay for troops to fight off barbarian invasions. Thus, we see Visigoths sacking Rome as early as 410 CE and establishing their own kingdoms by the end of the 5th century (Isbouts, 2010).

Media expert Dr. Marshall McLuhan identified another tipping point—the depletion of papyrus, which crippled Rome's vast communication system (1964). If you want to get a feel for the kind of effects this might have produced, imagine that one day the Internet, cell phone service, and mass media suddenly ceased. In the absence of the communication channels needed to maintain centralized authority and the rule of law, what would probably follow is chaos, survival of the fittest, and an intense localism.

In fact, that is what happened when Rome fell. Historians call what followed "the Dark Ages," lasting between 500 and 800 years, during which citizenship vanished in a legal sense, as did most of the recorded concern for the philosophical debate that supported its existence. As power coalesced, it was held by the Church and privileged classes who were more concerned with obedience to their authority than citizenship.

My apologies again to historians as I skip over several hundred years, but the reality is that citizenship was a vague concept with little support during the dark days and even into the Renaissance. We see sporadic experiments in citizenship in the city-states of Italy, such as in Florence, which reestablished the concept of "citizen" as a *res pubblica* (literally, "the public matter" or "commonwealth"). This was all the more surprising as most other city-states in the Italian *Quattrocento* (15th century) were either military or feudal dictatorships. Inspired by humanistic principles, particularly Plato, the Florentine chancellor Leonardo Bruni conceived of a true democracy whereby Florentine citizens enjoyed the protection of the state and its laws against the licentiousness that had ruled in Italy in prior centuries (Cronin, 1972). The House of the Medici, who ruled Florence for the remainder of that century, continued to honor these Platonic principles, even though in practice voting rights and the right to hold office were limited to the upper mercantile and financial classes (Strathern, 2005).

While Florentine's experiment with citizenship would serve as a powerful example for later generations elsewhere in Europe, it was the exception, not the rule. In retrospect, we can see just how fragile a concept citizenship was. It is fully understandable that its resurrection would require the bloody revolutions of emancipation during the late 1700s.

Citizenship as most of us would recognize it is based on the efforts of philosophers, writers, and politicians living during the Age of Enlightenment, which spanned the 17th and 18th centuries. It was an age of science and reason, and stood in stark contrast to previous centuries built on faith and superstition (Faulks, 2000). We might look at what emerged during this time as the beginning of the modern critical thinking movement. Philosophers like Rousseau and Locke looked at citizenship in logical terms. From their perspective, reason demanded that citizenship be based on an end to privilege, freedom for all, and the establishment of government structures that encouraged and facilitated everyone's involvement in their communities. Note the shift in emphasis from civic duty to individual rights and privileges. Citizens not only had obligations to fulfill, they had entitlements to enjoy. More important, citizens were to have a say about what their obligations and rights were. The new social covenant that began to emerge was that the state would protect citizens and their freedoms in return for which citizens would support the state and the laws and structures upon which it was founded (Heater, 1999, 2004).

It is no surprise that it was the work of philosophers like Rousseau that supplied the philosophical foundation of the French Revolution or that it was the words of Thomas Paine and Jefferson that inspired the American Revolution. After all, both revolutions were primarily about the redefinition of citizenship. In fact, the document that the French created in 1789 to support their revolution was called the *Declaration of the Rights of Man and of the Citizen* (2010).

The essence of both the American and the French Revolution was the replacement of a tiered society based on social privilege by a legal structure that theoretically favored no one. In essence, tradition was replaced by reason, which led Enlightenment-era philosophers and nonphilosophers alike to conclude that a society in which some people were more equal than others could be neither just nor stable. The redefinition of citizenship was driven not only by reason but also by a belief in the "inalienable rights" of freedom and equality. Thus, reason and belief converged on the creation of an approach to community and citizenship that was based on universal equality, state responsibility to its people, and the individual's responsibility to serve the community.

How impressive humanity would have been had the citizenship revolutions of the late 18th century secured citizenship status for everyone. But they didn't. The American War of Independence secured full freedom basically for white males. The Civil War, much legislation, and many court battles awaited the United States before it could secure what most would recognize as citizenship today. When more complete forms of citizenship do emerge in modernity, it is within the context of a debate about how to balance the obligations and rights that resulted in postrevolutionary times, particularly in the following three areas described by citizenship scholar T. H. Marshall (in Heater, 1999):

1. Civic—personal freedoms of speech, religion, assembly, thought, faith, the right to justice, own property, to contract with others

2. Political—the right to participate in the political process

3. Social—the right to live a civilized life being in accordance with the standards prevailing in society

The debate about how to balance the obligations and entitlements associated with citizenship is—and should be—never ending. The current health care debate in the United States is a testimony to how this plays out in real terms. It is the duty of each generation to revisit these three areas of citizenship in light of social and technical evolution and ask the questions, *Does our current concept of citizenship balance the needs of individuals, society, and government? Does it allow us to be all we can be?* If not, then we need to adjust some combination of our goals, expectations, and social structures to adapt to our new vision of society.

What do we glean from the march of citizenship that will help us understand the challenges of digital citizenship today? The following:

- **Citizenship requires individual "virtuous" behavior.** Effective, creative, fair communities cannot be fully legislated and prescribed. In the end, they are dependent on each of us setting individual priorities and making personal decisions that make our communities work. Thus, throughout history, so-called "virtuous behavior" has been viewed as a key element of citizenship. This is no different for digital citizens.

- **Citizenship requires balancing personal empowerment and community well-being**. A particular kind of behavior required for effective citizenship is the ability to balance both individual and community needs. This is particularly problematic for denizens of the infosphere, who are often physically disconnected from the communities they impact.

- **Citizenship requires education**. "Virtuous behavior" is taught, not inherited, and needs to be addressed through some kind of educational rigor, with an emphasis on literacy and character education, topics covered at some length in Part III of this book. Thus, society needs "a system of general education, which shall reach every description of our citizens from the richest to the poorest" (Jefferson, 1818) in order to produce an educated populace. Without such a system, citizenship is impossible. There seems to be universal recognition that full citizenship be withheld from people until young adulthood. Thus, we have until that point to formally educate our children about the basics of what it means to be a citizen and community member.

- **Citizenship requires our participation.** Without our participation, citizenship cannot take advantage of society's single most important resource: the ideas and creativity of its people. Without our participation, citizenship becomes static and unable to evolve in response to changing social conditions. The digital realm is above all a participatory one. It is up to society to help students use their tools of participation effectively, creatively, and wisely.

- **Citizenship is constantly evolving, and thus requires our ongoing debate.** Citizenship requires a particular kind of participation: our willingness to debate and revise what citizenship means and how it plays out in real life. Citizenship is not just about "doing the right thing" as it is often portrayed. It is equally about deliberately reexamining our cultures and communities in order to cast new light on what the right thing is. In other words, citizenship is as much about perspective as it is about behavior. If we want the participation of our students, then we need to actively engage students in discussions about how the nature of citizenship can or should change. In fact, having them cultivate a metaperspective about their digital activities will help them self-regulate and engage in a reflective, creative reinvention of culture as we know it.

- **Citizenship must be inclusive**. There can be no more *Animal Farm* (Orwell, 1946) approaches to citizenship, in which some citizens are more equal than others. When that happens, instability and revolution ensues. This speaks very directly to the issue of socioeconomic disparity, often referred to as *the digital divide*, that currently excludes some from citizenship. It also speaks to the issue of crafting school policy that balances protecting students from the more pernicious aspects of the Internet with giving them room to practice digital citizenship through their successes and failures in navigating the freedom of the infosphere. This is particularly tricky for K–12, which addresses the needs of the very young, adolescents, and young adults, all of whom have varying "rights and privileges" based on a mixture of culture, law, school policy, and parental concern. That is, we offer students a sliding scale of Internet access as they progress in their citizenship education. The question for policy makers is, *How do we calibrate that scale?*

- **Citizenship is a result of media evolution.** In many ways, this book is about media evolution, thus I didn't dwell on it during my brief history of citizenship. But suffice it to say that citizenship depends on revolutions in media to expedite and spread new ideas. The Age of Enlightenment was highly dependent on the printing press and the resulting spread of literacy in order to facilitate the proliferation of revolutionary ideas. Similarly, the era of inexpensive, widely distributed social media has facilitated and in many ways defined our current discussion of digital citizenship.

- **Above all, citizenship is tied to community**. That is, citizenship arises because people gather in groups and inevitably ask the question, *What does it mean to belong here?* This leads to issues of group ethos. In particular, it leads to discussions of how a group defines itself socially with regard to beliefs, customs, and practices, as well as which behaviors are expected, encouraged, tolerated, debated, restricted, and prohibited.

The last point about citizenship's tie to community is key. We have seen from the preceding discussion that the drive toward community is the result of the innate desire of humans to congregate in groups in ways that serve everyone's needs individually and collectively. We carry that "ancient human" (Dertouzos, 2001) with us into cyberspace. Once groups formed within the online world with enough focus and cohesion, the issue of citizenship naturally arose. As we study this phenomenon, three questions drive our inquiry:

1. How do the great changes in community caused by digital technology and networking change the nature of citizenship?

2. What perspectives do we need in order to understand, use, and evaluate the new communities in which we participate so that we can do so as informed citizens?

3. What behaviors and codes of conduct are befitting citizens who occupy these new communities?

These questions can never be resolved, only debated. But it is our awareness of them that will help us involve our students in the world of digital citizenship with a sense of purpose and perspective. After all, we want our students to be critical thinkers, meaning that we want them to think about what they are doing in ways that are informed, reflective, intelligent, contextualized, proactive, and compassionate. These three questions need to guide our critical thinking efforts as we help students pursue issues of community and citizenship in the Digital Age.

THE EVOLUTION OF COMMUNITY: FROM FARMLAND TO FACEBOOK

Kinds of Community

Citizenship is tied to community. It is an expression of our understanding of what our community expects of us and we expect of it. Thus, we take a brief look at the rise of digital communities so that we can better understand how the issue of digital citizenship evolved.

We begin by reminding ourselves that the Internet has been a fixture in our daily lives for only 10 to 15 years. When I make this point in public presentations, a hush of astonishment settles on the audience. Only 10 or 15 years? Yet can we remember life without it? Prior to the publicly available Internet, intrepid cybernauts used very slow e-mail, BITNET, Usenet, and other adventures in commercial and egalitarian social media. These early days gave us mail lists—still known as listservs—user groups, and a number of attempts at distributed resources and social media long since forgotten. It was an interesting time, similar to the early days of automobiles in that it often required participants to fend for themselves technically. The few who were willing to make this commitment could explore new lands that others simply could not.

Social media began during the 1960s and 70s with e-mail, basically one-to-one communication, and was followed by listservs and electronic bulletin boards, which facilitated one-to-many communication in that they allowed users to send one message to a list of recipients. Soon after came "computer

FYI
Honoring Pioneers
If there are a grandmother and grandfather of the field of social media studies, they are Roxanne Hiltz and Murray Turoff. Their book _The Network Nation_ was published in 1978, preceding the publicly available Internet, as well as my own study of online community, by nearly 15 years. Their vision, research findings, and perspective about living in a connected culture are still prescient even today.

conferencing." It was an immense step forward that gave digital community its first real breath of life because it facilitated many-to-many communication. It allowed users to congregate and communicate in groups that participants defined in terms of membership, ethos, and purpose. It allowed them to gather in ways that reminded us of communities.

In 1990, I undertook a study of an online community, which consisted of studying the activities of approximately 400 people who were using a computer conferencing system on a regular basis for social, professional, and educational purposes. Note that this was pre-Internet, so participants were pretty much on an electronic island by themselves with very limited access to outside information sources. They were tethered to the mainframe that housed their electronic community by slow dial-up modems connected to their desktop computers at home. Wireless megabit transmission was still far into the future, as was the use of images, video, or many of the other kinds of media we take for granted today. The world of online communication was a text-only world for many years.

I was drawn to this research topic because many of the conferencing system participants referred to the system as a community. Thus, my research sought to answer a seemingly simple question: Is this a community? Suggesting that a virtual congregation could be considered a community was largely viewed as heresy by established academia. Communities were physical, period. Thus, my journey through the project was largely uphill. It began with trying to define community, which, as it turned out, was a complex and nearly impossible task.

To give the reader an idea of how difficult community is to define, Wikipedia opens its article on community with the following: "In sociology, the concept of community has caused infinite debate, and sociologists are yet to reach agreement on a definition of the term. There were ninety-four discrete definitions of the term by the mid-1950s" (Community, 2010). This was certainly the situation I encountered as I began my research.

However, there was one theme within academic discussion that provided useful direction for my study: defining community in terms of how it had changed before and after the industrial revolution. Basically, three models of community emerged in the research literature, which were identified aptly by sociologist Barry Wellman as solidary community, neighborhoods, and personal networks (Wellman, 1988; Wellman & Leighton, 1979). What follows is my interpretation of these concepts in light of our current discussion of digital community:

1. **Solidary community—preindustrial**. The word *solidary* is defined by Dictionary.com as "characterized by or involving community of responsibilities and interests" (Solidary, 2010). However, from my

perspective, solidary community also captures a mythic sense of community that supposedly existed prior to the industrial revolution. Communities were largely agricultural, place based, intensely local, and personal. Think Disney—or for AARP members, the Waltons—and you get the idea. The implication is that life was good because communities were small, interpersonal gatherings with common cultures, concerns, and "responsibilities and interests." The reality of course was much different. Life was often hard, short, and subject to the whim of whatever despot was in charge. But the idea of this kind of community persists and is often alluded to by the elders of any generation who begin sentences with, "Back in my day . . ."

2. **Neighborhoods—industrial**. As people migrated from the fields to the cities to work in factories during the industrial revolution, solidary community began to fizzle out. If you want to impress friends and family with your sociology background, you can tell them that *gemeinschaft* yielded to *gesellschaft*. Those terms roughly translate into "community" and "society," respectively (Tonnies, 1988/1957). However, community wasn't destroyed. Instead, it resurfaced within cities and towns as neighborhoods. A few important shifts define this kind of community. First, while it was still localized and personal, it was no longer isolated. Instead, it was set within a larger community that was surrounded by outsiders. Second, life and work were separated in the shift from solidary to neighborhood communities. While you both worked and lived on the farm during the days of solidary community, you now split your life between two places, going to work at the factory and then retreating to your neighborhood after the work day was over.

3. **Personal networks—postindustrial**. With the advent of modern transportation and communication technology, each of us began to build our own personal communities based on our own personal networks. To visualize this, see yourself as a hub of a wheel, with each spoke representing a person in your community to whom you are connected via communication or transportation technology. Thus, we can belong to a family or network of friends whose members are completely geographically dispersed, many of whom might not even know each other. The result is that your community and the basis for your legal, geographically defined citizenship could be completely separate. Historically, this was a truly revolutionary idea, which has been further brought to life as social media has come into use.

Even though each of these kinds of communities are idealized and hard to pin down in terms of specifics, they serve as emotional archetypes in that they capture some fundamental idea about what community provides the human experience. As such, we see in the evolution of community the gradual separation of community and geographic citizenship. With solidary communities, everything happened in one location. With neighborhoods, community was still localized but set within larger geographic entities. With personal networks, the separation is potentially complete. Your community can be in one place, while your geographic citizenship can be elsewhere.

TRY THIS

DRAWING YOUR NETWORK

With yourself as the hub of a wheel, draw your personal network, using spokes to connect you to the major people, places, and things in your life. If you want to make it interesting, use spokes of different lengths, widths, or colors to depict the importance of each person or element in your network. If you are a teacher, have your students do this with the specific instruction to include the digital components of their network. Lead a discussion on how their networks evolved and where they think they are going. Of particular interest is how technology has redefined what it means to be an acquaintance, friend, and confidant.

My study concluded in 1993. Since then, a good deal has happened in terms of how we can connect with each other in the infosphere. Personal networks were largely individually based because the technology used at the time—mostly phones, transportation, and some early e-mail—did not easily facilitate the group communication that has become the hallmark of digital community today.

But personal networks persist today because each of us is still at the center of our own network, regardless of how interconnected its members may be. For example, the term *personal learning network* (PLN) is commonly used to describe the network of electronic resources we individually maintain to keep up to date in our professions. Mine consists of a number of listservs (mailing lists), Twitter, and blog and RSS feeds (largely automatic webpage updates). Yours might consist primarily of information gleaned from wikis and YouTube or mail received through your professional organizations. No matter how we structure our PLNs, each of us is at the center of our network, much like the original personal networks born out of first-generation communication technology.

In retrospect, personal networks allowed us to wade into digital community gently by providing opportunities to live in different communities at the same time and to be active members in communities that had little geographical basis. As such, personal networks provided the foundation for much of digital culture as we know it today. In many ways, personal networks were the calm before the social media storm.

THREE LEVELS OF COMMUNITY IN ISTE STANDARDS

We use the term *digital citizenship* as a catch-all phrase to describe an ideal for our students with regard to understanding their opportunities and responsibilities in the Digital Age. If we look at it as simply meaning "what it means to be a citizen in the Digital Age," then it works fairly well. After all, issues of local, global, and digital community are always at play these days, so digital citizenship would therefore seem to embrace all of them as well as the citizenship issues associated with them.

But before we adopt the phrase *digital citizenship* in this way, let's understand what the different kinds of community identified by the new ISTE standards add to the issues associated with being a citizen in the Digital Age.

Recall that ISTE's refreshed standards refer to three kinds of community with regard to citizenship: local, global, and digital. Students and educators need to be able to understand and participate effectively within each in order to be fully engaged citizens. Like Wellman's (1988) three kinds of communities, those mentioned in the ISTE standards are also difficult to describe in terms of specifics. They overlap a good deal and function more as descriptions of our emotional experience of community than of places or activities, whether real or digital. However, the terms *local, global,* and *digital* are widely used because they resonate with the human experience and thus provide a portal into how we view community. That is, somehow these terms are very useful to us as we tell stories about a world that has been made very complex by our digital technology. Thus, our job isn't to determine how accurate they are but what is meant by their use. Below are my descriptions of what I think they address in a general sense.

Local community. Local community is "old-fashioned" community in that it consists of people who can communicate directly with each other without too much effort. This typically involves interaction of a geographically immediate and often personally meaningful nature. In terms of groups and locales, this refers to families, classrooms, schools, or the neighborhoods or towns in which we live. In some ways, local community is the

Digital Age equivalent of solidary community in that it can often involve groups with whom we share common cultures, concerns, responsibilities, and interests, reinforced by geographic proximity. However, note that these attributes can also apply to digital, geographically distributed communities. Thus, one of the most distinct attributes of local communities is that we can experience the effects of our own actions up close in a relatively unmediated fashion.

Global community. Strictly speaking, this is anything beyond local community, which covers a tremendous amount of territory. However, as the term *global community* is most often used, it has little to do with geography as a primary consideration. Instead, it describes a sense of affiliation that means "beyond self" and is inclusive of a much broader social and environmental setting than we can immediately perceive. We can think "more globally" by thinking about the ripple effects of our actions beyond ourselves, whether they are felt in a neighboring town or half a world away.

In its broadest sense, global community is an attempt to put a human face on abstract concepts like "humanity" and "earth as ecosystem." This has become important because technology has gathered us into a global village and forced us to look at the effects of our actions in much broader terms. Doing so highlights the fact that we live on a very interconnected but culturally diverse planet and that addressing issues, opportunities, and problems that cross political and cultural boundaries will require building new kinds of social bridges.

The subtext here is that the the world is now inextricably interconnected in three ways: ecologically, technologically, and humanly. If we are truly trying to prepare our students for the real world, as workers and citizens, then we need to pay attention to all three.

Digital community. Digital communities are the groups to which we belong that are primarily sustained through electronic rather than geographic proximity. They are highly adaptable in that they can serve as extensions of local community, solely as global communities whose members will never share a common geography, or a combination of the two. Of primary importance is that people gather in digital communities by choice rather than due to geographic default. They are driven to do so largely by common needs and curiosities, from sharing a common interest in someone's YouTube channel, to enrollment in an online course, to membership in a listserv devoted to the Red Sox, to engaging in a blog-based educational project to study international issues, to pure exploration of a common curiosity via a wiki. Digital communities might not be local, but they *feel local*. Members of digital gatherings feel they belong to a real community, and thus project themselves into cyberspace in ways that have meaning and emotional significance.

It is because digital communities feel local that global community becomes less abstract than it might otherwise seem in two ways. First, it adds an emotional dimension to global community through participatory social media. That is, we talk to people—whether through text, voice, video, avatars, or other media—and in the process experience emotional connections and intellectual engagement that are quite real. Second, digital community maintains an ongoing scrapbook of resources that provides context for all the things we do. We inform our community activities by reading reports, watching videos, and researching the cornucopia of materials that the web provides. All of these resources are equally available to each of us. Thus, in digital community we are simultaneously living in a community center and museum that is constantly updated by us all.

Digital community can also be viewed as a place in metaphoric terms, in that we use the language of local community to describe many of our activities—we "go" online in order "to hang out and visit" with Facebook friends and virtual "neighbors" whom we miss and want to get to know better. In fact, one primary finding of my online community study was that people engage in their online community primarily for two reasons: to make new friends and meet new people. In the case of the group I studied, members were often local. Thus, making new friends and meeting new people offered real, added value to the local community experience. Those who were not local still experienced many of the emotional benefits of a local community through the interpersonal connections they made.

Virtual worlds take the idea of "digital community as place" to new heights and depths. For example, in Second Life we actually see artifacts that remind us of RL (Real Life), such as tables, campfires, houses, and people with whom we sit and chat. These things and activities are all borrowed from local community and adapted to the medium of cyberspace. But in Second Life, you get to do something you can't do in RL, other than be perpetually thin and attractive: You can fly. Nice improvement.

It is a good time to pause and reflect about just how different these concepts of community are from those we might have grown up with. When I was in school, we didn't talk about issues related to global community except when we read *National Geographic* and were moved to discuss how bizarre and unlike us the rest of the world seemed to be. And in my day, *digital* meant you were doing something with your fingers.

Yet it is also a good time to realize how much digital citizens resemble their ancestors. We clearly project ancient needs into new territory. We invent new behaviors in the service of time-honored ideals. In the process, we reinvent our future as we rediscover our past.

YOU: WHERE LOCAL, GLOBAL, AND DIGITAL COMMUNITIES INTERSECT

To help us understand how we identify and align ourselves with multiple communities, try using the following activity that I first experienced as a child. Even though I describe it as an activity to be used with students, it works equally well with anyone.

Ask students to describe their own personal network by drawing a series of concentric circles, with themselves at the center, and with each circle describing their membership in a group that is important to them. It works well as a thought experiment as well as an actual exercise using paper and pencil.

Because community is a vast idea, you can help steer the exercise by defining community in different ways to produce different results. For example, you might want students to produce concentric rings showing their membership in legal communities, in which case you might see something that looks like the image below. Depending on the students' grade level, you might want to model what you mean by "legal community" by identifying the first two as "family" and "town in which you live." This is represented in Figure 1 and can be rightfully considered a representation of community membership, 1.0.

Try directing this exercise in other ways by asking them to draw circles representing such things as "information sources" or even "food sources."

Now remove any direction and ask students to draw circles of communities that *feel* most important to them. What they produce might be based on the following hierarchies of groups presented below. Note: I am presenting this in linear fashion rather than as circle diagrams to save paper:

Self—Family—Circle of friends—Basketball team—Local artist group . . . Country . . . Etc.

Or more recently, like this:

Self—Family—Circle of friends I text with—Facebook friends— Basketball team . . . Etc.

Self—Family—Town—County—State—Country—World

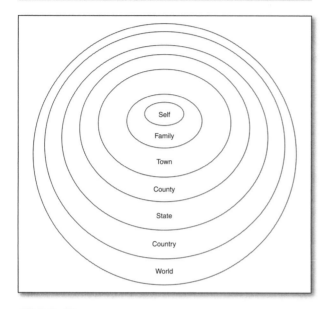

Self

Family

Town

County

State

Country

World

Figure 1 Community Membership Diagram 1.0

Teachers might produce something like the following to describe the professional communities that feel most important to them:

Self—School—Language arts community—Book club—School community—State language arts association—NCTE (National Council of Teachers of English) . . . Etc.

Or for younger teachers:

Self—Classroom—School—Online language arts community—Wiki members . . . Etc.

There would be many permutations to be sure, and everyone's citizenship circle diagram would look different. But most would mix legal, professional, and personal associations and draw their circles based on which groups *felt the most important to them*. In the process, they would draw upon local, "beyond local," and digital groups to describe their sense of association with the important groups in their lives. These are roughly akin to ISTE's three communities: local, global, and digital. You will also notice that as participants mix all three kinds of communities, their use of mutually exclusive circles becomes more difficult to do. For many of us, thanks to digital communication, our associations cross a number of community boundaries. Concentric circles don't adapt to this very well.

A few important points emerge from this.

First, depicting our associations using concentric circles may work well to describe geographic or legal kinds of citizenship, but they don't work nearly as well to describe most other kinds of association in the Digital Age. For example, local family may be my first circle, but the next circle may consist of all my family members who are on Facebook. However, only some of my family members are on Facebook, and only some of my family members are local, perhaps because of a divorce in the family or the ability to include geographically dispersed, extended-family members using electronic media. In addition, because digital community feels local, friends of family members who live in Thailand or Florida who are active in my Facebook community *feel* like local family. And then there are Uncle Ted and Aunt Edna, whom I haven't heard from in over a decade even though they live only five minutes away. To describe all of this pictorially, you would need to use a creative approach to diagramming, such as one of Edward Tufte's informational graphics, which use an array of visual rhetorical tools (www.edwardtufte.com); or perhaps a social network diagram, like the one shown here created by architecture student Nicholas Ng to depict the groups of friends he has on Facebook based on their distance and relationship (view original at archithesis .wordpress.com/page/2/). Whatever you used, producing an accurate diagram would be challenging.

Second, my very informal research tells me that most students won't naturally include "world" or "global community" as one of their communities. As I mentioned earlier, global community is an abstract concept for most because it deals with issues like "global ecosystem" or "humanity." Thus, given that community identification is mostly driven by feelings of association, it is understandable that most would not list the world as a primary "community of feeling." Yet many of us would include digital communities, which may be global in geographic composition.

Thus, it is our job as educators to help students see global issues if they are to address them. In figure-ground terminology, the world needs to become figure. This seems counterintuitive. Surely the world—the great encompassing environment that contains everything—is always ground. Not so, if we are to help raise global citizens—or at least local citizens with global awareness. It is hard enough to see the impact of our actions a block away. Seeing them half a world away takes real work.

Facebook Relationship Diagram by Nicholas Ng

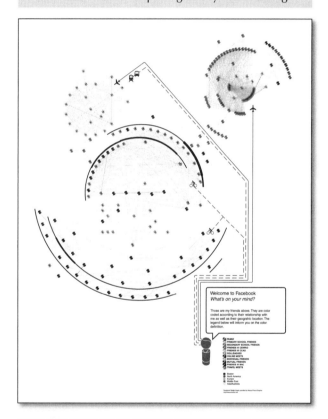

Figure 2 Community Membership Diagram 2.0

FYI

Global community feels local when it goes digital.

Each of us is the center of a personal network that connects us to a number of communities that are personally meaningful. The task for teachers is to help students to connect their personal networks to global realities that are personally meaningful and academically important. There are several options for doing this:

- **Deepen the time spent on the inherently global web.** Students already experience the world through the web. We can take advantage of this fact and help them mine their experiences to produce a deeper understanding of the world in which they live. When the world becomes the backdrop for what you see and do, it can also become the backdrop for what you think about.

- **Directly connect with others in a more global context.** This can include informal international e-pal relationships, formal study groups consisting of an international cadre of students, and everything in between. Presumably, this happens digitally, using social media and any of the wonderful activities on the web that promote this, like WebQuests and structured e-mail collaborations. But it might also happen by actually visiting other places in the real world. Again, this shift in background will help produce a shift in foreground.

- **Directly inquire into global issues.** By this I mean that we should deliberately include content and methodology in school curricula that consider issues of global significance. Until we do this, thinking globally and acting locally remains a rather blurry concept to most. The newspaper, whether paper based or web based, is a wonderful source to mine for curriculum possibilities that tie directly to real global issues. Imagine curriculum built around understanding climate change, intercultural communication, or innovative energy development. The possibilities are exciting and abundant.

- **Focus on everyone's ripple effect.** Imagine once again the personal network diagram, with each of us at the hub of a wheel and with spokes that reach out in many directions. In this case, the spokes connect with our impacts on the world. There are many activities that promote this perspective. For example, every year my students conduct research about their energy consumption habits in order to better understand how their individual energy use can reduce unwanted impacts on their communities and the world of natural resources. They do this by studying the ripple effect that begins with their own energy use choices and by using a spreadsheet program to play "what if?" with changes in their lifestyles. The results are always illuminating. This activity is detailed in Chapter 6 of this book.

- **Use site-based learning to promote connections to place.** This might seem counterintuitive given that site-based learning has an intensely local focus. But the reality is that understanding local impacts is an effective launching point for understanding them in a broader context. That is, everyone has a home. Understanding your home in greater detail might help you better understand the relationships that others have with their homes and their local communities. By extension, this should help you connect with others through the ecosystem, the tEcosystem, and the greater world of human activity.

- **Focus on what is unique as well as what is universal.** Behind any global movement, whether in education, charity work, or even business, is the sense that each of us is somehow different and somehow the same, and learning to balance these two realities will allow us to move forward in more socially productive ways. I have been part of school projects involving this theme in which students from several countries made inventories of assumptions they had about their foreign counterparts in terms of the food they ate, clothes they wore, issues they considered important, and so on. Then they would swap inventories. Two realizations, equally powerful, were always present: (1) They were much more alike than they had imagined, and (2) they were also much more different than they had imagined. In fact, it was the universality of this realization, rather than the details they discovered, that provided students their most important connections with each other.

A Word About Multiple Identities

While living in many communities and integrating a number of identities might have the potential to confuse us, it also has the potential to improve our understanding of our world in two ways. First, because we are no longer isolated in our physical communities, we can travel to other parts of the globe electronically and begin to gather the perspective we need to live successfully in a connected, multicultural world. Second, as we merge and integrate our own multiple identities, we are compelled to synthesize many viewpoints, which is crucial to being a global citizen.

> **FYI**
>
> ### There's a Lot Going On
>
> There are many global projects and organizations that take advantage of living in digital community. To begin, look at Kiva.org, the NetGenEd Flat Classroom Project, and The Global Education Collaborative. If you are interested in others, see my digital citizenship wiki at jasonohler.com/dc, where you can also add your own.

Thus, we rightfully have many hopes for living in a digital world, one of which is that we may be able to use the global and multicultural nature of digital community to manage our identities so that we can collectively build bridges and develop resources in VR (Virtual Reality) that could help us in RL (Real Life). After all, if digital community has helped us discover our ability to get along, then the only thing that prevents us from doing so in RL is old thinking.

The bottom line is that we are reminded by the thoughtful work of writers like Amartya Sen (2009) that each of us has many identities because we belong to many groups, a fact that is amplified in digital community. We have identities that are local, nationalist, and global, as well as personal, professional, and familial (Sen, 2009). Which ones predominate typically depends on the situation, but it is always a matter of choice. At times of conflict or opportunity, we can choose to emphasize our differences or our connectedness. It is up to us.

3 Gathering Digitally

In this chapter, I look at two aspects of becoming a digital community member: How we alter our persona as we enter cyberspace and how we gather once we get there. As always, although what we will look at is very new, it is grounded in behavior that has been with us for some time.

CHANGING MINDS: THE ALTERED SELF

We have always been capable of managing many personae. We speak authoritatively about professional matters within the confines of the work place, whisper intimate secrets with confidants at home, and scream and yell in public as we cheer on our favorite sports team. This is all considered very normal behavior.

With the introduction of cyberspace into the human experience, identity management takes a leap into the realm of identity invention. Our ability to hide our RL (Real Life) identities by using obscure user presences—from chat room names to avatars who look nothing like us—allows us to literally reconceptualize ourselves. The result is that we can become a very new blend of self. We can try on new selves to see how they fit. We can outright lie or be more honest than we have ever been. And we can say and do things that would not be tolerated in RL.

However, in our current concern with overt identity management we have lost sight of the fact that identity reinvention came of age during the earliest days of cyber communication when we actually knew who we were talking to online. It was facilitated by a phenomenon known as "disinhibition," which cyber researcher Nancy Willard (2007) defines as what happens when the "use of technologies interferes with the recognition of connection between action and consequences" (p. 4). In the absence of RL's familiar social and contextual cues, as well as the tangible feedback we are used to receiving in more direct interaction with others, we cultivate a sense of being invisible and anonymous, when in fact we are neither. This false sense of concealment allows us to say things that we simply would not otherwise.

As an early adopter of electronic mail with an abiding interest in the social sciences, I noticed the impacts of disinhibition at once. In colloquial terms, we called this phenomenon then, as we do now, "entering the zone." We see it in body language, as people lean forward in their chairs with glazed looks on their faces while they tap out e-mail or stare into space as they talk on the cell phone, oblivious to the world outside their own heads. Essentially, their body language is telling everyone nearby that they have entered a very personal zone and that they "do not want to be disturbed by the conventional sociality with physically proximate individuals" (Turkle, 2008, p. 122). The lack of the presence of "the other" in RL forces us into our own minds, where the familiar outer social landscape is replaced by an interior landscape. Our new environment is sculpted largely by our own imaginations, which find paying attention to the immediate details of our surroundings confining and annoying.

Most of us are well acquainted with the downsides of disinhibition. Communicating through cyberspace can delay, obfuscate, and distort communication. In addition, we do not often witness the local repercussions of our actions reflected in the people we see at school, work, or in our neighborhood. We have all sent e-mail messages that have been misinterpreted, largely because we were not present to explain them. Anonymity didn't make this happen, because everyone involved knew each other. The medium massaged this misunderstanding.

Yet disinhibition has quite an upside. A lack of directness in communication can actually mitigate prejudice and liberate those who might be reticent to communicate in RL due to a number of factors, including shyness, intercultural misunderstanding, and even stuttering. I have witnessed many of my students who were reluctant to participate in a physical classroom come to life in an electronic venue for these reasons. One said to me once, "I finally get to speak!" I also witnessed an increase in thoughtfulness online. The actual time it takes to type forces a time lag between thought and communication, which gives speakers—typers in this case—time to actually consider what they have to say.

> **TRY THIS**
>
> *UNDERSTANDING METADATA*
>
> *To drive home the power of voice inflection, have each member of a group of people inflect the words, "What do you mean?" to produce a different meaning. I have asked 25 students to do this and been amazed as each managed to say something different. Emoticons and brevicons were born out of our need to compensate for a lack of meta-info, like inflection and facial expression. But they are only partially successful in doing so.*

The result is that digital venues can bring out the best or the worst in its citizens. What follows are two kinds of disinhibited communication I have witnessed in digital venues that explore the different kinds of communication that we need to help our students and ourselves understand and harness.

Special Case 1: Reading Yourself and the Need for Meta-Information

"I can't believe he said that to me!" cried one of my colleagues as he read his e-mail. I looked over his shoulder and read the message that basically said, "Why don't you teach that unit, if you think you are up to it." I saw nothing wrong, but my colleague was livid. "Why wouldn't I be up to it?" my colleague bellowed. "This is my area of expertise; of course I would be up to it!" I then reminded my colleague that he had been sick for a while, and that perhaps this was an inquiry into his health. Silence. "Perhaps," he said sheepishly.

All communication is composed of a combination of content and meta-information, which gives the content its true meaning. Without meaning, communication is experiential chaos. Thus, in the absence of explicit meta-information conveyed through such things as voice tone, context, and body language, all of which are notoriously absent or muddled in cyberspace, we have a choice: risk chaos or supply the meta-information ourselves. We typically choose the latter, as is the case here. The result is that sometimes when we read text in cyberspace—whether e-mail, blog comments, or avichat (avatar

> **FYI**
>
> *When We Read E-mail, We Are Reading Ourselves*
>
> In the absence of meta-information in digital communities, sometimes when you read messages from others, you are actually reading yourself.

conversation)—we are reading what we have projected into the communication rather than what is necessarily present.

We have come up with interesting ways to compensate for the flat or distracting world of virtual interaction. For example, we can be explicit with our words (god, I'm angry!) or use emoticons [;-) or :-0] or brevicons (LOL or IMHO). It is all an attempt to compensate for what we lose when we use mediated communication. It is interesting to note that even in media-rich avatar worlds, a good deal of communication is still typed. Thus, much of what we are talking about here is still in play.

So what drives us to interpret communication as we do?

In the absence of any explicit guide for interpretation, such as the use of emoticons or brevicons, communicators will imbue a statement like, "Why don't you teach that unit, if you think you are up to it" with the tone, and thus the meaning, that builds on previous knowledge of the sender, whether from previous RL or VR interaction. This allows the use of conversational tones that ordinarily don't translate well among strangers in digital communication, like subtlety and sarcasm, among people who understand each other. Perhaps my colleague didn't have a good relationship with the person who sent him the e-mail, which caused him to put a negative twist on the message he received.

But what about people who don't know each other? Or mistakenly think they do? Perhaps my colleague did not know the sender and was simply projecting a personal insecurity into the e-mail he read. Perhaps he was just having a bad day. Whatever the case, because we are meaning makers we will imbue messages with some meaning, however unrelated it may be to the intentions of the sender. In supplying the meta-information needed to make a communication whole, we create a reflection of ourselves.

Bottom line: While we need to teach students about the issues associated with hiding behind an online identity, we also need to help them understand that the very nature of the media they are using already imposes the potential for misunderstanding into the communication process. When they go online, they change.

Special Case 2: "Interlational" Communication

Another interesting side effect of the lack of familiar social reminders in cyberspace is what I call "interlational communication," which I define as communication across social distances. Although it is not a phenomenon particular to cyberspace, electronic communication facilitates it very well.

I have seen many instances in digital community in which people cross social distances by stepping out of roles defined in RL. This happens in a number of ways, including communication among strangers or those "out of reach" due to social convention, as well as among friends about otherwise forbidden topics. Sometimes, interlational communication is intentional; sometimes it's not. Sometimes, the communicators know it is happening; other times they don't. What is important is that it is a truly new addition to the pantheon of communication that digital community has afforded us. The result is that there is a good deal of conversation that was not going on before.

The first time I witnessed interlational communication was during the mid-1980s. A high school teacher and a dozen or so students had taken a field trip to our university's computer lab to use our computer conferencing system. As students became more comfortable with the medium (don't forget—digital natives did not exist yet), they sometimes addressed their teacher by his first name within the computer conference, though they still addressed him by "Mr. Smith" when they talked to his nonvirtual persona sitting just feet away. They crossed the social distance that separated student and teacher within digital community but not outside it. Fascinating.

I then watched two students sitting next to each other exchange e-mail within the conferencing system, saying things they would never turn to each other and say directly. Clearly, they were not crossing a physical communication barrier. After all, they were sitting next to each other and were aware of the fact that they were communicating with each other. They crossed some kind of social barrier. Fascinating again.

My next foray into interlational communication was deliberate. I invited our local representative in state government to connect via computer conferencing with a fifth-grade class that was less than a five-minute walk from her office. What resulted was something no one expected: very real, ongoing communication about issues of the day that affected elementary students. The medium allowed everyone to step out of their roles as adult and children, or politician and nonvoter, to enter very real dialogue on a much more equal footing. Had the representative visited the class physically, she would have talked for a half hour, fielded a few questions, and left. There would have been none of the follow-up communication needed to really explore an issue. The medium facilitated crossing social distance, resulting in a qualitative leap in the value of the experience.

The next interlational project was global in scope. It involved establishing an e-mail connection in 1988 between high school students in Juneau, Alaska, and Moscow, USSR, for the purpose of discussing world issues. While this would hardly be considered news today, it was so extraordinary at the time that it attracted CNN coverage.

Younger readers will need to talk to AARP members for a more complete geopolitical overview of life during those times, but basically the

United States and what was then the USSR were sworn enemies, a relationship that persisted until the 1990s. They maintained nuclear arsenals pointed at each other that were capable of destroying each other's countries many times over. The world called it MAD: Mutually Assured Destruction. In the event of nuclear holocaust, the rest of the world would have been collateral damage.

In this drama, average United States and Soviet citizens were cast in the role of each other's enemy. However, while students from the two countries discussed a number of mutual ecological concerns, they quickly morphed into global citizens with little interest in politics or the supposed differences that separated them. One can't help but wonder what might have happened had electronic communication been fully deployed during the times of the Montagues and the Capulets. Perhaps Romeo and Juliet would have lived (Shakespeare, 1975b/1599). One can't help but also wonder what might happen today if adherents of different political philosophies and religions routinely used similar means of communication with the expressed desire to explore areas of common interest within a more global context. All we hear about are the extremists. The rest of the population needs to start talking. Electronically facilitated interlational communication could play an important role.

I was so fascinated by the potential of interlational communication that I tried to get lawyers and therapists to use electronic communication in the service of conflict resolution. Clients on both sides of an issue were typically inhibited by the presence of RL social cues, which is a professional way of saying they couldn't stand the sight of each other. The result was that they would power up or shut down in each other's presence, cutting off any kind of communication flow. I thought electronic communication might defuse that somewhat, and allow them to cross a social boundary they had created by casting each other in the role of adversary. A number of therapists and lawyers heard me give presentations about this and expressed great interest in the possibilities of using this kind of communication for conflict resolution. But as one honest lawyer (that's what I said) explained to me, "But I don't see how we would make any money doing this." Ah yes . . . the money thing.

These examples are taken from personal history that happened some years ago. In them, we can see the beginnings of identity management that is commonplace today. Since that time, the potential to cross social boundaries and role barriers has grown immensely. The use of e-mail, texting, blogging, avatars, and new technologies we can't foresee present many opportunities to use electronic communication to circumvent prejudice, destructive role play, and overcome many barriers to communication. In not seeing each other, we may see each other more clearly. In the process, we learn we had the ability to communicate all along.

As we reflect on the results of disinhibition in cyber communication, we should go forward with the following understanding: Alterations of self in cyberspace happen by virtue of interacting with the medium. Our deliberate recasting of identity through the use of obscure IDs and other means of hiding our identities simply builds on this fact. Once again, the medium is the message. And the message is that when we enter cyberspace, we become different people whether we intend to or not, regardless of how we identify ourselves.

PERSPECTIVES ON ORGANIZATIONAL COMMUNICATION IN DIGITAL COMMUNITY

It is due in no small part to our disinhibited existence online that we require a certain amount of moral and perceptual evolution to project the consequences of our actions through the nebulous ether of the Internet. Facilitating students in this evolution should be one of our main goals as we help them cultivate the sensibilities of digital citizens. To help lay some groundwork for this, let's consider how communication space has been rearranged in the infosphere by considering the work of Joshua Meyrowitz (1985). Then we will consider the work of Edward T. Hall (1966) in order to distill some practical guidelines for understanding and practicing communication in the virtual realm.

Many years ago, I read a transformational book that has stuck with me ever since, *No Sense of Place* by Joshua Meyrowitz (1985). It is a dense book, full of many ideas that made me pause and ponder. But I will focus on two that are germane to our discussion of how electronically mediated culture changes the nature of human communication.

First, as highly dispersed citizens of a networked culture, we have lost our sense of "here." As we simultaneously crawl the web looking at pictures from Thailand on a New York travel website, while watching a TV show shot in California pretending to take place in Mexico, while contributing to an international wiki that involves students from 10 countries, while texting a parent three time zones away, where is our local center? What is our sense of place? Where do we consider our home to be? Perhaps this expanded sense of self is mostly for the better. Nonetheless, it is different. We now have personal identities that must merge several different kinds of communities that span many places, time zones, and kinds of communication. The result is that we may owe allegiance to several different communities at the same time. Sorting all this out is a core issue of digital citizenship.

Second, a mediated culture changes a number of traditional roles, causing "a very discernible rearrangement of the social stages on which we play our roles and [that causes] a resulting change in our sense of 'appropriate behavior'" (Meyrowitz, 1985, p. 4). I addressed this somewhat through earlier examples of "interlational communication." As Meyrowitz notes, boundaries that once distinguished children from adults, traditional authority figures from those lower in the hierarchical pyramid, and "onstage" from "backstage" behaviors have dissolved in our electronic ecosystem, changing the "situational geography of social life" (Meyrowitz, 1985, p. 5).

FYI

Leaky TVs

During my childhood, the world of TV was leaky, while the domain of books was utterly nonporous. I could watch TV many places, most often without adult supervision. However, book distribution was tightly controlled by publishers, libraries, and our personal gatekeepers: our parents. In high school, obtaining my first copy of Lady Chatterley's Lover, *an explicit adult love story by D. H. Lawrence (1957) that was banned in many countries until it was generally recognized as exceptional literature, was not easy. Once I finally got a copy, I had to hide it and read it quickly, so I could pass it on to whomever was next on the subterranean reader's list I had managed to join. This situation has flipped as of the web. The infosphere now provides books on demand quite easily. Books too are now leaky.*

In modern times, this happened to us first as consumers of broadcast media. Thanks to radio and TV, the social boundaries that separated us became instantly leaky because everyone had radios and televisions that received ubiquitous public broadcasting. When I was not allowed to watch television at home, I simply watched it at a friend's house. At a young age, my worldview was shaped by the white, blissful, upper-middle-class family portrayed on the TV show, *Leave It to Beaver* (Cadiff, 1957–1963). But then, that same medium introduced me to my first urban ghetto, which I discovered was only 15 miles away. The result was, as Neil Postman (1982) put it, "the disappearance of childhood."

Now we cross social boundaries as creators, not just consumers. In fact, we have become our content. The mediascape used to be dominated by programming produced by professional mediasts with big budgets and well-protected, proprietary communication channels. Now it is populated by a great deal of user-generated materials from YouTube videos, to Second Life communities, to blog material, to a plethora of twitter tweets, much of which talks about us, our lives, and our perspectives.

While we welcome the shift from the centralized broadcast communication model of one-to-many to the more inclusive social media model of many-to-many, being able to speak rather than just listen comes with a price, namely, we are responsible for what we say. It is our job to help students understand that when they post content on the web that they are rewriting the world. In fact, taking responsibility for what they say is a key point in their development of effective digital citizenship skills.

EDWARD T. HALL AND THE PROXEMICS OF VIRTUAL SPACE

To help untangle the different digital venues in which students and the rest of us interact, as well as the responsibilities associated with them, we consider Edward T. Hall's (1966) four kinds of communication space. Among his many accomplishments, Hall founded the field of *proxemics*—the anthropological study of how people interact with space. This led him to define four kinds of communication that he associated with four kinds of physical space. As we shall see, they are easily adapted to four kinds of virtual space encountered in the mediasphere. Hall's four kinds of space are

1. **Intimate**—very private communication and/or intimate interaction that is typically one-to-one or one-to-very few in nature;

2. **Personal**—private communication that occurs among just a few people or in small groups; typically participants need to be invited or granted access to participate;

3. **Social**—group communication that is open to the public; examples include a party, meeting, or other kind of gathering in which everyone can speak; and

4. **Public**—one-to-many group communication in which there is a clear separation between speaker and listeners, such as a lecture, concert, or media broadcast; typically there is no expectation of or desire for interaction on the part of the listeners.

These are not mutually exclusive, and they interact quite readily, largely because communication has such a ripple effect. What may begin as a lecture (public communication) might spawn sidebar conversations (private communication) or group conversation around the water cooler at work (semiprivate, semisocial) or an intense discussion at home (intimate communication). Despite the permutations, the four basic kinds of communication venue are helpful in describing much of the communication in our lives, particularly in cyberspace.

TRY THIS

SEEING PROXEMICS IN YOUR LIFE

Make a list of all your digital communication. Don't forget to include your spam mail, the news feeds you receive about your favorite sports team, the updates you receive from your family listserv—everything. Then identify each in terms of Hall's four levels of communication. Does it cover everything?

I was fascinated by Hall's taxonomy because the computer conferencing system I was studying in the 1990s consisted of all four of Hall's social spaces. In fact, I see them in every digital community, usually in the following ways:

1. **Intimate**—one-to-one conversations in virtual environments (e-mail, IMs), cell communication (voice, texting)

2. **Personal**—closed, invite-only digital gatherings; cced messages to a select few; closed listservs

3. **Social**—open conferences; many Nings, wikis, blogs, listservs, chat groups; public conversations in virtual environments

4. **Public**—read-only webpages, blogs, video broadcasts, public postings, one-to-many e-mail announcements; newsletters

As in RL, these social spaces are not mutually exclusive. One can post a movie on YouTube (public space) and invite viewers to comment about it using either private e-mail responses (intimate space) or by posting general reactions on the YouTube site that everyone can see and respond to (social space). Also, someone could post the link to the video on an invite-only blog (personal space), a blog that invites public discussion (social space), or a website that primarily publishes and does not seek public interaction (public space). These permutations and many others exist for wikis, blogs, Second Life, you name it, and they are largely controlled with security tools, like restricted access and passwords, as well as by our interests and time limitations.

What is truly different in digital community is how fluid and intersecting these communication domains have become. All of the possibilities I described would require no more than a few minutes of my time and no heavy lifting. Try replicating any of them in RL without digital communication. The amount of paper, video tape, stamps, and envelopes this would require—not to mention time, money, and access to a photocopying machine—would make it prohibitive.

What Hall (1966) provides us is a structure for talking about what we do in cyberspace with our students in terms of the following two aspects of communication:

1. What kind of space is your communication appropriate for? That is, who *should* see this?

2. What are the potential issues if someone steps outside of that space? That is, who *can* see this?

Addressing these questions helps us think about who we should be talking to and why. In the thumb-twitching world of text messaging, such reflection is much needed. The reality is that when we are online, we are "in the zone," absorbed into the world of digital community. We don't often stop to think about what is appropriate. We just talk, and we do so without the social cues that we are familiar with in RL that remind us of what to say, how to say it, and who is listening.

Web lore is replete with numerous accounts of people who didn't think before sending electronic communication and have suffered the consequences. In Hall's (1966) communication terms, most of them used public or social space when intimate or personal space would have been more appropriate. I read about another example today, in which someone posted a message on Facebook about her boss being a jerk (my translation of her words into something more suitable for a general reading audience), forgetting that she had made her boss part of her social network. He read it and promptly fired her. Even if she had not made him part of her network, a friend of her boss might have read it and copied and pasted it into an e-mail to him, in which case he probably also would have fired her.

I warn my students, most of whom are studying to become teachers, that hiring committees routinely scan the web looking for inappropriate behavior in digital communities that may reflect inappropriate behavior in local communities. To see some examples, simply Google "Facebook Faux Pas." Reading your cuss words or a detailed account about how drunk you were when you danced the merengue at the office party rarely plays well in public, whether in RL or VR. While hiring committee members might claim that their concern is with your activities, what also bothers them is the fact that you didn't have the good sense to keep it to yourself—you went digitally public and social when you should have gone digitally personal or, better yet, digitally intimate. That is, you were not adept at using the proxemics of digital community.

The perspective that Hall (1966) offers is really helpful only when we are dealing with "virtuous" people whose worst cybercrime is an inept use of social space. For those who have more nefarious intentions, intimate and private space can be a breeding ground for stalkers, phishers (identity thieves), and others of dubious character. This translates directly into concerns for safety for children in cyberspace. It also translates into concerns about kids who might be engaged in playful but inappropriate activity through private or anonymous communication. This issue is taken up in Part III of this book.

For adults and children alike, what vexes us is the question of who might see what we post, regardless of how careful we are about the social space we use to post it. This is due to the fact that digital technology is highly leveraged. That is, you can create great impacts by expending a very little amount of energy. This is a very sharp double-edged sword. Forwarding a memo about someone's arrest for drunk and disorderly conduct is just as easy as forwarding a memo about his award for academic achievement. This issue also vexes us because despite our best efforts, any communication can be innocently or deliberately forwarded, crossposted, or misposted. Cyberspace is so fluid that anything can show up anywhere.

GUIDELINES FOR VIRTUAL BEHAVIOR

The default is simple: In order to protect ourselves and each other, we must assume anyone can see anything. We then screen what we say as though it might be presented out of context on the nightly news by a politically unfriendly news analyst. However, the result would likely be that we would say very little or only talk trivia, ending thoughtful communication as we know it.

There is another perspective: Keep talking but use some common sense. While some filtering of Internet content makes sense for K–12, the reality is that students will be far better served if parents, teachers, and civic leaders engage them in conversations about using common sense in cyberspace than by our largely abortive attempts to prevent them from using large portions of the Internet. Coaching students about issues of safety and responsibility is the only way to help them develop what many cybersafety professionals consider the best Internet filter available: the one between their ears. Needless to say, the balance that is struck between filtering and coaching is largely determined by the age and developmental stage of the students involved.

The points below constitute some of the common sense I have gleaned during many years of facilitating education in cyberspace. They are more concerned with fostering community than some of the more hot-button issues currently in the media like sexting and cyberbullying. (See Part III of this book for a treatment of those issues.) Also, see my Digital Citizenship Resource Wiki (jasonOhler.com/dc) for web links to some guidelines for safe online behavior. What I present here are tips about managing your online neighborhood.

1. **Use the appropriate communication venue**. Be sure you are using, in Hall's (1966) terms, the appropriate social communication "distance." Do this not just to protect yourself but also to be effective in your communication. While you shouldn't use public space when private will do, there are times when you should use public space because private space limits your good ideas to an audience that is too small. Common sense will guide you.

2. **Consider "proxemic" trade-offs for students.** There are plenty of inappropriate sites that are public and social in nature. But it is the intimate and private sites that pose a potentially greater risk, simply because they are out of public view. When considering limiting private and intimate communication for this reason, be aware that the trade-off here is that students cannot develop personal relationships, which may be very healthy and academically legitimate. Be informed and reasonable in what you do.

3. **Understand the role of strangers in digital community**. We tend to teach students to equate *stranger* with *danger* in cyberspace. The reality is that networked culture would not exist without communication among strangers. I'm probably typical in that I learn far more from people in cyberspace whom I have never met and probably will never directly meet in RL, than from those I know firsthand. Therefore, rather than outlaw communication with strangers, engage students in common-sense conversations about it. Are the strangers they are talking to asking for personal information, or are they interested in their views on a school topic or current event? Do they want to know where they live—or what their favorite book is? As

---

FYI

Guidelines for Managing Your Online Neighborhood

- Use the appropriate communication venue.
- Consider "proxemic" trade-offs for students.
- Understand the roles of strangers in digital community.
- Inquire about membership.
- Inquire about disclosure.
- Post only what you would sign.
- Personally disclose only with permission.
- Practice conditional trust.
- Observe context.
- Be deliberately vague at times.
- Wait a day before sending a flame.
- Ask, "Am I reading myself?"
- Expect and use "interlational" communication.
- Ask for permission—or perspective—to join digital communities.
- Use RL metaphors to describe VR environments.
- Engage students in developing online guidelines.

always, the goal is to help students learn how to balance safety, common sense, and opportunity within digital community.

4. **Inquire about membership.** What are membership requirements for the particular digital community you want to join? Do they ring true, with ways to enforce accountability? Or does it sound like the community directors are simply covering themselves in the event of legal action? It may be time to read the disclaimer we all click past on our way to using a new piece of social media software.

5. **Inquire about disclosure.** Can you contact the director of a group list, blog, or online project? Is the participant list public information? What are the policies for disclosing names and conversations? It may be that because you are part of a middle school math listserv, you want your name to be public. But you may not. It is best to find out what your options are.

6. **Require students to post only what they would sign.** This point is easier to make when the online identity that students use reflects their actual RL identity. But students may use obscure online names or be prevented by school policy from revealing too much about themselves. Thus, it is up to us to help them understand that the same responsibility is attached to whatever they add to infosphere, regardless of how identifiable they are. If students use obscure online names in cyberspace, the questions to ask them are, "Would you sign it if the world knew who you were? If not, why not? And if not, should you post it?" Bottom line: Our students need to attach a sense of personal responsibility to everything they do, in local, global, and digital community. This means sending some things and not sending others. However, it does not mean students should disengage from constructive public discourse just because others might disagree with them. Debate about important topics is to be encouraged.

> ### FYI
>
> ### In an Age of Info Overload, Reputation Is Everything
>
> Daniel Solove's (2007) book, <u>The Future of Reputation</u>, is instructive in this regard. He begins by recounting a story by journalist Don Park about the "dog poop lady." When a young woman refused to clean up her dog's poop when he relieved himself on a South Korea subway, passengers took her picture, pitched it to the rumor mill of the web, and the story instantly went viral, making the rounds of blogs, chat rooms, and other Internet media outlets. She was so globally shamed that she dropped out of the university she was attending.

7. **Personally disclose only with permission.** A companion issue with the one above is the issue of how much to disclose, to whom, and for what reasons. Again, common sense will guide you. There

may be perfectly legitimate reasons for students to identify themselves within the context of academic pursuits. But it isn't a bad idea to require students to always check in with teachers and other adults in charge about what is safe and responsible in terms of personal disclosure. Some districts allow first names but no last names. Some allow pictures while others expressively forbid it. Know your school's policy, and feel free to challenge it if it seems too restrictive or permissive. Disclose judiciously, but be open to doing so when it makes sense to do so. When in doubt, seek a second opinion.

8. **Practice conditional trust**. Once in a digital community, trust but verify. Does anything seem funny in an odd way? Do you find what you are saying elsewhere on the net? Do responses "make sense" and observe the kinds of behavior you expected? Check in with others in the same community to see what they are experiencing.

9. **Observe context.** Nothing on the web appears by itself. If your students are posting to a video service, then typically their video link will be surrounded by links to advertisements, related services, and other videos. Do these provide an appropriate context for your students' work? We are judged by the company we keep.

10. **Be deliberately vague at times**. Saying, "It was difficult to engage in last week's conversation because it was dominated by a few speakers" is very different than saying, "Don't Bob and Jenny ever shut up?!" Think twice if not three times before identifying specific individuals, events, or organizations. Communication in the digital world is like toothpaste—once out of the tube there is no putting it back.

11. **Wait a day before sending a flame**. This follows from the point above. Flaming used to be what the online community called a tirade by e-mail, that is, beating someone up verbally with text. I sent out one flame in my life—just one. It was many years ago, and I have regretted it ever since. I have prepared flames since that time, but always waited a day before sending them. The result: My better judgment always prevailed, and I didn't send any of them. In digital community, we can use time to compensate for the lack of space. That is, we can regain some of the perspective we lose in not having spatial cues in VR by waiting in RL. Blustering is rarely our true goal in these situations. Being informative is. No one can hear you when you are yelling at them.

12. **Ask, "Am I reading myself?"** This also follows directly from the point above. Recall the earlier discussion about this topic in regards to a lack of metainformation. The point here is that when we react overtly to someone in VR, we need to ask ourselves whether our reaction to a communication is warranted by the

information contained in the message or whether it is more a projection of ourselves into the communication in order to compensate for a lack of meta-information. Are we reading the sender or ourselves?

13. **Expect and use "interlational" communication.** We need to remember that interlational communication in virtual space helps us cross social boundaries in positive ways. Be aware of the power of interlational communication, and use it reflectively and deliberately.

14. **Require students to ask permission—or perspective—before joining digital communities**. Permission for students can come from parents or teachers in charge. Older students may bristle at needing permission to join an online community because they feel they are mature enough to make the decision on their own. However, I have found that they will more readily accept your perspective about what to consider before joining. The goal, as always, is to have a conversation that helps them make their own decision, informed by some aspects of digital community they might not readily see.

15. **Use RL metaphors to describe VR environments.** When creating an online venue for students, use a metaphor drawn from RL to describe it. Doing so allows you to import familiar behavioral expectations into a VR situation. Calling your online environment a zoo or a seminar room invokes two very different kinds of behavioral expectations. More on this in the next section about online learning communities.

16. **Engage students in developing online guidelines.** There are many benefits to this. First, it compels students to speak aloud a number of the concerns about the online world that they may be keeping to themselves, perhaps because they don't want to appear uncool among peers or divulge too much about their subterranean cyberculture to those outside the culture, primarily adults. Second, the reality is that they have the most informed idea about what they are experiencing. Adults have a great deal to learn from them in this regard. Third, a public discussion about this issue involving adults and that seeks to balance safety, responsibility, opportunity, and respect allows students to think differently about the topic by placing it in a reflective context. That is, just as we can benefit by listening to them, they can benefit by listening to us. We have more interpersonal experience and the potential to have a more objective viewpoint because we are from outside their culture. And last, like adults, they will think very differently about breaking rules they have developed versus rules that have been imposed by others. Making them part of the power structure can be very beneficial in this regard.

GUIDELINES FOR CREATING ONLINE LEARNING COMMUNITIES

Thanks to online learning, education is now a buyer's rather than a seller's market.

This is a dramatic shift that has happened relatively recently due to the Internet and the evolution of networked tools. In order to appreciate the significance of this shift, imagine that you were allowed to shop only at the department store nearest you. Because Wal-Mart was only two miles away, you were not allowed to go to Kmart, which was three miles away in the opposite direction, even though Kmart was stocking exactly the designer jeans you have been looking for. It's a crazy idea, yet this is how we have approached sending students to school for decades. Attendance has always been geographically based, and we felt lucky to live close enough to school to attend. Education was a seller's market.

Not anymore. This is due in part to more flexible options in public schooling, including charter schools and more parent choice about which schools their kids can attend. But it is also due to the fact that online learning opportunities have reached into every nook and cranny of the educational experience. Education at all levels has competition from the online sector.

> ## FYI
>
> ### Online Education in K–12 Is Booming
>
> According to a 2008 Sloan-C report, 66% of school districts responding to a survey who had students enrolled in online or "blended courses" (combining onsite and online education) anticipated their online enrollments will grow. The overall number of K–12 students engaged in online courses in 2007 to 2008 was estimated at 1,030,000. This represents a 47% increase compared to 2005 to 2006 (Picciano, 2009).

When I started teaching online using e-mail and listservs, circa the early 1980s, the idea of online learning was brand-new. There were no how-to manuals to tell us how to proceed and there was no Internet to help online teachers share their ideas. All that I had was common sense, the ability to persist through a great deal of trial and error, and the willingness to be adaptable and creative as the tools evolved and opened new methods of communication. It didn't hurt that I found virtual teaching fascinating, incredibly fun, and that I considered my involvement in it to be my contribution to making the world a more equitable place.

Things have changed dramatically since then. Google the phrase *teaching online* today, and stand back—you will be hit by a spray of information that has the force of many fire hoses. In 25 years, we have gone from information underload to overload on topics like these. Now the problem is sorting through the plethora of tips, tricks, approaches, activities, resources, class structures, media-blending formula . . . and on and on.

I continue to teach online today, and do my best to take advantage of the cornucopia the web has to offer in terms of resources and social media. Yet despite the growth in tools and opportunities, I find that the ancient human is alive and well. That is, there is still one guideline above all that remains constant for me: Use online tools to create online community.

Students' greatest pleasure is interacting with each other, and their greatest asset is their collective intelligence. This perspective was reinforced in 2003 when Dr. Lynne Schrum and I conducted a comprehensive study of attitudes toward distance education at my university. We found, among other things, that the primary complaint on the part of students was the lack of interaction with other students. They wanted the experience of community, but they were basically treated as individual students who were separately tethered to the instructor, largely because most teachers used broadcast technology rather than social media for class delivery. The result was a dissatisfying social experience.

If students are taking a class that is delivered primarily online—versus a blended onsite class that uses online communication to extend or expand class—then their class is essentially their community, and their classmates constitute the members of that community. Treating their experience as such helps compensate for the lack of onsite interaction. It also introduces many opportunities for communication that might not be present in an onsite learning situation, many of which were described in previous discussions in this book. What I present here are some guidelines for teaching online based on those discussions, as well as nearly 30 years of experience as a virtual teacher.

FYI

Guidelines for Managing Your Online Learning Environment

1. Treat every online learning community as a special situation.

2. Use as many of Hall's (1966) communication venues as possible.

3. Teach the unfamiliar in terms of the familiar: Use metaphors.

4. Use many social setting metaphors.

5. Use multimodality when developing online communities.

6. Blend media to personalize space.

7. Require collaboration when appropriate.

8. Tell stories.

---

1. **Treat every online learning community as a special situation.** There is no "one size fits all" approach to addressing the needs of each online learning situation. Each class is its own unique

subculture with its own character and requirements. It is up to each online teacher to use an anthropological perspective in order to determine the unique needs, limitations, and expectations of each learning group. Sure, posting lessons on Moodle or Blackboard and asking students to engage in weekly conversation works as a fall-back. But your class will come alive when you know more about your students, including their level of Internet access, how your class fits into their overall learning objectives, what kind of previous experience they have had learning online, what interests them in the class topic area, what social media they use and online communities they are a part of, and so on. In retrospect, I am amazed at the many different approaches I have used over the years to teach similar material, all because the needs of each learning community were so different.

2. **Use as many of Hall's (1966) communication venues as possible.** This idea is further explored in points below, but I wanted to state it clearly and unequivocally. Students benefit from a multimodal approach—in terms of media and communication space. The more kinds of Hall's communication you use, the more it feels like a real community.

3. **Teach the unfamiliar in terms of the familiar: Use metaphors.** You can tell kids to be respectful, but don't forget that their grandparents told them the same thing when they took them to church. I'm not sure how much it meant to them. Transferring respect from one situation to another is a fairly abstract concept that requires lots of modeling and practice. If we want kids to practice respect in virtual classrooms, we need different strategies. Recall the earlier discussion about how the lack of familiar social cues in cyberspace can confuse virtual behavior. This becomes particularly important in educational settings, where behavioral norms are especially important. Not only do you want behavior to be respectful, but you also want it to be productive. What makes social orientation difficult is that when we enter digital communities, we enter a mental space I call "mind void." We really don't know where we are, and because of that, we tend to go forward as explorers in a new land in which local customs don't seem to exist.

An effective way to address this proactively is to use RL metaphors to describe VR situations. That is, describe the blog, wiki, conference, or virtual reality space you have set up for your class in RL terms. The result is that you can then call on familiar social perspectives, customs, and behaviors that are associated with that space in RL.

Perhaps your online environment is best described as a discussion occurring in a quiet seminar room with a lake view, a newsletter production activity occurring in your classroom after school, group research being conducted in a museum, individual portfolio development occurring in the privacy of each student's room . . . whatever it is. Be sure to mention both place and activity in order to fill in as many mind void blanks as possible and thus imply as many kinds of behavior as possible.

4. **Use many social setting metaphors.** This provides practical considerations for using as many of Hall's (1966) communication venues as possible. Consider the communication that transpires in an average day at school. Some of it happens in classrooms, but much of it happens in hallways, after school, in between classes, via twitters, texting, or good old-fashioned gabbing. In addition, students work in small groups, confer privately with teachers for help, and maybe talk to resource teachers alone or in groups. The fact is that when we characterize education as something that occurs just in the classroom, we miss a good deal of what actually happens at school. Beyond the obvious virtual presence for your online class—like maintaining websites and discussion groups—here are a few other suggestions:

   o **Set up "hallway" venues**. I used to set up conferences for my student teachers to which I did not have access. I would then encourage them to use it to talk about me, the class, life in general . . . whatever they wanted. I called it a "hallway conference" because it reminded me of the way students confer in the hallways, informally and out of the watchful eye of authority figures. It is a good example of Hall's (1966) private form of communication in that it was a closed conference, open only to certain people. As always, make sure that activities like these conform with school policy.

   o **Hold virtual office hours**. I also set up virtual office hours, which is easy to do these days with Skype, virtual environments, and even simple texting. In Hall's (1966) terms, I used an intimate communication venue so that students could talk just to the instructor. In addition to scheduled office hours, I held rolling office hours via e-mail. Wikis and blogs are ideal to use as social space for ongoing class "maintenance" discussions about where to find resources, resolve technical issues, and so on.

○ **Use small groups and whole groups**. Divide the class into small groups to tackle particular issues, which they then report back on to the whole class. This is easy to do with a number of social media and blends private and social space nicely.

5. **Use multimodality when developing online communities.** There is a general sense among educators that learning will appeal to more students if we offer them multiple pathways to the same information. Therefore, in much the same way that you want to use as many of Hall's (1966) communication venues as possible, you want to use as many kinds of media as possible. Some kids are more visual learners, others more acoustic, others more textual, and so on. But just as important, the more senses you appeal to, the more your online community begins to look like real-world community. The value in a multimodal approach to education is that it reflects RL, which is inherently multimodal as well.

6. **Blend media to personalize space**. A specific application of the above point is using blended media to personalize and extend personal space. We alleviate mind void by using artifacts from RL. Beyond metaphors that remind us of places and things in physical space, we can use images, audio introductions, video, and other kinds of media that tell about who we are. As always, caution needs to be observed with regard to school policies about posting personal information.

I find that any kind of RL contact, whether live meetings at the beginning of a class, or live conferencing during the course, helps to fill in the blanks caused by mind void. I also find that using common metareference points, like resources or news reports, helps create a sense of shared awareness of the world and thus a sense of community. If you work at a site-based school that also serves online students, then find ways to include online students in some of the activities of your school. One idea from my experience as a virtual teacher at the University of Alaska: We recorded visiting lecturers and concerts and made those available via the Internet. Opportunities like this are abundant.

7. **Require collaboration when appropriate**. In real terms, collaboration translates into a community of interdependence, which can be an effective way to keep students involved with each other. However, beware: Sometimes students don't want to be interdependent. After all, when you take a class as an individual student,

the only challenge to your success is yourself. But if you work in an interdependent environment, you sacrifice your independence for a more complete experience of community. It's a trade-off. Earlier, I reported that Dr. Schrum's and my research discovered that distance students' primary concern with their experience was the lack of interaction with other students. Note that they did not say they wanted to work with them, just interact with them.

There are many ways to encourage interdependence, including delegating roles and responsibilities and using collaborative pedagogy, including peer review, cooperative learning, jigsawing, joint projects and research, and study and presentation groups. If you are reluctant to manage group projects virtually, you can certainly encourage nonbinding kinds of interaction, such as peer review or informal communication about class assignments. You want students to keep talking, even if they aren't collaborating. It all helps develop a sense of community.

8. **Tell stories.** Learning communities are storytelling communities. Groups of students who learn together often want to share what they learn and how they learn in many forms, including tips and tricks, anecdotes, research findings, and detailed accounts we might call stories. We want to encourage the use of stories because they are very effective information containers and transmitters. Stories compel tellers to synthesize information that is important to them. In the process, they make what they know more understandable to others.

All of my student teachers, many of whom I teach completely at a distance, create two pieces of media for my classes: a video story about their educational philosophy and a digital story that crystallizes some concept in their professional content area. The fact is that we forget lectures, but we remember stories. And having students tell each other their stories is an effective way for the tellers to truly synthesize what they have learned and share it with their colleagues.

SOME CLOSING NOTES ON REORGANIZING OURSELVES

Even in the very early days of social media, the technology changed how we talked, what we could say, and how we could organize, providing a classic case of the medium being not only the message but also *"the massage"*

(McLuhan, 1967). Those early days stood in stark contrast to the world of broadcast communication media that directly preceded it in which few talked and most listened, and audience members had a very difficult time organizing.

The social mediascape that we take for granted today adds immensely to this shift from broadcast to community-based communication. Twitter, blogging, and so on have pitched us into a period of creative chaos, in which individuals have usurped power once reserved only for formal organizations (Shirky, 2008). Individuals can now launch a cause, facilitate a public conversation, or create a community without hiring a single person, creating a board of directors, or investing in technology beyond their laptop and a wifi connection. These individuals don't need organizational affiliation to set up virtual shop, nor do they need an FCC license to use a $300 camera and their home Internet connection to create a television channel.

The result is that adhocracies threaten hierarchies. As it appears on Wikipedia, Waterman defined adhocracy as "any form of organization that cuts across normal bureaucratic lines to capture opportunities, solve problems, and get results" (adhocracy, 2010, para. 3). This serves as a very apt description of human activity on the web in general.

A significant difference between hierarchies and adhocracies is that adhocracies value community members on the basis of their actual contribution rather than their ability to follow traditional lines of command. The focus in adhocracies shifts from supporting the organization and maintaining its viability to successfully completing whatever project is at hand. There are many benefits to workers in this situation. No one needs to show up at work at a single location to serve a single organization. We can parse our time as we see fit, divvying it up among many companies, projects, personal pursuits, or social efforts, without needing to leave home or clock in with one particular authority. And bonus: We can basically wear whatever we want.

As social communication media become pervasive and invisible to us, there is yet another result that is quite vexing, namely, that anyone can organize for any reason, including reasons that worry and threaten us. This didn't use to be the case. Organizations used to go through a social vetting process. Public involvement and attention, not to mention hiring people and developing mission statements, made them a very visible, tractable public event. Not so anymore. As Shirky (2008) explains, we now understand that networking is neutral, at least in the sense that those with access to it can use it for whatever they want, from showing how to be mean to how to make meaning. Thus, terrorists, cat haters, and those who support the sports teams you despise can organize as easily as businesses, school districts, and your favorite charities.

While society has grudgingly adjusted to this breadth of freedom for adults, they have not done so for minors or K–12 education. For children, the buck stops with whatever adult is in charge, not with the child. The bottom line for educators is that teaching digital citizenship to our children needs to include addressing why we organize as well as when organizing is in the public interest, and when it is not. While the idea of children organizing in cyberspace might be a scary thought, it will happen with or without our blessing. Therefore, the essential question that should drive us here is simply: How do we help students develop a sense of perspective about how to use online space? Once again, we are forced to consider among problematic options as we revisit the question proposed in the Preamble of this book: When it comes to teaching our students, do we consider them to have two lives or one?

Part II

Seeing Technology

4 What Bothers Us About Technology

FEAR IS THE MIND KILLER

Someone once told me he felt like we were all just props in technology's movie. Every now and again, technology allows us to make cameo appearances in a patronizing attempt to keep us around. After all, for the foreseeable future the machines still need us to give them life. However, to paraphrase *Macbeth*, after we strut and fret our lives

upon the stage for a moment or two (Shakespeare, 1606/1975a, p. 1068), we recede into the background, as the great digital machine churns away.

These are feelings, not facts. But they are real feelings based on at least some real facts, and they are the subject of this chapter.

There is plenty to be excited about with regard to technological advancement. In fact, I have spent a lifetime trying to play to technology's strengths and avoid its weaknesses by helping educators integrate technology effectively, creatively, and wisely into teaching and learning. But the fact is that whenever I engage groups in discussions about digital citizenship, sooner or later I begin hearing about what scares them about technology. Sometimes, I hear overt annunciations of fear, such as teachers afraid they will become obsolete to their students, or average consumers afraid to use credit cards because they are worried that their identities will be stolen so convincingly that they will lose their reputations forever. But most of the time, what I discern is a continuous, low-level infection of the spirit that keeps us constantly yet subtly apprehensive. The result is that we are just uncomfortable enough that we can't confidently chart a course using technology, especially when it involves providing a leadership role for our children.

And lest we think that techno angst applies only to the current generation of digital immigrants, we are reminded by the quotations in the FYI box that fear about new technology is universal. It may be true that our kids are currently so immersed in digital technology that they are tacitly, if not blindly, accepting of it. However, we can rest assured that they will have their day to be adults and parents and worry about what their kids are doing with technology that will be so powerful that it defies current imagination. They too will find reasons to be uneasy and perhaps afraid.

We should not be surprised that a highly technological society is bothersome to many. After all, modern citizenship evolved from the need for the general populace to obtain some level of control over its destiny, a right it had been denied until very recently in historical terms by other human beings. Thus, the subtext of the fears that "ancient humans" feel about technology surfaces as something like this: "After all our struggle to achieve a sense of control over our own lives, why would we want to be citizens in a land that technology has made too complex to

---

FYI

Techno Angst is Forever

"Students today can't prepare bark to calculate their problems. They depend upon their slates, which are more expensive. What will they do when their slate is dropped and it breaks? They will be unable to write!" (Teachers conference, 1703)

"Students today depend upon paper too much. They don't know how to write on slate without chalk dust all over themselves. They can't clean a slate properly. What will they do when they run out of paper?" (Principal's Association, 1815)

"Students today depend upon these expensive fountain pens. They can no longer write with a straight pen and nib, not to mention sharpening their own quills. We parents must not allow them to wallow in such luxury to the detriment of learning how to cope in the real business world, which is not so extravagant." (PTA Gazette, 1941)

"Ball point pens will be the ruin of education in our country. Students use these devices and then throw them away. The American virtues of thrift and frugality are being discarded. Business and banks will never allow such expensive luxuries." (Federal Teacher, 1950)

"Students depend too much on hand-held calculators." (Anonymous, 1985)

All quotes from the collection of Fr. Stanley Bezuska, as cited in Thornburg (1992, pp. 58–59).

understand, that we feel we have no control over, and that scares us to death?" It is understandable if our digital lifestyle feels like a step backwards.

FACING OUR FEARS

Don't worry. I am not going to suggest you sit on a pillow in an empty, dark room, light a candle, and get in touch with your feelings. But I am going to ask you to consider the specter of technology as many experience it. Doing so will help you understand the fears of others in your educational community.

Developing this understanding is particularly important because much of what has prevented positive forward movement in educational technology has been based on fear and anxiety rather than clear concerns born out of deliberate, reflective consideration. When we identify what bothers us, it loses its power to completely control us. So let's identify what bothers us about technology. In the chapters that follow, we will then look at ways to see the technology in our midst with fresh vision so that we can plan for technological change constructively.

What bothers us about technology? A number of things, which I group into the following areas that I have synthesized from my many conversations over the years with parents, educators, students, and concerned citizens: ubiquity, invasiveness, vulnerability, amplification, reduction, misreality, ephemeralness, permanence, indisconnectability, overwhelment, vulnerability, sovereignty, dehumanization, and obsolescence—complex-sounding words that represent some fairly rudimentary feelings.

Although these areas of concern are interconnected and hardly mutually exclusive, each approaches the unease we feel about technology from a different vantage point. Interestingly, each carries with it an opposing "accompanying delight," as it were. Thus, our fears are accompanied by a counterweight that provides at least some ambiguity, thereby mixing perceived benefits with vague anxiety. In the pages that follow, at least one delight is identified for each area of concern.

UBIQUITY

Before I earned a PhD, I would have described technology as being "everywhere" instead of "ubiquitous." Sorry about that. Occupational hazard. But they mean roughly the same thing.

I begin with ubiquity because most of our fears about technology flow from the fact that we couldn't escape our tEcosystem—that is, our technological ecosystem—even if we wanted to. If we truly desired to live off the grid, we would probably get there in a motorized vehicle using four-wheel drive and Global Positioning System (GPS) technology. Once there, we would begin digging in the dirt with hand tools that were crafted by precision machines that are run by computers. At night, we would curl up in our sleeping bags filled with a synthetic fiber created by the petrochemical industry. And as we dozed off, we would look up at the stars, only to see a few satellites and airplanes pass overhead now and again. Technology now massages us so completely that the human-machine symbiosis has become more of a continuum than a partnership, making it difficult to perceive where we leave off and our technical extensions begin.

There are specific elements of ubiquity worth noting. First, unlike the natural ecosystem that has evolved through random processes, the tEcosystem is there by our design. This is particularly important because technology carries with it biases, some obvious, some subliminal, some we are aware of, and some we are not. Biases ultimately give voice to perspective, ethos, worldview, and, ultimately, citizenship. More about technology's inherent bias in Chapter 6, Becoming a "De-Tech-Tive."

Second, ubiquity has changed our relationship with time and space completely. When something is everywhere all the time, it tends to obliterate time and space, or at the very least commodify them and make them so portable they seem irrelevant. Think hotel chains, network television, and boxed cereal in supermarkets, and you get the idea. No matter where we go, from Los Angeles to London, there they are, creating a technological infrastructure that envelops us in a continuous, familiar stream of experience. The net result is that time and space seem somehow less relevant than they used to. I still cherish going to another culture and eating food I haven't tasted elsewhere or enjoying a unique experience that is particularly local. When I savor those experiences, I am savoring a palpable sense of time and space that is otherwise lost to me within my normal technological support system.

FYI

Technology: The Ultimate Time and Space Machine

The obsolescing of time and space is not strictly a digital-era phenomenon. Consider a pre-iPod activity, like drinking water from a ceramic cup, circa 3,000 BCE. Compared with sticking our hands into a stream, using a cup substantially changed how we moved in the time-space continuum. Because we could fill a cup with water, carry it wherever we wanted, and leave it there, we turned an ephemeral activity into part of the permanent, ubiquitous infrastructure. And because many people began using ceramic cups, we could begin to gather in communities, the ultimate conquest of time and space.

Third, technology's ubiquity is due in large part to the fact that the tEcosystem is so interconnected that pulling on one thread of the technology tapestry causes everything to unravel, often rather quickly. One line of botched code, one malfunctioning relay node as an e-mail message makes its way from sender to receiver, one downloaded virus-riddled e-mail attachment—and the tEcosystem begins to fail. But the myriad of diverse, specialized parts that are fused together into an intricate pattern of interdependency virtually assures the system's perpetuity. Whenever something important to us fails, we build a more robust version. In the long run, the cat and mouse game that hackers and demanding consumers play with service providers and digital developers only makes the system stronger and more ubiquitous.

Accompanying delight: Technology is nowhere, so I don't have to deal with it. That is, it is invisible, yet I can continue to count on it. Perfect, because I don't really care about how my refrigerator works; all I want is cold food. Woe to me, however, should there be a power outage . . .

INVASIVENESS

The individual bits that make up the ubiquitous tEcosystem often go undetected until they are suddenly upon us, like sci-fi invaders suddenly stripped of a cloaking device. They show up in our lives one day as an invitation to twitter, a cell phone that doubles as a movie camera, a synthetic life form whose parents are a computer (Venter, 2010). It is as though the tEcosystem is run by a vast, invisible subculture that we can neither join nor overtly influence. Its mission is to keep invading our lives by reinventing the future through technological advancement and to make the next generation of must-have things—whether we asked for them or not. Modern citizens, who cherish the right to participate in important decisions that impact the community, recoil at this. Why weren't we consulted? Where is the militia to counter the invasion?

Accompanying delight: Technology can be such a welcomed intrusion. Technology brings us surprises we have come to love, like junk mail that tells us just in time about airfare specials to Hawaii or gadgets that segue effortlessly into our approach to digital problem solving by, for example, allowing us to post all of our vacation pictures on one website, so we don't have to send them to each of our friends individually. Every time we exercise the choice to buy whatever invades our lives, we *are* consulted. And we keep saying, "Thank you." But I do wish those telemarketers would stop calling me . . .

VULNERABILITY

Invasiveness comes in other forms, such as surveillance and personal information collection. They produce a new kind of vulnerability based on reversed abandonment—we are never alone, nor can we be.

Built into RL are physical probes, cameras, and sensors that watch us and collect information about us. Whenever we enter a store, there is a good chance we are being recorded. And we are tracked in the tEcosystem as well. Every time we fill out a form, perform a search, join a social website, or engage in the dozens of other ways we routinely identify ourselves to total strangers in the infospere, we help populate someone else's database. We often have no idea where our information is or whom to contact about it, and we have very little control over what happens to it or how it is used.

Even Google admits that it tracks our searches and other user information, but it also promises that it "anonymizes" it by removing our names. However, it does not delete the relationship between the content of our searches and our IP addresses, which identify where we connect to the web and thus, in most cases, who we are. The result is that Google has plenty of information to identify users and their interests. AOL demonstrated how this works in 2006 by releasing the results of over 600,000 searches in "anonymized" form, which led easily to the identification—and the profound embarrassment—of a number of its subscribers. This was a surprise to AOL, who truly thought that anonymization would protect its subscribers (Kantor, 2006).

Remember, whether or not the government can spy on people may be up for debate, but third parties have pretty much free rein in this area. We are left to trust that information companies will "not be evil," as Google promises via its motto, and that they will never allow the government, the health care industry or commercial interests, as well as whatever enemies we may have, to lessen their commitment to honor the trust we have placed in them.

But even if Big Brother could become a benevolent uncle, doing only good and only when we wanted him to, we would still be bothered by the fact that he exists. Citizens in a democratic society like to be informed and in control. They don't like to be watched without permission, and they don't like feeling vulnerable in their own communities. It reminds them too much of life before true citizenship arrived.

Accompanying delight: Technology watches over me. Thanks, globally interconnected network of information, for knowing that my airbag was activated and where my accident occurred. And thanks for telling the paramedics ahead of time about my blood type and the fact that I am allergic to penicillin—you may have saved my life. Most important, thanks for tracking and catching the bad guys of the world. I realize that in order to watch them, you need to watch me now and again. But given I am not a bad guy, could you turn the camera off?

AMPLIFICATION

Technology would not be so problematic if it were merely ubiquitous and invasive. It is the fact that technology so significantly amplifies human action that gives it teeth. After all, what happens when you give glasses to the visually challenged? The same thing that happens when you give bigger amplifiers to bad guitar players. They become superhuman in some small way, for better or worse. I see the amplification effect at work all the time when I conduct workshops in new media narrative, aka digital storytelling. Those projects without a compelling story to tell are made worse when amplified through the megaphone of technology. Those with solid story material have the potential to become amazing.

McLuhan's (1964) flagship book about technology, *Understanding Media,* is subtitled *The Extensions of Man.* Our tools and our media have always extended and amplified us. An ancient example is the lever. It survives today in many forms, including a tire jack, which allows the average person to lift a car off the ground, extending raw muscular power through engineering insight.

Today, our levers are largely mechanical and electronic. A car extends our eyes at night through headlights, our ears through radio, our back by allowing us to carry much more than we could on our own. Digital technology amplifies us even further. An intercontinental cell phone call, music software that easily translates what you hear in your head into what others can hear aloud, a Twitter posting chronicling the revolution in Iran—each of these amplifies human activity in a way that was inconceivable not long ago. Every generation's scientific fiction becomes the next generation's reality.

Perhaps the most enduring example of a technology amplifier is "the button." During the Cold War era, "the button" was widely understood to refer to the ability of both the United States and the Soviet Union to unleash nuclear warfare with the push of a button. Much like the tire jack in principle, the button used a little bit of human power to create a large effect. Their difference is largely one of scale. The tire jack represents a modest amount of engineering and produces a modest effect, relatively speaking. In contrast, the button is the tip of a great technological iceberg below which is a massive amount of engineering that can produce a holocaust.

Much of the nostalgia that permeates the social critique of technology focuses on the halcyon days of simple tools when life moved along at a leisurely pace and amplification was not the threat that it is today. Tools used to be rather subtle in nature, and their effects were confined to a rather limited sphere of influence.

In contrast, today's machines leverage human action in godlike proportions. Pushing a button, posting a video, or making a phone call can result in an awesome display of the power of the few over the many, both near and far away. We have, to paraphrase *Star Trek*'s Captain James T. Kirk, the power of the gods without the wisdom. The fallacy in this reasoning of course is that history has seen very few wise gods.

Amplification concerns citizens because communities need to use power wisely, in a distributed, publicly accountable fashion, or they risk regressing to earlier times, when the few tyrannized the many. The result is that the art of citizenship often involves balancing the rights of individuals with our collective notion of the common good. Often, the essential question that citizens have to answer is this: At what point are the potential risks so great to the community that citizens are willing to forgo their individual liberties to ensure the safety and integrity of the community?

Accompanying delight: Technology makes me godlike! Too much fun. Thank you, technological infrastructure, for my eyeglasses, wheelchair, car, microwave oven, as well as for guns, airplanes, elevators, computers, and cell phones. And thank you for life-extending medicines and surgical procedures as well as pills that restore my hair and virility. But to be honest, I am a little worried. I know I can handle being amplified, but I'm not sure about other people . . .

REDUCTION

Reduction turns amplification on its head. While levers amplify us, they also tire us out. While cars amplify us by allowing us to go faster, they also reduce our ability to appreciate the here and now, given that we are whizzing by both en route to somewhere else. While the button amplifies us, it also reduces us to being a miniature cog in a decision-making machine. As such, we are required to provide yes-no answers that are out of place in a highly complex world that is full of shades of maybe (more about amplification and reduction in the next chapter).

Accompanying delight: Less is more. Reduction often translates into slowing down, humbling ourselves, and moving away from the general flow of madness, so we can spend more time with ourselves and families, smelling the roses and enjoying life. After all, this is something we have been meaning to do for years anyway . . . right?

MISREALITY

A specific form of ubiquity is the misreality that swarms around us. It consists of the great body of information that we ingest daily that is slanted, false, or so subtly transformed that we don't think to question it. But even when our suspicions are aroused by things we see, there is no time to follow up on them. Thus, we live in a constant state of slight apprehension, wanting to trust, yet wondering whether what we are seeing is at all true or real. In the case of deliberate forgery, we are left to wonder what purpose led the forgers to lie to us in the first place.

Here is a simple example of misreality made all the more poignant by the fact that I, with no discernible art skills, managed to create it very easily. If you connect to jasonOhler.com/deception, you will see a picture of me with both hands at my sides, smiling brightly into the camera. Next to it is the original picture, in which I am also smiling brightly, but have one hand jammed into my pocket, looking unprofessional, and not at all web-ready. The process I used in order to go from sloppy to preppy involved about a half-hour's work using a simple digital retouching program. I copied my good arm, inverted it, superimposed it on my "bad arm," did a bit of digital doctoring, and voila! There I am, representing a moment in time that never existed. While I was at it, I took care of a few areas on my rock-washed jeans that looked like wet spots. After all, there's no sense in needlessly embarrassing myself in the infosphere.

I often show these photos to my students and ask them if they think what I did was wrong. They invariably say no. Then I ask, "Does what I did bother you?" They invariably say yes. It is a unique kind of neurosis in which we are bothered by something that isn't wrong.

Behind the unease created by misreality is the uncomfortable feeling that something has slipped in underneath our radar and penetrated our personal space undetected. We don't like it because we weren't consulted beforehand. Nor were we informed afterward. Citizens want to make informed decisions about their communities. And they can't do that if they don't know what is really going on.

Accompanying delight: Metareality brings us a greater truth. And yet misreality breeds a kind of hyper-reality or metatruth about the way things really are. E-mail and avatars can sometimes encourage honesty in communication that eludes us in face-to-face conversation. Similarly, the picture I massaged is actually more representative of my sensibilities about self-presentation than the original. After all, had I known the photograph would show up on the web, I would have posed differently. The result is that we are left to wonder whether our RL selves are actually the masks we use to hide our true identities, which emerge only when we can edit who we are. Besides, you edit your pictures on the web—don't you?

EPHEMERALNESS

Misreality wouldn't stand a chance if we had time to investigate it. But the next aspect of technology that bothers us makes that impossible: ephemeralness. This is akin to brevity and transience, but neither really captures the sense of living in a period of exponential change in which things don't just move along, they disappear entirely to make room for whatever is replacing them. Tools, information, and media change so quickly that innovation has the feeling of a drive-by, inducing a fear of imminent obsolescence in many of us.

Modern citizens are just now adjusting to the speed of change. After all, in retrospect, history seems to have been kind. We were allowed a few millennia of relative downtime between the agricultural and industrial revolutions and then a few centuries' respite before the Information Age urged us into overdrive. Now the changes come so quickly that we live in a constant transition zone in which change never slows enough to coalesce into anything as solid as an age. Our invention comes with an ever-decreasing half-life. One of the most difficult challenges Digital Age citizens face in a world gone ephemeral is trying to maintain a solid core of values while remaining open to change. Typically, citizens want their communities to last. But in order to do that in this day and age, they need to cultivate a new personal relationship with change in which they need to be solid but supple, lasting but lithe, fixed but unformed, immutable but innovative, eternal but elastic. Today's goal is to try to be at peace in the eye of the change hurricane and, on a good day, even enjoy the ride.

Accompanying delight: Change fixes all things. We can't wait for the next version of software. It always works so much better. So the sooner it gets here, the better! But could you take a week off sometime?

PERMANENCE

The ephemeral nature of things has given permanence a kind of retro nostalgia value. The genuinely old have a palpable understanding of this. Those who are too young to have experienced the slow rate of change nonetheless have memories provided by the media that recall simpler, slower times.

However, there is one kind of permanence that most digital citizens fear: permanent overexposure from having their words and actions committed to digital community's eternal memory. Earlier, I mentioned AOL's release of personal search information. Now add to this the efforts of each of us, with movie cameras and trigger-happy copy-and-paste fingers, who delight in posting what we want, wherever we want. Whether we do it for fun or spite, or out of a genuine sense of duty to inform others, once we post something on the web it is toothpaste out of the tube. Worse, everyone can copy the spilt toothpaste and repost it, making any desire you have to clean it up potentially irrelevant. The reality is that whether the memories that others create about us are true or representative simply won't matter. Any defense we may offer will be so much less entertaining than the original story that it will get lost in the noise. In community, character matters. Citizens are judged by what they do. As I am writing this, I am trying to remember what it was that Tiger Woods did for a living, amidst the media hoopla about his dalliances. Ah yes, it was golf.

Accompanying delight: I'm immortal because the infosphere will never forget who I am! Thanks, citizen journalists, for copying, pasting, and reposting all of the good stuff about me. Now I know my grandkids may learn all about me. But could you leave out the stuff I did in Vegas?

INDISCONNECTABILITY

At the intersection of transience and permanence is the fact that we are largely unable to unplug from the unlimited number of communication channels that scream for our involvement. A neologism to describe this might be *indisconnectability*—which may simply be another name for loneliness.

We experience this in two respects. First, we are perpetual consumers of the content created by others. Content comes in many forms but can roughly be divided into what is produced by professional mediasts (TV programs, movies, made for web production, etc.) and the renderings of amateurs like ourselves who contribute to the many social media venues, websites, and video repositories.

We need to pause and appreciate just how different this is from even 20 years ago, when there were very few TV channels or other information outlets and no real social media to speak of. In those days, content creators competed fiercely to occupy the little bandwidth that existed. Fast-forward to now, when channels are begging for content, giving many professionals a commercial venue, as well as giving each of us amateurs 15 minutes of fame that will forever be embedded in the collective memory of the infosphere. Living in and among the overpopulated infosphere brings with it a nudge to contribute ourselves. It is our duty as citizens.

Second, we can't unplug from our personal social networks in which we *are* the content. We are, as Sherry Turkle (2008) puts it, tethered selves. We carry our geographically dispersed network of friends, family, and acquaintances with us wherever we go via the cell phone that fits unobtrusively into our pockets. As a result, we always travel in "cell space," using technology that is "always-on/always-on-you" (Turkle, 2008).

Again, we need to pause to appreciate how different this is when compared with life just 10 years ago. When we wanted to ignore others in public, we occupied ourselves with a book, our own thoughts, or some other private, solitary pursuit. Now we do so by entering a communication space in which we talk to invisible people who are simply "elsewhere." While once thought to be rude, it is perfectly acceptable to text, talk, or blog while in an RL social situation (Turkle, 2008). Dead air time, once the concern only of professional mediasts, has now invaded our private lives, and understandably so. We are now constantly onstage as both actors and audience in a play without end.

Behind indisconnectability lies the fear that we may miss something, however trivial, that may connect to something else that may not be so trivial. We live in a state of constant insecurity that can be addressed only by "reaching out and touching someone" through text messaging, sharing a common media experience, or even—as prosaic as it sounds in this day and age—actually talking on the phone. The concept of being alone seems to have evaporated—while loneliness persists. It is as if we have returned to a preindustrial state in which being continually embedded in community has returned to challenge the push for individuality that characterized the previous century. The ironic twist here is that our community is spread throughout the world and is reachable only via a stream of 0s and 1s. It is temporally available while being spatially distributed.

Accompanying delight: Thanks to being always plugged in to the greater digital community, I can serve my community by being everywhere all the time. As I write this, I am texting with my niece and downloading a consulting contract while the weather channel is sending updates that advise me about my travel prospects for tomorrow. Fortunately, this occupies me so that I don't have to talk to the guy next to me on the subway. What will I do if he says hello?

OVERWHELMENT

Our inability to unplug leads directly to our overwhelment. So much is produced so quickly these days that slow, plodding, serial-processing human beings can't begin to keep up with it no matter how networked or adept at multitasking we are. Keep in mind that it is a goal of modern citizenship to participate in the events of our community in an informed manner. The sheer amount of changing information makes that impossible in any ideal sense. Case in point: I just Googled "global warming" and received over 35 million hits in less than a second. No doubt I will have time to explore only a few and will unconsciously cultivate the mistaken notion that I am informed.

Everyone has a favorite overwhelment story. Mine focuses on Firefox, my web browser of choice these days. Firefox recently turned five, and has become so popular that third-party developers have enhanced Firefox's power by producing add-ons, including e-mail clients, link organizers, social networking tools, pop-up blockers, and so on. How many add-ons have been created? Firefox says there are—get ready for it—5,000. Only 5,000 add-ons

> **FYI**
>
> ### Overlinked and Understaffed
>
> *Just out of interest, I counted the number of links sent to me today via e-mail by friends, colleagues, strangers, and organizations. It came to well over 200. Each link led to something at least interesting and possibly useful, like a newsletter, article, video, or information-rich website. And each link linked to other links . . . and so on. Like everyone else, I need three or four clones to stay on top of things. And they need to be able to get along. Incidentally, the development of the Semantic Web (SW) is a direct challenge to overwhelment. It may help turn future searches into reports rather than lists of web hits that we have to slog through. We shall see.*

to read about, install, and try. If you give each 10 minutes of your life, that would take only 833 hours, or about 35 days. This assumes you are working nonstop, without sleeping, eating, or spending time with your family (no big change to our techno lifestyles there). Thus, I often hear the cry, "I simply can't keep up!" And, in fact, we can't. The result is that frequently we substitute feelings and superstition for knowledge and understanding simply because it saves time and feeds basic emotional needs.

Accompanying delight: There's so much to choose from! It's like Joseph Weizenbaum (1976) explicated, tongue in cheek, in his "pig principle": If something is good, more of it must be better. So bring it on! After all, the only thing worse than having 1,000 channels of television is having only one. But I sure wish my remote could click through channels faster . . .

RESOCIALIZATION

If we are losing our way, whom do we turn to for help, guidance, and perspective?

It used to be simple. As I mentioned earlier, when I was growing up, my parents, teachers, minister, and *Leave It to Beaver* (Cadiff, 1957–1963) converged on a life outlook. Life was fairly well contained within a fairly well-defined perspective.

Not so anymore. Children have access to as many media channels as they have time to explore, all of which promote different viewpoints and challenge whatever upbringing school and family have provided. Information is now conflictual rather than convergent. Children, as well as the rest of us, have been seriously resocialized. Those who provide the foundation for our life perspective change constantly. And we adapt.

Accompanying delight: There're so many neat ideas out there, including my own! Now I can find as many viewpoints as I want. I can even find viewpoints that agree, so I don't have to do too much heavy thinking. This works for me, but I encourage others to keep browsing . . .

SOVEREIGNTY

The cumulative result of all that bothers us about technology is that we wonder who is in charge, ourselves or our machines. That is, who is sovereign?

This issue has been in play since our earliest tools. I illuminate this fact when giving presentations with the following demonstration. I hand a hammer to someone in the front row of the audience and ask him to hold on to it for me. This is an odd request to be sure, and no doubt some who receive the hammer think to themselves, "If he doesn't feel comfortable with the hammer, then maybe it's a good idea that I take it." Much to my surprise, no one has ever summoned security.

Back to the person holding the hammer. In about five seconds, I often witness something amazing: The person with the hammer begins moving it, as though unconsciously searching for something to hit. When I point this out to hammer recipients and ask if they had a desire to hit something before I gave them the hammer, they typically say no. Then, I explain, the hammer must have told them what to do. That is, the technology controls them. The technology is sovereign.

This is an uncomfortable realization for most. But the reality is that if I give you a car, you think about driving; an Internet connection, and you think about surfing. This is not a new concept. As Postman (1993) noted, "simply expressed in the old adage . . . to a man with a hammer, everything looks like a nail. Without being too literal we may extend the truism: To a man with a pencil, everything looks like a list. To a man with a camera, everything looks like an image. To a man with a computer, everything looks like data. And to a man with a grade sheet, everything looks like a number" (p. 14). We cannot come into contact with anything, whether animal, mineral, vegetable, or digital, and not merge with it at least a little. When we do, we are forced into a power-sharing arrangement, the result of which is that we see the world at least somewhat as it does.

Because a machine has such limited behaviors, we submit to it much more than it submits to us—it is much easier for us to understand a hammer than it is for a hammer to understand us. And because tools are just ideas with clothes on, we become not only like the tool but also like the social forces behind it. The thing we think we control actually controls us by our unconscious design. Until we see this clearly, technology is our sovereign. But once we understand this, we can negotiate a power-sharing arrangement.

Accompanying delight: Technology is often a benevolent ruler. Technology frees me to do many things I would rather do. And it gives me opportunities I would never have otherwise. Technology must like me! Thanks, technology. I appreciate your help and your input. But if it's alright, I would like to be in control once in a while—would that work for you?"

DEHUMANIZATION

If concern about sovereignty is our rational response to the troublesome qualities of technology, then dehumanization is our emotional response.

When the things we place in between us separate us rather than connect us, diminish us rather than improve us, amplify our frailties rather than challenge us to overcome them, we cry dehumanization. When a machine misspells our name, erases something we mistakenly told it to erase, or doesn't understand that a bomb dropped on a city kills everyone, regardless of their character, we cry dehumanization. And we should. This needs to become a rallying point for what kind of world we want and how we as citizens want to shape the communities we create. The modern citizen emerged from millennia of dehumanization at the hands of other humans who were often equipped with powerful, controlling technology. Thus, our concerns about dehumanization are based on years of accumulated experience.

Rehumanization of the human-technology symbiosis is not a simple goal because technology is often an all-or-nothing affair. The eyeglasses and word processing software that allow us to write poetry also allow us to write hate mail. But one citizen's floor is another citizen's ceiling. It is very difficult to keep just the things that we consider beneficial to humanity or to limit the use of technologies to specific applications because there are plenty of people who want what we don't like and vice versa. In order to leverage our humanity, we must allow others to leverage theirs. Pull on one thread of the tapestry, and it begins to unravel for everyone.

Accompanying delight: It is good to be reminded that I live in a pluralistic society. While what others want may be repugnant to me, it ensures my right to have what I want—which may be repugnant to them. Thank god for mutually assured repugnance, and the freedom it assures for all of us. I just wish others had better taste . . .

OBSOLESCENCE

The most immediate fear for teachers with regard to dehumanization is obsolescence, specifically the fear that they will be overtaken by machines, kids, or younger teachers with more digital know-how. Although some teachers are genuinely excited about the challenges and opportunities of teaching digital kids, others feel uneasy, overwhelmed, and irrelevant.

The reality is that the more technological we become, the more important teachers become. Machines don't teach citizenship—humans do. Teachers mistakenly think they need to be advanced technicians to be effective in today's classrooms. They don't. What *is* important is that teachers become advanced managers of their students' talents, time, inquiry, and productivity. Teachers need to be able to articulate standards of quality and provide feedback that students can use to meet those standards. They need to be the guide on the side rather than the technician magician.

Now more than ever, students living in the overwhelming and often distracting world of technical possibility need the clear voice of a teacher who can help them develop the perspectives that will be important to them for a lifetime of citizenship—locally, globally, and digitally. Now more than ever, students need teachers who can help them sort through choices, apply technology wisely, and tell their stories clearly and with humanity.

My advice to teachers concerned with the possibility of obsolescence? Focus on citizenship first and technology second—and everything will fall into place.

Accompanying delight: I get to reinvent myself. Thank you, obsolescence, for forcing me to reexamine my goals, teaching practices, and commitment to the field. Thanks for the push into new areas of exploration, the offer of new, imaginative tools, and the opportunity to rethink teaching and learning at their most fundamental level. But can I still have summers off?

5 Seeing Technology

A Primer

Fish can't see the water.

—An old proverb

Our response to what bothers us about technology needs to be to see technology. We need to try to see it as clearly as we can so that we can evaluate it and make informed decisions about its use. In addition, once we see it clearly, we can ask leadership to make decisions that reflect our understanding of technology's trade-offs and our priorities as citizens.

But as Dr. Karen Dill (2009) explains in her book, *How Fantasy Becomes Reality: Seeing Through Media Influence,* just being aware of technology's effects does not mitigate many of its unwanted impacts. Instead, we need to be actively engaged in deconstructing technology and making connections between what it does and how it changes us. Doing so is an ongoing, never-ending process.

NOTICING TECHNOLOGY

Recall our earlier discussion about figure versus ground. Technology is so pervasive that it has become what McLuhan and Powers (1989) call "ground." That is, it's so embedded in the environment that it's basically invisible to us: We are fish, and our tEcosystem is the water.

When do we notice technology? There are a few times.

We notice technology when it's new. Whenever I finish remodeling some part of my house, I like to sit and appreciate the new environment I have created because I know it is a short matter of time before it becomes background—the new ground. Same with technology. We see it when it's new . . . but only briefly. Then we depend upon it and take it for granted as though it had always been there.

We notice technology when it breaks. Remember when your refrigerator broke, and you had hundreds of dollars of spoiled food and a big mess on your hands? Suddenly, you saw your refrigerator in great detail. But shortly after it was fixed, it became just intelligent furniture again.

We notice technology when it's upside down. One day in class, Marshall McLuhan told us all to turn a book upside down. As we sat staring at our upside-down books, he told us we were seeing the book as an object for the first time because we couldn't engage with the content—that is, we couldn't read what was on the page. It is similar to an exercise used by Dr. Betty Edwards (1999) in *The New Drawing on the Right Side of the Brain* in which students are asked to draw a picture of something that is turned upside down, so they can see the object using the right side of the brain rather than engaging with the content of the object using the skills associated with the left side.

It was a pivotal moment for me, as I imagine it was for others in McLuhan's class. In turning the book upside down, we were able to see the book as medium because we weren't distracted by the message it carried. Book as medium, rather than story. Book as thing, rather than an invisible information container. What a concept.

We see things when they are upside down or out of context. Things out of context become figure as they rise above the ground . . . until we get used to seeing them that way.

SEEING EXERCISES

Here are a few exercises that can help you to see the technology in your midst. Do them yourself as well as with your class. They're worth doing just for the "ahas"—your own and your students'.

Rearrange the Technology Timeline

Turning the book upside down in McLuhan's class jolted our perception of a technology by rearranging it spatially. What would happen if we rearranged technology temporally?

Steven Johnson (2006) describes an effective method for doing so in his book *Everything Bad Is Good for You:* Flip the order in which technologies arrive, and imagine how you would feel about the new technologies upon their arrival, that is, while they were figure, before they became ground. As he explains via McLuhan, our natural tendency would be to find fault with the new technology: "As McLuhan famously observed, the problem with judging new cultural systems on their own terms is that the presence of the recent past inevitably colors your vision of the emerging form, highlighting flaws and imperfections" (p. 18).

To clarify this point, he invites us to try a thought experiment in which we ask ourselves the following question: If video games were popularized before books, how would we view books when they entered our cultural landscape? Given the all-too-human, conservative inclination to favor existing cultural systems over new ones, he suggests we would find much wrong with books, including the following:

- Books understimulate the senses because they use only one kind of media (words) while games stimulate and integrate many senses due to their use of so many kinds of media.
- Books are tragically isolating while games involve social interaction.
- Books force readers to follow a linear path while games invite users to participate in controlling the narrative of a story through active problem solving. This limitation of books suggests that readers are powerless to change their circumstances, and must follow paths created by others rather than those they create themselves (pp. 19–20).

Flipping technologies in time is an engaging idea. It forces us to confront the fact that often how we feel about technology has less to do with its actual value and more to do with our emotional response to the ways in which it jolts our cultural equilibrium.

Your Turn

Flip any two technologies (radio and TV, the plane and the car, folk remedies and modern medicine) and write a few paragraphs that capture your response to the emergence of the "new" technology. Feel free to send it to me. I would love to read it and, with your permission, post it on my Digital Citizenship Resource Wiki (jasonOhler.com/dc).

Develop a technology metaphor. There is no better way to determine whether students understand something than to require them to translate it. Translating Shakespeare into street English, or geometry into a personal project, requires that they truly understand the material.

Developing a metaphor requires translation because it involves, according to Robert Frost (1946), "saying one thing and meaning another"

(p. xvi). Developing a technology metaphor compels you to see technology clearly in order to compare it to something else.

Here are some examples I have collected over the years. It is often a groundbreaking and poetic experience for the teachers who create them because it helps them get in touch with their overriding concerns, hopes, and perceptions concerning the role technology plays in their lives.

A Fog . . .

Technology is a fog. It covers its inventions, so when one gets close to them, they are seen clearly. But the pathways leading to them are cloudy, sometimes completely concealed . . . This fog causes me to move carefully, unsure of where the next step will take me, hiding the "big picture." I want someone else to see through the fog and find my best path.

A Chameleon . . .

Technology is always changing its hardware and components, but its intended purpose or reason for being does not really change. There is always the chance that something bigger or better will come and destroy its existence. Technology moves quickly and stealthily and never stays in one place for long.

A Fountain of Youth . . .

Technology is like the fountain of youth. Sought after since the early days of time . . . [It] promised health, vitality, and even immortality. In other words, the fountain of youth is equated with the perfect life . . . we buy a bread machine to bring back the aroma and flavor of homemade bread—something we had as a child without the fancy equipment. Today, we have the fresh bread minus the memories of baking with mom or grandmother . . . Like the various charlatans of the 1800's traveling around in their wagons touting the latest elixir that would cure all ills and in a way be someone's "fountain of youth," technology promises things it cannot always deliver.

Your Turn

Describe a technology metaphor. Create your own metaphor about technology. Send it to me—I'd love to read it. You can see more technology metaphors created by teachers, as well as post your own, at my Digital Citizenship Resource Wiki: jasonOhler.com/dc.

Seeing Technology Traps

The term *technology trap* comes from James Burke's (1978) excellent television series, *Connections*, which explored the rise of civilization in terms of the interconnectedness of technological innovation. To Burke, all technology is potentially a trap because it fails after we become dependent on it. Yet without our dependency on technology, civilization would not move forward. Thus, we all live inside a vast, interconnected set of traps.

Remember the day the printer stopped working while you were trying to print out a grant that was due by 5 p.m.? While the printer was working, it was just furniture—it was ground. When it broke, it became figure—a trap that you saw in great detail. Describing traps helps us see the technology all around us.

Your Turn

Describe a technology trap. In one page, tell a story about a time technology "trapped" you. Discuss what happened, how you saw it at the time, and how life changed for you thereafter. You can read about some technology traps created by teachers, as well as post your own, at my Digital Citizenship site: jasonOhler.com/dc.

> ### FYI
>
> #### Air Controllers Forced to Type!
>
> On 11/19/2009, a single circuit board in a piece of FAA equipment at a computer center in Salt Lake City malfunctioned, resulting in a communication blackout among air traffic control computers throughout the United States. As a consequence, air traffic controllers had to type in flight plans rather than relay them digitally, causing widespread delays throughout the entire air industry. Murphy's delicious irony here is that the air industry was reduced to moving only as fast as air traffic controllers could type. The fact that the malfunction of one tiny cog of the great international air traffic machine can create such an immense ripple effect reminds us of the traps that lay in wait for us everywhere.

Seeing Technology Miracles

A miracle is the reverse of a trap. Remember the day technology made it possible for you to do something you have always wanted to do—or never knew you wanted to do—but couldn't because you didn't have the tools? Perhaps music software allowed you to write your first song, Facebook allowed you to find a long-lost friend, or an online discussion put you in touch with an expert from another country who gave you a great idea for an exciting unit of instruction.

Your Turn

Describe a technology miracle. In one page, tell a story about a time that technology allowed you to do something "miraculous." Discuss what happened, how you saw it at the time, and how life changed for you thereafter.

You can read about some technology miracles created by teachers at my Digital Citizenship Resources Wiki (jasonOhler.com/dc). I would love to hear about the traps and miracles in your life. Feel free to post them on the wiki yourself; or pass them on to me, and I will do so.

Live Without Technology, and Study What Changes

Technology Blackout Day was an actual event in 2005 that encouraged teachers and students to live without technology for a day and share their experiences with the Internet community. All in all, it was a very interesting experiment.

FYI
An Apt McLuhanism
"A primary method for studying the effects of anything is simply to imagine ourselves as suddenly deprived of them." (McLuhan, 1974, para. 3).

Rather than living without all technology, try living without a particular technology, preferably a simple one. You can probably guess what life would be like without your cell phone. But try living without a fork for a day or, for dramatic effect, an entire week. Good luck.

Your Turn

Live without a technology for a day. Identify technologies that you use frequently, and choose one to live without for a day. Keep a journal in which you reflect on how you adapted to living without it. In addition, reflect on how not having the technology interrupted, redirected, or improved your lifestyle, perhaps by challenging you to become more creative in the technology's absence. If you do this with students, please involve parents in the decision about which technology to forgo.

Ask Your Parents, Grandparents, or Elders
About Life in Earlier Times

Like everyone in every era, my grandmother grew up during the best and worst of times. She used to talk to me at length about the good old days before the widespread use of the telephone, automobile, and television, and of life during simpler, more predictable times. During her day, adults were respected, children knew their place, and community was more cohesive.

But they were the worst of times as well, not because she didn't have 500 channels of cable TV or the riches of the Internet at her disposal, but because it was a dark period of history in some ways. Women made half what a man did for the same work, African Americans still didn't really have the right to vote, and "environmental degradation" was only something rabble rousers talked about. Given the state of media during her day, she may well not have known much about any of this.

As we came of age, her unconditional love for us endured despite the fact that she often saw us as disrespectful. No doubt we were. Besides being pesky young adults with all our biological meltdowns and attitudinal challenges, we began to have access to a good deal of information that had been denied her during less networked times. The result was that our information environments were fundamentally different: Hers was convergent while ours was conflictual. She didn't question much because the narrative of her generation was so controlled and consistent that it didn't leave much to question.

On the other hand, my information environment was more informed and thus far more confusing. As radio and TV evolved, it began to produce new programming that brought realities about inner-city poverty and civil rights into our living rooms in shocking detail. I watched war unfold on the nightly news while radio pushed me to be rebellious and dance to rock 'n roll. The result of the new information environment was to directly challenge notions of social equanimity and convergence that were the bedrock of my grandmother's America.

Yet I grew to appreciate how much her generation did with the little they had. It fought holy wars, built an empire, and developed a free society that would eventually give my generation the right to question everything hers had created. And despite her lack of material possessions, she had been very happy, owning less and somehow having more. I doubt the next generation will say that about mine.

The point is this: It is every generation's job to inform the next, not because they are better, but because they are different. They honor different perspectives and often different values. Above all, they see community and citizenship differently, and we have everything to gain by understanding how their view differs from ours.

Talk to your elders. Talk to your grandparents, parents, or other elders in the community about how they lived without the technologies we now take for granted. The point is to look at the past through the perspectives of people you know and trust so that you can better understand what you are gaining and losing as digital technology permeates your life. Don't look for just the good stuff or just the bad stuff. Be an anthropologist. See what is there. Try to understand their era not only as a culture unto itself but also as one from which you emerged. Young kids are in a particularly good position to mine this assignment for nuggets of insight because they may have many generations of elders accessible to them.

SEEING BY GETTING PHILOSOPHICAL

I have come to appreciate that the word *philosophical* is viewed with suspicion by teacher practitioners often because they hear it in association with a new administrative initiative that will lead to the formation of yet another afterschool committee that will generate great ideas that will ultimately go nowhere.

But I think teachers are some of the best philosophers we have, when we give them a chance. Like taxicab drivers, bartenders, and hairdressers, they have a unique viewpoint that draws upon a wealth of experience that is unavailable to most of us. Unlike the other professions mentioned, theirs is publicly funded and under constant assault by media pundits. In addition, they have a task the rest of us don't: to carry out Thomas Jefferson's dream of preparing effective citizens through education.

Providing teachers opportunities to reflect upon their great wealth of experience allows them to touch base with the philosophy that guides them as they teach our children. Doing so is essential for their well-being as well as for the well-being of the educational system. And it gives them a chance to tell media pundits what a bunch of idiots they are—in nicer language than that, of course.

That is why I welcome ISTE's Standard 4 about digital citizenship. It calls upon teachers to "zoom out" and get philosophical about living digitally, so they can then "zoom in" and get practical about addressing the issues related to digital citizenship in real ways. For now, we are going to zoom out. A bit later, we will zoom in.

Developing a Technology Philosophy

Do you have a personal philosophy about using technology in your classroom?

Most teachers actually have a technology philosophy, but they may not know it. It shows up in the ways they use technology with their students and in the questions they ask about when, why, and how to use technology personally and professionally. If you want to know what your philosophy is, examine the decisions you make during the day that you don't have time to think about. They externalize what you believe with regard to many things, including technology.

If you're like most teachers, your philosophy addresses issues beyond technical proficiency, like respect and safety, as well as developing a balanced perspective about technology's advantages and disadvantages. After all, you want your students to see "the big picture" of technology so that they can be informed citizens as well as educated students. You want them to use technology not only effectively and creatively, but also wisely and responsibly.

Creating a philosophy about being a digital citizen is a challenging, compelling, and enlightening thing to do. All of my educational technology master's students, most of whom were classroom teachers, developed an educational technology philosophy to discover how technology use resonated with their core. They modified this throughout the program as their use of technology changed how they viewed the world.

Citizenship is not just something we practice—it is also something we embody. As such, we need to understand our philosophy as digital citizens. Doing so will help us see technology more clearly. It will also help us think about, affirm, or modify our philosophy as it applies to being a teacher practitioner.

Your Turn

What's your philosophy about educational technology and digital citizenship? In a paragraph or two—a page at most—articulate your philosophy about using technology in teaching and learning. Be sure to address the responsibilities and opportunities associated with digital citizenship for yourself and your students. Put it aside. Let it percolate. Go back to it in a week. Still sound good? Then revisit it at least every year to make sure it still captures what you think and feel.

Questions to consider as you flesh out your philosophy:

- Do you articulate concern as well as hope? Responsibility as well as opportunity?
- Do you leave room to learn about new technologies and the new "big picture" issues that may accompany them?

- Does your philosophy reference or imply the past as well as the present and the future?
- Does your philosophy address others as well as yourself?
- Does your view of citizenship address local, global, and digital community?

Your Turn

Make an educational philosophy video. Every year, I require each of my preservice students to create a short video about their educational philosophy as a teacher, particularly as it relates to using technology with students. It helps them learn media production while developing an understanding about how to use technology in a considered, reflective manner. Students are encouraged to spend no money on the project and, whenever possible, to use the same free media development software that is used in their schools, typically iMovie on the Mac and Moviemaker on the PC. Although students are allowed to shoot video, I prefer they use still images with voice-over narration because it is easier, leaving them more time to focus on the narrative. I emphasize using simple, solid content and forgoing glitz. Productions should not exceed two minutes.

Most students tell me that synthesizing their philosophy into a few recorded paragraphs was much harder than harnessing the technology. This is as it should be. This project compels students, most of whom are just months away from being in charge of their own classroom, to come to grips with who they are as technology-using teachers, something most of them have not done.

I think it is reasonable to assume that had I not required them to consider their philosophy this straightforwardly, they probably would not have done so on their own. And had I not asked them to create something as compelling as a media production, the experience would not have been nearly as enlightening. After all, while it is easy to change text, it is not at all easy to change media. The result is the assignment is a very clarifying activity for them as teachers as they consider precisely what it is they want to say and capture with a medium that is relatively fixed in nature. While my students do not have to post their final presentation on a video service like YouTube, most do. This project is a wonderful blend of all three communities. They talk globally about how they view their local classroom and then post that in the digital community for the world to see.

Many past students have told me that they have translated this exercise into "Who am I?" projects for their own students. Their students get to use the media they love in the service of serious reflection about what is important to them as people: win-win. Visit the Digital Citizenship Resource Wiki to see examples of teacher philosophy videos. And feel free to add links to your own.

WHAT'S YOUR TECHNOLOGY MANTRA?

Philosophies and mission statements tend to be lengthy. On the one hand, there is nothing wrong with this, as length engages the writing brain, that part of us that slows down, reflects, and focuses. But on the other hand, there is a downside to lengthy philosophies: They are too long to memorize, thus we tend to forget them. A good way to address this is to synthesize your philosophy into a mantra.

Guy Kawasaki (2007), a futurist and engaging keynote speaker, is all over mantras. I once heard him say that most people within an organization didn't know what the organization's mission statement was. Why? It was too long! No one is going to memorize a page of information. At best, they will remember the bullets that synthesize the really important stuff. He recommended that companies create mantras, simple one-sentence descriptions of their core philosophy or mission.

So view your philosophy statement—which might be many paragraphs in length—as a prewrite for your mantra. Get all the ideas and concerns out there that are rattling around in your psyche. Then try to find the essence of your philosophy—the fractal or koan that distills your longer statement and presents it in highly synthesized form.

Educational Technology Mantra Examples

My students—most of whom are teachers—often extract mantras from longer philosophy statements. Here are two mantras created by teachers that I have always liked.

> *"To use technology the way I use any of the tools I own: with respect and care, as well as with interest and excitement."*

> *"To honor the power technology brings to my life by using it with the responsibility it requires."*

These would still be a bit long for a mantra purist, but they work fine for me. Here's a mantra that is a bit too long that guided me for some time:

> *"To use today's tools effectively, creatively, wisely . . .*
>
> *To reflect on the past and prepare for the future . . .*
>
> *To balance personal fulfillment with community well-being."*

This eventually was distilled to:

> *"To use technology effectively, creatively, wisely."*

I haven't touched this mantra for many years except to add "funly" in 2003:

"To use technology effectively, creatively, wisely, and funly."

What's the Value of a Mantra?

Your mantra becomes your touchstone. When you are lost and trying to get your bearings in your digitally overdone world, this is what you refer to in order to see if you are on track. As sometimes happens, you find that your mantra must change because it simply does not capture your understanding of the world anymore. Such was the case when I added "funly" to my mantra, as described above.

Developing a technology mantra is a great activity for you as well as your students. Adjust this for your age group as needed. If you have students create mantras, keep their work, and give it back to them years later. I have found that doing this never fails to astound.

Your Turn

What's your mantra about educational technology and digital citizenship? You have one sentence to address this. The fewer words you use, the more powerful and memorable your mantra will be. As with your philosophy, put it aside. Let it percolate. Go back to it in a week. Still sound good? Then revisit it at least every year to make sure it still captures what you think and feel. As always, feel free to add yours to the others at my Digital Citizenship Wiki (jasonOhler.com).

WHAT'S YOUR SCHOOL'S PHILOSOPHY?

Not only do teachers have educational technology philosophies, but so do schools, school districts, organizations, and departments of education. Each educational environment is a unique technology culture driven by its own unique perspective about digital citizenship and the use of technology in teaching and learning. The technology culture of your school will determine what is possible, supported, encouraged, expected, and discouraged for you and your students. It will determine everyone's rights and obligations, as well as limitations and opportunities, as digital citizens.

Formal versus informal philosophy. Typically, a school has a formal philosophy in the form of a vision and mission statement that sets the direction for an entire school community. Unfortunately, they rarely have mantras. Some schools and districts take digital citizenship seriously and address issues of technology and learning in some detail. Others don't. The quality of leadership in an organization in large part determines how importantly technology is viewed in an organizational context. This is addressed in much more detail in Part III under the topic of character education for the Digital Age.

A second, less formal philosophy can be inferred from classroom and school activities. The formal philosophy describes intentions and policy, while classroom activities provide a "dashboard" reading of a school's actual health. Just as you expose your belief system in the decisions you make that you don't have time to think about, an organization exposes its core beliefs in the operational decisions it makes about what it supports in classrooms.

Your Turn

What's your school's technology philosophy? To understand your school's technology philosophy, become an anthropologist who seeks to understand the nature of your school community as a technology culture. Find out what technology your school has, who uses it and why, who the technology leaders are, what policies and standards guide technology's use, and what customs and rituals are observed in relation to using technology in teaching, learning, administration, and interacting with the public.

I have taught technology infusion classes for preservice teachers for many years. This is one of their first assignments. The goal is to have them see the technology culture in which they work and to understand how technology and digital citizenship are viewed by that culture. Once they have gained that perspective, they have a much better chance of being a successful practitioner.

If you are interested in this, try using the observation instrument I provide for my preservice students, "Knowing Your School's Technology Culture." It appears below, but it can also be downloaded through the Digital Citizenship Wiki (jasonOhler.com).

Understanding Your School's Technology Culture

    I. Technological Capacity and Capabilities

        A. What kind of technology is available to you?

        B. What Internet capability is available?

C. How is computer and Internet access provided? Dispersed computers? One to one? Labs? Can students use their own equipment?

D. What kinds of filters are in place, and how do they restrict what you might want to do?

E. If resources like social media are blocked, are there "intranet" options? Are there ways to get special permission to use blocked resources?

F. Who has the specialty gear (cameras, scanners, etc.), and can you use it?

G. What is your best sense of the technology that your students have at home? To what extent can you expect them to have access to technology and the Internet outside school so that they can work on school projects?

II. Leadership and Policies

A. Does your school have a mission statement and an educational technology plan? If so, when were they last updated?

B. Are missions and plans used and generally valued at school? Do you use them?

C. Do the missions and plans address the issues of digital citizenship or of developing a balanced view of technology adoption?

D. Is technology well funded at your school? Do you see signs of technology rotation, professional development, and ongoing maintenance of existing equipment?

E. Does your school have Internet use and parent permission policies? When were they last updated?

F. Does your school have policies about using cell phones, PDAs, and other personal technology at school?

G. Does your school have policies regarding issues like cyberbullying, sexting, and other activities related to cybersafety and respect?

H. Has your school adopted or established competencies for students? When were they last updated?

I. Who are the ed tech leaders within your school? Does your school have an ed tech committee? Is it active? What are its responsibilities?

J. Who are the student leaders in technology? Are there programs that allow them to use their expertise to help teachers and other students? Are there special programs that allow them to pursue their interests?

K. Are community members involved with regard to using technology in your school?

L. If something breaks, who fixes it? How do you contact them? Is corrective and ongoing maintenance well supported?

Reflection

In a few paragraphs, summarize your assessment of your school as a technology culture by addressing the following questions:

- What is the current status of your school as a technology culture?
- What is the overall attitude about and level of support concerning the use of technology at your school?
- Which areas are doing well?
- Which need improvement?
- How can you become involved?
- If you had a budget and authority, what would you do to improve your school's technology culture?

Whether you use this instrument formally or informally, doing so will help you to see more clearly what kind of local, global, and digital community your school supports.

Bottom line: To change your school's culture, first see it as a community with an ethos and underlying philosophies that guide its activities. Once these are visible, they can be discussed and changed. Without altering the foundation, you can't truly change the nature of the community.

6 Becoming a "De-Tech-Tive"

Helping Students Understand Technology's Impacts

A MATTER OF BALANCE

If we had to use one word to describe our desire for students in their use of technology, it is *balance*. We want them to cultivate balance as kids so that they might carry that sense of balance forward into their adult lives. Balance implies that multiple perspectives need to be synthesized into an integrated view of community. That is exactly what we want our students to do.

The subtext of ISTE refreshed Standard 4 is that it asks teachers to balance—*and help their students balance*—many things:

- Opportunity as well as responsibility
- Excitement and empowerment as well as caution and consideration
- Personal fulfillment as well as community and global well-being
- Global perspective as well as local action
- Hope for themselves as well as the world

Balance: It is the heart of digital citizenship.

In previous chapters, we addressed how to see technology in philosophical terms. In this chapter, we learn how to see it in very practical terms, focusing on the details and impacts of the technology that permeate our lives. To do this, we become "de-tech-tives." Doing so helps us and our students deconstruct technological power, see the present and future impacts of technology, and have fun all at the same time.

BECOMING DE-TECH-TIVES

Recall from Chapter 1 my suggestion that we should consider adopting the following standard to guide students in becoming digital citizens:

Students will study the personal, social, and environmental impacts of every technology and media application they use in school.

It is this standard that drives our desire to turn students into de-tech-tives.

A theme throughout this book is that in order to help students become effective digital citizens, we must help them see technology that is largely invisible to them. Recall that we are fish trying to see the water—and just how difficult that can be. Our mission as de-tech-tives is to see technology's characteristics and impacts as figure rather than ground—that is, as things and events we focus on. We must reverse the trend of making technology invisible that educational technologists have been championing for years. Sure, we don't want to stumble on our tools as we try to use them. But once we make them invisible, we don't think to question them. Thus, for the exercises in this chapter, we need to focus on them.

Ideally, we should be able to see impacts that are not only past and present but that also may occur in the future. After all, there are plenty of pundits talking about technology's impacts after the fact. However, truly enlightened digital citizens should be able to project evolving impacts of current technology as well as predict new technological trends. Doing so will enable them to think more clearly about the future they want for themselves and their communities.

I must quickly add that I appreciate that predicting our technological future already confounds truly smart people with a good deal of experience in this area—who often have very bad track records. Thus, we are not looking for students to be "right"—we will leave that for the proponents of No Child Left Behind. Instead, our goal is to involve students in discussions about the future as critical thinkers and caring citizens. Without their interest, the future will happen to them rather than because of them.

What Do De-Tech-Tives Do?

They work for the Science and Technology Administration (STA).

To engage your students in the de-tech-tive process, involve them in this hypothetical situation. Suppose there was a Science and Technology Administration that was charged with determining the potential impacts of technologies before they were released into mainstream society, much like the Food and Drug Administration is charged with determining the potential impacts of new foods and drugs before they are allowed to be sold. Students can consider existing technologies in terms of their existing or future impacts as well as new technologies they speculate might exist one day. As an exercise, all approaches work very well.

Incidentally, I am not suggesting that the government create an STA, at least not one with punitive powers. Doing so would probably end innovation as we know it. But I am suggesting that each of us could voluntarily become our own STA and begin looking at technology in a more investigative, long-range way. Critical thinking, I believe it is called.

The STA works as the basis for short mini-lessons, longer units of instruction, and everything in between. But more important, teachers can use the STA as a continual touchstone topic in literally any area of study. As appropriate issues arise, teachers can ask students, "So what would the STA say about this?" In this way, the STA works as a crosscurricular thematic perspective that doesn't always require a separate, focused assignment.

TECHNOLOGY CONNECTS AND DISCONNECTS

The heart and soul of our technology assessment perspective is the fact that every technology connects and disconnects. It is not unlike Newton's first law of motion: Every action has an equal and opposite reaction. De-tech-tives must be able to see how each technology they study connects and disconnects in order to analyze a technology's impacts and potential impacts in a comprehensive fashion.

The connections and disconnections are always present. For example, consider eyeglasses. They connect us to a world we could not otherwise see. In the process, they make us more mobile, capable, and productive. How, pray tell, do they disconnect us? By reducing our reliance on those whose help we would otherwise depend in order to get around, by reducing us to an individual when we would have otherwise belonged to a group.

It is hard to argue against eyeglasses, and it is not my intent to do so. In the spirit of full disclosure, I have had corrective surgery for distance vision, and I use reading glasses to see what I am doing up close. In fact, I buy reading glasses by the case because I lose them so often. But don't think we have adopted glasses free of charge. Don't think it was all gain, no pain. They cost us a social connection, which, on balance, we are quite willing to pay.

ESSENTIAL QUESTIONS OF THE DE-TECH-TIVE PROCESS

Recall that the essential question that drives the mission of the STA is mantra-like in its compactness:

- How does technology connect and disconnect?

Believe it or not, some find this question too value laden to be appropriate for some uses. Another way of asking this question, which seems more neutral to some, is:

- What are a technology's short-term and long-term effects?

Both questions will yield similar results.

What confounds our ability to clearly see connections and disconnections, or short- versus long-term effects, are the following:

- Connections are immediate, obvious, shiny, helpful, and fun . . . and it isn't fun to question them. In fact, you sound like a party pooper at the technology extravaganza when you do.
- Disconnections are harder to see because often they are camouflaged. Also, typically they are appreciated only in hindsight and only when we focus on them. After all, it is hard work to follow a trail that started in the past, crosses our present, and extends into the future. In addition, we have an emotional aversion to seeing technological disconnections because doing so is not nearly as much fun as just enjoying the connections. Doing so can lead to buyer's remorse.

As I mentioned earlier, typically we are not very good at projecting the impacts of our technology. For example, few anticipated that the microwave oven would obsolesce the need for family dinner. Yet that is exactly what it has done. Microwave ovens create instant food, much of which a child can cook without parental help. The microwave connects us to time, which translates into ballet class, foreign language lessons, and extra sports for our kids, much of which we trade for family dinner hour. The microwave oven connects us to individual lives because we can eat alone, and it disconnects us from a group gathering.

We see this now, but we didn't see it when microwave ovens were being mainstreamed into our daily lives. Would we still have bought microwave ovens had we seen this proactively? Probably. But seeing this now might help us reconsider the value of eating as a family. It might make us consciously consider what we have gained and lost so that we can evaluate one small aspect of our technological lifestyle. And it might just compel us to find more time for family dinner.

> **FYI**
>
> ### The Microwave Versus the Dining Room
>
> *Recently, my wife and I went house hunting and noticed something interesting. In most new homes, there was no longer a dining room. There were family rooms, entertainment rooms, and living rooms, as well as eating areas adjoined to the kitchen. But the dining room was gone. This is pure conjecture on my part, but I believe we were seeing the influence of the microwave oven on space planning. No doubt needing somewhere to put a 48" flat screen TV also had something to do with it. In the age of the microwave and overwhelming home entertainment options, the dining room has become wasted space.*

THE DE-TECH-TIVE PROCESS

STA de-tech-tives investigate, analyze, and make recommendations about how to address the personal, social, and environmental impacts of technology. What do they wear to work? Unimportant, as long as it looks professional.

The de-tech-tive process has three steps:

1. **Investigate.** Scrutinize the technology, collecting data the way detectives do.

2. **Analyze.** Analyze, debate, brainstorm, reflect, collect corroborating data—whatever the class activity calls for. The goal is to do so in relation to our questions about the impacts of technology and the issues related to digital citizenship. These are discussed later in this chapter.

3. **Evaluate and Recommend.** Produce a final evaluation that leads to one of the following recommendations:

   o Keep the technology.
   o Don't keep the technology.
   o Keep the technology but with conditions or modifications.

You will note that most of the activities I suggest in this chapter are very low tech. This is on purpose. You don't need technology to explore this topic, though its use can certainly enhance how your students conduct their investigation and express what they discover. I like creating low-tech environments to discuss these issues because doing so shifts the focus from using tools to thinking without them, a metamessage of the STA perspective.

STA De-Tech-Tive Process—Step 1: Investigate

In what follows, I describe seven areas of inquiry to help guide the investigative process. Time and circumstance may dictate that you use just a few or collapse several into a single theme. That's fine. These areas were developed so that you could use what you need as you need it. The areas are not mutually exclusive, and they can be adapted as the situation demands. Remember, the STA doesn't have to be a unit or even a lesson. It can simply be a mini-lesson or a perspective that you raise in class with your students, however briefly. A little bit of technology evaluation is better than none.

The STA's investigative activities fall into the following *Inquiry Areas:*

1. Physical characteristics—how is the technology made, what is it made of, how is it used?

2. Enhancements/reductions—how does it amplify and diminish us?

3. Predecessors/next steps—what did it replace, and what does it imply?

4. Social contexts—what are the social expectations that produced our desire to have it?

5. Biases—who does it favor, and who gets left out?

6. Benefits—what are the qualities of this technology that drive its creation and adoption?

7. Impacts—what are its connections and disconnections?

Each is addressed in turn.

Inquiry Area 1: Physical Characteristics

In much the same way that McLuhan helped his students see a book as a thing rather than a story container by having them turn it upside down, we want to help students see technologies as "things made of stuff" by looking at them out of context. If the technology under consideration is small enough, I will often place it by itself on a clean white sheet of paper, raising it from ground to figure rather dramatically. Sometimes, I will do so while playing the theme from *2001: A Space Odyssey.* A little bit of histrionics never hurts.

Students can make a list of the materials that comprise "things," research where they came from, and try to find out who actually crafted them into the things we buy. The point is for students to see the things in their lives as the result of a global network of raw materials, labor, ideas, engineering, manufacturing, transportation, and merchandising before they appear on a store shelf, either physically or virtually. Digital citizenry respects not only the global network of communication but also the global network of stuff.

Question: What is it?

Have your students examine common technologies and ask:

- What is it made of? Where did the materials come from?
- Who designed it?
- Who made it?
- Where was it made?
- How was it made?
- How did it get here?
- Can I fix it, or does someone else need to do that?

Suggested Activity

Assign small groups to investigate technologies as things. Their goal is to produce a list, bubble diagram, or other suitable artifact showing the process that was used to create the technology, from mining the natural resources to shipping the final products to stores.

I am a big fan of the *History Channel*, the *Discovery Channel*, and other programming resources that routinely feature programs about how things are made. They provide a good model for this exercise, and perhaps a good resource for your class, if you can overcome copyright hurdles.

In addition, a simple web search will yield a great deal of resources about this topic, including the following:

- Made How. This site explains how common technologies are made. Go to www.madehow.com.
- MIT's Sourcemap project. Its mission statement, to quote its webpage, is the following: "We believe that people have the right to know where things come from and what they are made of. Sourcemap is a platform for researching, optimizing, and sharing the supply chains behind a number of everyday products" (n.d., para. 1–2). Go to tangible.media.mit.edu/project.php?recid=111.
- Track My T. "This site lets students type in the unique lot number on their T-shirt and then go through an amazing interactive journey

FYI

A Special Note About Nonthings, Like Social Media

In what way is Facebook, a cell phone call, or an avatar in Second Life a "thing"? The reality is that everything we experience in the infosphere is built upon things. You can focus on any part of a media experience in order to flesh out the things that are involved, including the main object itself (like a cell phone), a part of the object (just the screen), or some part of the communication path it depends on (like the towers, the transmitters, and the computers at cell provider headquarters). Use whatever fits.

tracking their T-shirt from its very beginning as a cotton seed on a farm to every step before they bought it" (iLearn Technology, 2010, para. 2). From the iLearn Technology website: Go to ilearntechnology.com/?tag=track-my-t.

Check the Digital Citizenship Resources Wiki (jasonOhler.com/dc) for more resources in this area. And feel free to add your own.

Inquiry Area 2: Enhancing/Reducing Characteristics

Recall that in Chapter 5 I identified two of the common fears about technology to be amplification and reduction. In a sentence, every technology extends or amplifies some part of us, while reducing another part. This area of inquiry is intended to help students see this quality of technology in terms of empowerment and disempowerment. Enhancement and reduction basically constitute connection and disconnection in very physical terms.

We briefly considered the car in terms of enhancement and reduction in Chapter 4. Let's take a more detailed look at it here. My car's wheels amplify my feet by allowing me to go faster, but they reduce them by disconnecting them from the ground. My car's trunk amplifies my back by allowing me to carry more, but it disconnects me from using my own muscles. My car's headlights extend my night vision while reducing my ability to develop the use of my hearing to know what is ahead of me. My car's radio extends my ears by connecting them to faraway places, but it disconnects them from the sounds in my immediate environment. My car's speed takes me to places I would not otherwise visit while preventing me from seeing the things around me in detail because I am moving too fast.

And we are just getting warmed up. Understanding the car in this way provides a wonderful means for us to hone our investigative insight in terms of how technologies enhance and reduce us.

Whenever possible, I like to take students through an historical journey—history lessons under the radar, I call it. Start with something simple and preindustrial age, like a pencil. Engaging students in "deconstructing" a common, simple technology is fun, inexpensive, and eye-opening. Then tackle something predigital that they use every day, like a microwave oven or a car, before talking about the stuff of digital life, like cell phones and computers. If you are working with young students, you might ask them if they have ever seen a pencil before proceeding.

Question: How Does the Technology Extend and Reduce me?

Choose a technology, and address the following questions:

- Which of the five senses does it extend and reduce?
- What part of our body does it extend or reduce?
- What technology that I already have does it extend or reduce?
- What experiences do I gain? Which do I lose?
- Does it extend and/or reduce our ability to think or remember?
- For younger kids, the questions become—how does the technology make me bigger or smaller, smarter or dumber?

Suggested Activity

Create a simple table, like the one below, that compares and contrasts the extensions and reductions of a particular technology. The example below is adapted from my preceding example of the car:

Table 6.1 Technology Extension and Reduction

Characteristic	Extension	Reduction
Wheels	Feet	Not feeling the ground
Trunk	Carrying capacity	Not using my muscles
Headlights	Seeing at night	Not using hearing to "see at night"
Radio	Hearing music from faraway places	Not hearing sounds of immediate environment
Speed	Taking me places I cannot otherwise go	Not seeing my immediate environment because I am moving too fast

Inquiry Area 3: Predecessors and Next Steps

There is very little that is totally new in the technology world. Invention is a cumulative process, with ideas and technologies building upon each other. If this is so, what did the first technologies build on? Ourselves. As explained earlier, we can consider a cup to be Version 2.0 of the technology used to scoop water out of a stream. Version 1.0 was our hands.

As I look at the things in my house, whether cell phone, coffee cup, or pencil, each is somehow an extension of ourselves. However, more important to this inquiry area is the fact that each of these is probably an improvement of technology that came before it and an indication of technology that will replace it. Each technology, from cups to cell phones to social media, sits at the center of a timeline that stretches in both directions.

Question: *What does the technology replace? What will replace it?*

Choose a technology and address the following questions:

- Did your parents, grandparents, or previous generations have it? If not, how did they live without it?
- Did your parents, grandparents, or previous generations have an earlier version of it? What was it?
- How does this technology represent an improvement over its replacement?
- What do you think it will be replaced by? How soon do you expect that replacement to happen?
- What improvements will the technology offer over the current technology?

Suggested Activities

Have students consider household objects that do similar things. This might involve "everything used to write," which could include pencils, pens, markers, and the family computer. Have them place these on a timeline that indicates how they evolved. Also, have them develop a timeline that places a technology they are studying in relation to its predecessors and whatever new versions may exist or that they project might exist someday. The results might look something like this:

Wagon train -> car -> antigravity vehicle?

Telephone -> cell phone -> telepathic transmitter?

Talking in the hallway -> Twitter -> spoken shorthand?

Or in terms of environmental impacts of their cell phone:

Then	Last year's cell phone—useless. Threw it out.
Now	I think I can recycle this one, but what do the recyclers do with it?
When	Future cell phones should be biodegradable or be reusable.

Inquiry Area 4: Social Contexts

Technology adoption often happens because of social expectation. The goal of this inquiry area is to help students see that the technology and information sources they use are often the result of influence or pressure from family, friends, educators, colleagues, and the all-pervasive media-sphere. At one point in our not-too-distant past, having a TV or a car was considered a luxury. Now these things are considered necessities. In fact, not having them is often considered irresponsible. When did that happen? More important, how did that happen?

Because we are dealing with kids, we are particularly interested in the role that peer pressure plays in technology adoption. Buying clothes, acquiring new gadgets, and maintaining a Facebook presence often begin as lifestyle enhancers, before they become necessities, often because they become part of "the uniform" of a social group. One year, your kids just had to shop at the Gap. Next year, it was Old Navy. Where do those shopping imperatives come from? Sure, it may have been an advertisement that kicked it off, but eventually the expectations surfaced as hallway conversations and unspoken dress code requirements at parties, as well as a peer mandate circulated via Facebook. Parents, administrators, and teachers are then left to ponder whether to ban the latest great thing in our kids' lives or figure out how to adapt them responsibly to the school environment. Once again, we are faced with the question asked in the Preamble: Two lives or one?

This is certainly not all a bad thing. In many cases, the expectation to have technology can be extremely positive. Many of the technologies students add to their lives can create opportunities and make life more enriching.

But that is not always the case. And whether it is the case or not, it is always a good idea to know why we are buying whatever we are buying. It's the same for our kids.

Ultimately, our goal is to help students understand why they adopt technology so that they can more objectively evaluate how they do so. That is, we want to help students view technology adoption in much the same way we hope they view the food they eat, the drugs they ingest, or the way they spend their time: as lifestyle choices.

Question: Why do you own that gadget or use that social media site (or wear those clothes or eat that food)?

Choose a technology or information resource, and address the following questions:

- Do friends or people you admire expect you to have it? Are you joining a community of users? Will you be excluded from a group, formally or informally, for not having it?

- How do you use it in your classroom? At home? At work?
- Does it have practical value or primarily enhancement value?
- When did you first decide you wanted it?
- How did you decide what style of it to buy?
- Other than cost and features, what figured into your decision to buy the particular brand and model that you bought?

Suggested Exercise

Have students trace their decision to buy a particular thing in their lives. The more recent the purchase, the better, as recall will be more effective. Also, ask them to trace a decision about what to wear to school or at a party. The idea is to have them see lifestyle choices as deliberate, albeit largely unconscious decisions, driven by factors that can be uncovered with a little bit of de-tech-tive work. Their conclusions can be presented in many forms, including a simple list, a bubble diagram, or a decision tree that identifies specific decisions in the adoption process. Needless to say, they could also use wikis, video production, and a number of other digital tools to capture and present their findings.

Inquiry Area 5: Technology Biases

Everything created by us contains our bias. Thus, every technology has bias. That is, every technology encourages some behaviors and activities and not others. A book encourages a private story experience and discourages community storytelling. A web browser encourages us to browse the web and not the library: connect-disconnect.

In addition, technology also favors those who can use it, and disadvantages those who can't. A right-handed baseball mitt favors the right-handed. A book written in English excludes those who read only Spanish.

Question: What is the bias implicit in the technology?

Choose a technology, and address the following questions:

- What does it encourage or inspire you to do that you can't or wouldn't do without it?
- What does it discourage you from doing?
- What activity does it displace or replace?
- How does it favor you and not others or vice versa?
- Who gets left out, and what are they missing out on?
- Could it be modified to include more people?
- For younger students, the questions might be: What can you do with this technology, and what can't you do? Can all of your friends use it?

Suggested Activity

Have students create a t-balance that details who benefits and doesn't benefit from a particular technology. The table below shows this with regard to particular characteristics of a few of the technologies already discussed in this chapter.

Table 6.2 Technology Bias

Characteristic	Who benefits?	Who doesn't?
Pencil, in terms of writing (vs., e.g., drawing)	The literate, those with access to education	The illiterate, those without schools
Right-handed mitt	Right-handed people	Left-handed people—are their mitts more expensive? Harder to find?
Book written in English	English readers	Non-English readers—include anyone you know?
Cell phone	Those who can afford them and have access to networks	Those who can't afford them—who might these be?

Inquiry Area 6: Technology Benefits

We pay special attention to a technology's benefits because technologies are created to add value to our lives. If they didn't add value, producers wouldn't make them, and we wouldn't buy them. As STA de-tech-tives, the more we understand about why a technology is seen as valuable, the more thorough our investigation will be. Technology is a mirror. We see who we are in the technology choices we make.

Question: How does the technology benefit us?

Choose a technology, and ask which of these qualify as reasons we might adopt it:

- To save time or money
- To provide comfort, ease, or freedom from toil
- To avoid being left out
- To protect ourselves
- To become healthier or live longer
- To provide opportunities
- To add power to our lives
- To become educated or better prepared for the workforce

- To have fun or be entertained
- To feed an addiction or habit
- To improve communication
- Anything we missed?

Suggested Activity

Use the list above as a "check the box" checklist. Have students identify each benefit that fits the technology under consideration, and explain why each is relevant. As always, the more students talk among themselves, the better. Their greatest asset is what they teach each other when they compare and contrast their experiences and insights.

Inquiry Area 7: Technology's Impacts

Having seen the benefits of a technology, we can now consider a more balanced viewpoint by considering its impacts. Recall the essential question that drives our inquiry: How does technology connect and disconnect us? A more thorough consideration of that occurs here as we consider specific impacts and disconnects.

Question: How does the technology impact us?

Choose a technology, and address the question: How does the technology impact local, global, and digital communities in the following areas?

- The environment
- The human body
- Work
- Education
- Society, family, friendships, community
- Your relationship with yourself, with others
- Your higher self or spiritual self
- Future technologies, technology convergence
- The power structure
- Other cultures
- Others?

Suggested Activities

The reality is that doing a thorough job investigating each of these is impractical given the time budget most teachers have. So here are a few suggestions for busy teachers.

- Limit students to considering just a few of the impact areas. Let them choose the areas that interest them.

- Identify a few aspects for students to focus on. Any two or three will do, but perhaps spread them out among the environment, self, and some aspect of society (work, education, etc.).
- Ask students to consider just one or two impacts, specifically as they relate to local, global, or digital community, or some combination of these.
- Connect this to whatever you are doing in class. As a technology arises in class discussion, pause to ask about its impacts. Doing so can take as little as a minute or two.

Remember, the STA is a perspective as much as it is an activity. A little bit of discussion about technological impact is always better than none.

Step 2. Analysis, Debate, and Brainstorming

The Great Debate

Under ideal conditions, teachers set up three teams for the final project. Innovators debate the agents of the STA, and judges render a final decision about the fate of the technology. Prior to that, they work in their groups, brainstorming and preparing their findings. Here is the basic structure of the debate:

1. **Innovators.** These students represent the people who invented the technology that the STA investigates.

2. **Agents of the STA.** These are the STA de-tech-tives, automatically at least a little concerned about how the technology might impact society and the environment.

3. **Judges.** These students will listen to both sides and render a verdict about the technology.

This can take place in many forms but typically all students investigate the technology and then choose whether they will join a side of the debate or become a member of the panel of judges.

Step 3. Evaluate and Recommend

The final step in the great debate is for the judges to render a final decision in one of three forms:

1. **Acceptance.** The technology is good to go, whether it is a technology that already exists or one that students predict will be developed in the future.

2. **Rejection.** The technology may not be allowed to enter mainstream society in its current form as well as in any modified form.

3. **Conditional acceptance.** The technology can go forward but with modifications or conditions related to its use. Students need to be specific about what their recommended modifications or conditional uses need to address.

As always, reasoning needs to be thorough and articulate. And of course, the innovators are always allowed to appeal!

Pressed for Time?

As mentioned earlier, feel free to adapt this exercise to the reality of your classroom. Students may work alone, carrying out each phase of the project themselves. Or they may work cooperatively, taking advantage of the local, global, and digital experts they consult. However it plays out, the goal is for students to investigate, analyze, and make a decision about how to view the impacts of technology on human communities.

The essential thrust of this exercise can be included as much shorter inquiry activities by simply focusing on one of the essential questions:

- How does technology connect and disconnect us?
- What are its short-term versus longer-term effects?

These questions could be asked about:

- The railroad, as you study American westward expansion in social studies;
- The microscope, as you study the microscopic world in biology; or
- YouTube or blogspace, as you study mass publication and the risk of personal exposure in language arts.

Final Output

In terms of final output, it may be appropriate for students to simply draw their own conclusions or to work in groups to create a position paper, video, or multimedia project explaining their findings. Or teachers may just want students to summarize their findings, using some of the instruments shown in this chapter to help make an oral presentation in class. Perhaps your students already keep a learning blog, or are active in a 3D environment, in which case you could have them blend activities about technology assessment into previous projects. Whatever works.

A Plug for the Debate

If you have time, the great technology debate is a wonder to behold. Some of my favorite moments as a teacher

FYI

The Lasting Effects of Technology Evaluation

I was in a department store one day when I saw a former student of mine staring at a blender. "Hi!" I exclaimed, genuinely glad to see her. She looked at me and scowled. "Every time I go to buy a piece of technology, I can't help asking myself how it connects and disconnects me!" That was a compliment, I think.

have been listening to students ardently defend a toaster oven or, as in the case study I present just ahead, argue for the development of a consumer awareness rating system for digitally retouched media.

Debates can be lively, whether about a pencil, a digital camera, or an imaginary technology that students predict will be developed in the future. By the end of the debate, students will have developed many important critical thinking capabilities. And they will be able to analyze and evaluate a technology in great detail in terms of its impacts on and potential for all their communities—local, global, and digital.

A CASE STUDY OF CONDITIONAL ACCEPTANCE: THE CASE OF DIGITALLY RETOUCHING PHOTOS

Like life, technology assessment is never black and white. Presented here is a case study involving middle school students that bears this out.

Middle school students were presented with a technology assessment issue that had received a great deal of publicity at the time: digitally altered photos that were appearing in major media magazines. *Time, Newsweek,* and even *National Geographic* had been implicated in altering published photos and not alerting the public. The public found out and began to object.

After collecting a good deal of information and considering the issue in light of some of the STA's inquiry areas, students were left to debate what to do about it. The innovators argued freedom of speech, and the STA agents argued responsibility in journalism. Ultimately, the class decided to give photo manipulation a "conditional acceptance" as long as photos that appeared in magazines and on journalistic websites included a number that represented the degree of manipulation. The scale they adopted was

1 to 10. Further, they said that readers should be able to click on web-published versions of photos and see the original as well as read a paragraph about how the photo had been manipulated.

Students then debated how to calibrate the scale. They decided a 1 (the low end of the scale) meant the following. I am paraphrasing their actual words:

- Not changing much of anything
- Changing colors of small things and removing red eye caused by camera flash
- Slightly moving or deleting a small object
- It didn't take too much time or alter too many pixels
- No one got hurt too much.

On the other hand, a 10 was the following:

- Seriously changing an object (putting Elvis's head on the Queen's body)
- Making it look like you can fly when you can't
- Changing the meaning of the picture
- Using a lot of cut and paste
- Changing evidence
- Someone was hurt badly

Who Should Rate the Pictures?

The students further reasoned that there would need to be a rating board to rate the pictures. The question became, What qualifications should the picture raters have? Students were borrowing the idea from the motion picture rating industry, and I was very impressed to see that they realized that determining rater qualifications was an important part of the system they proposed. In summary, they determined raters needed to be the following:

- At least 21 years of age (or at least 14!—see note below)
- The kind of person who wants to be a senator
- Someone with a good education
- Someone who is fair and impartial
- Someone who cares about the issue
- Someone who thinks about all circumstances
- Someone who thinks "correctly"

Note about minimum age requirements for photo raters. When students announced that they had decided that photo raters needed to be at least 21, everyone in the room—all of whom were roughly 14 years of age—loudly objected. The students immediately backed down and said that a minimum of 14 years old would suffice. It was a priceless moment for me, as I watched every student in the room declare they wanted the right to be part of the rating committee. They had researched the issue, and they had something to say about it.

Will There Ever Be Such a Rating System?

Like many good ideas that require us to submit to yet another set of regulations, a rating system for manipulated photos has been much more a good thought experiment than a real-world possibility. However, that changed recently in France due to concern for the health of young women.

The idea came from a group of French politicians, led by eating disorder expert Mrs. Valerie Boyer. She proposed warning labels for photos in magazines and advertising "to combat the idea that all women are young and slim." As of November 2009, the proposed wording for a warning label would read, "Retouched photograph aimed at changing a person's physical appearance." Mrs. Boyer suggested a fine of more than $16,000, or as much as 50% of the ad campaign's cost, for those companies not in compliance (Creamer, 2009).

Interested in this issue? Like so many areas of technological impact, this area of inquiry fascinates and haunts us. We enjoy the aesthetics of the web while expecting it to have journalistic honesty. The reality is that we haven't figured out how to have both and maintain a strong commitment to freedom of speech. Connect-disconnect. Thus, for now, the warning to digital citizens is currently caveat emptor—may the buyer beware. That being the case, here are some of my favorite resources in this area:

The Photoshop Effect

(www.youtube.com/watch?v=YP31r70_QNM&feature=related) This video features an interview with a professional photographer who talks about the prevalence of digital photo retouching in his profession and walks us through the process of digitally retouching the photograph of a model.

Girl Power

(demo.fb.se/e/girlpower/retouch) This interactive site allows you to deconstruct a digitally retouched photo. Be sure to click on the picture until you get the menu of photo changes. Then step through the changes to see how the picture was retouched.

Dove's Evolution of Beauty

This very popular video (www.youtube.com/watch?v=iYhCn 0jf46U) shows a time lapse series of a woman's face being prepared for billboard publication.

Automatic Beauty Software

And lest you think that photo retouching is something that only professionals can do, read "A 'beauty function' for a better look" (www.zdnet.com/blog/emergingtech/a-beauty-function-for-a-better-look/483). The article examines software that can automatically make you look "better."

Check my Digital Citizenship Resource Wiki (jasonOhler.com/dc) for updates in this area. Also, please visit the wiki, and add resources of your own.

ISSUES ARE EVERYWHERE

There is an endless supply of issues like digitally retouching photographs for students to investigate, explore, and debate. My suggestion is pick a newspaper—paper based or virtual—and draw from there. For instance, in today's Google Tech News (April 28, 2010) I read articles about Apple banning Flash on the iTablet, Facebook not caring about your privacy, and a decline in the earth's biodiversity. And that was just this morning. Each of these has tremendous connections and disconnections and can be investigated readily in light of the seven areas of inquiry detailed in this chapter. And most important, each of them will directly impact all of us in one way or another.

A FAVORITE PROJECT:
THE ENERGY USE SELF-STUDY

The preservice teachers in my technology integration classes come from many subject areas, including art, physical education, social studies, science, foreign language, math, health, and language arts. I am always searching for the perfect activity for them that will include as many of their areas as possible and stretch them into other content areas as well. Although perfection is always elusive, I want projects that do the following:

- Use a crosscurricular, project-based approach to content; after all, real life is project based and crosscurricular in nature;
- Model pedagogical and research practices that are effective and easily transferrable to other projects;
- Model practices that my preservice teachers can use with their own middle and high school students;
- Combine personal responsibility with broad impacts—that is, that combine thinking globally and acting locally;
- Focus on a real issue of the day that has the potential to be personally important to most people;
- Focus on a real issue in the sense that when students change their own lifestyle, there are real local and global impacts;
- Use a wide variety of digital tools to solve real-world problems; and
- Use and contribute to digital community in terms of making their findings available to other teachers.

That sounds like a tall order, but there are many opportunities available to us that meet these criteria. My favorite for the past five years or so has been the energy use self-study.

In this project, students use a version of what most scientists would recognize as the standard research process to study some aspect of their own energy consumption. They record their habits, compute their energy consumption, and then use a spreadsheet to play "what if?" in order to explore how changes in their lifestyle can impact energy use. They also use a perspective called "a factor of 10," so they can see what happens when they convince 10 others to adopt lifestyle changes they have made. It is a project that combines much of what is best in a unit of instruction in that it is a crosscurricular, project-based approach to understanding an important global issue in personal terms.

I should note that I am often puzzled and concerned about the fact that whenever I use what I call "the standard research process" with preservice teachers, many of whom have degrees in science, few have seen it before or used it frequently enough to embed it in their professional practice. To me, it is the most useful research framework in our inquiry arsenal. It can be used to address "Was Hamlet bipolar?" in language arts just as easily as it can be used to address "What are the impacts of global warming in your

FYI

Standing on the Shoulders of Giants

Like many of the activities I use in education, I adapted this from someone else's work. In so doing I am "standing on the shoulders of giants," to paraphrase Newton (Wikiquote, 2010a). I first heard about the energy self study in the 1980s as part of the work done by Beverly Hunter (1983), one of the very earliest pioneers in educational technology in the desktop computing age.

area?" in science or social studies class. Bottom line: Make no assumption about prior learning in terms of this process.

I should also note that I make no pretense to conducting rigorous research with this project—there simply isn't the time or equipment. The research projects are short and therefore limited in what they can do. Instead, we focus on the research process and in doing the best we can with the little bit of time and resources we have. The research process is described below.

The Research Process: Studying Our Energy Consumption

The basic steps are as follows. Please note that I have made some modifications to the standard research process to suit my particular needs. By all means, personalize this according to your own goals, the needs of your students, and the time and equipment realities of your classroom.

1. **Determine an essential question.** In our case it might be, "How can each of us conserve energy on a daily basis and thus help the overall energy crisis?" It is in many ways like an "essential question" used in learning by design (Wiggins & McTighe, 2005).

2. **Operationalize the essential research question.** Doing so should produce a simple, concrete, compelling question, accompanied by perhaps a few clarifying questions that look at your essential question in real terms. An example in our case might simply be, "How much energy would I save if I used compact fluorescent light (CFL) bulbs instead of incandescent bulbs?"

3. **Create a preconception inventory, allowing students to track their own learning.** Research tries to document change over time. In this case, this includes tracking what students learn during the course of the assignment. There is no better way for students to assess their own learning than to have them articulate what they think they know prior to beginning their research, and then have them revisit their preconceptions after the project is concluded. It is always eye-opening. This element of research was

popularized by I-Search pedagogy some years ago. In some formal research, it might surface as a hypothesis about what researchers expect to find.

4. **Google existing info on the topic.** This is the modern version of doing a lit review. It's not ideal, but it fits into the overall flow of a busy classroom much more easily. There is plenty of information available about subjects like converting from incandescent to CFL lighting, and it is important that students think in terms of what others have already discovered in this area. In so doing, they enter the larger research community, which is often digital and global in nature. Please note, understanding how to be a discriminating information consumer might be an appropriate pre-activity so that students can better understand the value of the information they find.

5. **Determine the data you need to answer the question.** In our case, the primary data students need is the number of hours they use their lightbulbs, the number of kilowatt hours they use and the cost of doing so, and the difference in electrical usage of the two kinds of bulbs. Anything else? How about how often they have to replace bulbs?

6. **Determine the methodology needed to get the data.** One of my students who conducted this research actually left a pad of paper and a pencil at each light and asked family members to log their on-off times. Again, this is not rigorous research. If it were, we would buy expensive meters that would log energy usage automatically. But don't let the perfect be the enemy of the good. Doing a reasonable job, and citing the limitations of your research design in your research report, is very acceptable.

7. **Conduct the research, and obtain and store the data.** Typically, students collect the data and enter it into a spreadsheet.

8. **Perform an analysis in light of the research question, playing "what if?" with your lifestyle.** Now the fun part. Students get to play "what if?" with their lifestyles using the powers of the spreadsheet to compare and contrast the energy used by the two kinds of bulbs. In so doing, they produce real results that apply to their lifestyles and their impact on the world. Rather than just comparing the two kinds of bulbs, you might also want students to play "what if?" with being more vigilant about light usage or with finding alternatives for low-use areas within their homes.

And don't forget "a factor of 10." That is, if each student convinced 10 others to be as responsible as they were, what would the results be? Real savings are produced very quickly.

9. **Present conclusions.** There are many ways to do this, but I usually require my students to stand and deliver their findings using a presentation created with PowerPoint, Keynote, or another suitable piece of presentation software. Given that art is the fourth R, I require students to use image metaphors, like pictures of barrels of oil, to show savings over a year, 10 years, or a lifetime. Without much effort, they produce a potential savings of several barrels of oil that they represent in visually compelling ways.

> ### FYI
>
> #### Watching Yourself Teach
>
> I will never forget the first time I watched a recording of my teaching. I was horrified. I walked around the classroom, constantly clicking a pen with absolutely no awareness I was doing so. It was so annoying, distracting, and embarrassing that I could make it through only the first few minutes of the recording before I had to shut off the video player. Ever since then, I have regularly recorded and watched myself—and braced myself for the worst. There is no question that watching myself teach has cleaned up my act immensely.

Because my students are going to be teachers, I also add another component to the project, which can only be considered cruel and unusual punishment: I force them to record their presentations, watch them, and critique them. Athletes and performers use this to improve their games. Teachers should too. There is no better way to see what their students see and hear all day long, including the ums, ahs, and strange habits, like calling on only boys in the back of the room for some unknown reason. Until you see these habits in action, you can't change them. It is an exercise in making your teaching practice figure rather than ground.

10. **Cite the limits of the study and describe the need for further study.** Part of the conclusion consists of citing the limitations of the study. The call for further study is considered a "handoff" to the next researcher who wants to build on your research. In this case, the study was limited because students could not collect data over longer periods of time and because they used imperfect data collection techniques. Thus, a call for further study might cite the need to address these issues. It might also cite the need to expand the study to include a wide range of lifestyles as well as perhaps different approaches to using natural light. In addition, their literature search was limited by the realities of the classroom day, which probably translated into some Googling and using Wikipedia.

11. **Revisit your preconceptions—what did you learn?** Students look at their preconception inventory created in step 3 and revise what they learned, citing misconceptions and misinformation. It is always illuminating.

12. **Post findings online.** All of my students keep blogfolios—that is, blogs they use as portfolios—to chronicle what they learn during their educational technology coursework. Results are presented publicly, using Google Docs, SlideShare, YouTube—whatever is appropriate to post the many parts of their project. Sharing results is what digital citizens do.

Hundreds of my students have completed this research project, studying such things as:

- Using a microwave instead of a convection oven to bake potatoes;
- Hang drying their clothes rather than using a dryer;
- Biking rather than driving to work a few days a week;
- Reducing the thermostat at night by just one degree; and
- Using a traveling cup rather than disposable paper coffee cups to reduce waste.

You name it. The result is always the same—aha. You don't know what you don't know, and you can't expand your knowledge until you raise an issue to figure that had once been ground. For most of us, the use of energy is ground in that we don't really think about it. This project raises it to figure.

Let's quickly review the benefits of a project like this:

- Students determine ways they can impact a global issue on a personal, and thus very local, level.
- They make this determination by using a time-honored research methodology that they can transfer to many projects in many content areas.
- They use crosscurricular, project-based pedagogy that focuses on understanding a real-life issue of great importance that appears in the newspaper in some form almost daily: our collective overuse of energy and the ripple effect that produces.
- They save not only energy but also money. Thus, there is a personal payoff for their investment of time.
- They combine math, research, current events, technology use, writing, and other skills. In the hands of a creative teacher, this project

can become the springboard for a unit in social studies and science as well as other areas. Incidentally, the math skills they use are very accessible to the nonmathematician. They are only slightly more advanced than those used in preparing a personal budget.

- They combine many kinds of technology applications in the service of research, including web searching, spreadsheet use, using presentation software, web-posting resources, word processing, blogging, and so on.
- Their lives as local, global, and digital citizens intersect meaningfully.

There are many projects like this that can be created using a similar perspective. Some are international in scope, comparing and contrasting issues like energy use among different communities and countries. Some look at the impacts of resource extraction and waste in terms of impact to human living conditions and environmental damage. Pick your topic, cast it into the research process above, and then avail yourself of the many opportunities that the digital community has to offer.

USING STORIES

Much of my professional life is spent helping teachers and students of all ages create media-based stories and other forms of new media narrative that are meaningful to them. I do this because stories are immensely powerful, not just as media we consume, but particularly as media we create.

The power of stories is well documented, and the opportunities to have students create stories and minidocumentaries about the connects and disconnects of technology are enormous. If you want to read more about it, I would refer you to my book *Digital Storytelling in the Classroom* (2008) or my web materials at jasonOhler.com/storytelling. Rest assured that having students create stories about any aspect of digital citizenship is a powerful and academically solid approach to engaging students in research and expression. However, I routinely assign another form of personal narrative that I find very effective: the letter. Descriptions of two of these assignments follow.

Letters for the Future

I have been using some version of "the letter for the future" ever since I was introduced to it about 25 years ago. In its simplest form, I ask students to write letters to themselves that they seal, address, and give to me for safekeeping. A year later, I mail their letters to them. I instruct students to write bold letters that ask hard questions about their lives, particularly about whether or not they had accomplished what they had hoped to during the past 12 months, as friends, students, and digital citizens. I don't read the letters, but my sense is that most accept that challenge. I have used this activity with high school students and graduate students. It never ceases to enlighten. Imagine using this activity specifically for purposes of digital citizenship training.

Letters From the Future

I taught a course for teachers for many years called "Thinking About Technology," which helped teachers consider technology's connective and disconnective properties. For the final assignment, I had students write "letters from the future" and read them in class at the end of the semester.

The basic approach to this assignment is as follows. After studying many of the topics addressed in this book, students project themselves 10, 20, or 50 years into the future and report back about how technology has evolved and impacted local, global, and digital communities. Students write the letter to someone they care about, and they are free to use vernacular writing as long as their writing is clear, well organized, and compelling.

Their task was twofold: to create a background snapshot of the future by providing details of everyday life, and to focus on one particular area that was related to their professional practice. Thus, for example, physical education teachers wrote about new gear they might be using in the future, while often social studies teachers typically focused on the social issues they thought would have become important in the intervening years, and so on. Students left their fingerprints of the class all over their work by applying technology assessment to a future world they created.

Besides being a very engaging and effective assignment, it also opened up writing avenues for students that often produced remarkable results. Students who didn't tend to write very good reports almost always wrote good letters. In their letters, their writing often improved in terms of grammar, organization, insight, and voice. Clearly, if students write better letters than reports, then this is indicative of an attitudinal issue rather than a cognitive issue. If it were the latter, they wouldn't do well with either assignment. I came to appreciate that the word *essay* or *report* created a kind of attitudinal blockage that could impede creativity, clarity, and writing ability. The word *letter* tells students "welcome home." In 25 years of teaching, no student ever wrote a bad letter from the future.

McLUHAN'S TETRAD

I close this section of the book by paying homage to the most comprehensive technology assessment model I have ever seen: the tetrad, created by Eric and Marshall McLuhan (1988).

It is a testimony to simplicity without sacrificing power. As such, it provides much grist for the mill even for novices who are trying to see the impacts of technology more clearly. It informs a good deal of my approach to assessing technology, including how I define the inquiry areas that I addressed in this chapter.

Basically, the model says that every new technology or medium does four things, as captured by the following four inquiry areas. The wording is adapted with permission from Eric McLuhan's (1998) *Electric Language*:

Enhance. What is enlarged, amplified, or increased (or miniaturized) or accelerated (if previously slow) or retarded (if previously fast)?

Obsolete. What is displaced, pushed offstage, or sidelined? What used to be the norm but no longer is because of the new thing?

Retrieval. What is renewed, retrieved, or reactivated? What old thing is updated? What comeback is made? What is revived?

Reversal or flip. What does the subject turn into when its enhancement process eventually becomes the norm instead of the unusual? What happens when the figure becomes the ground? What happens when you push the enhancement phase too far?

All four aspects of the tetrad are always in play. That is, every technology enhances, obsolesces, retrieves, and flips, all at the same time. Wikipedia offers the following example of how this works with regard to the radio:

- **Enhancement (figure).** What the medium amplifies or intensifies. *For example, radio amplifies news and music via sound.*
- **Obsolescence (ground).** What the medium drives out of prominence. *Radio reduces the importance of print and the visual.*
- **Retrieval (figure).** What the medium recovers which was previously lost. *Radio returns the spoken word to the forefront.*
- **Reversal (ground).** What the medium does when pushed to its limits. *Acoustic radio flips into audio-visual TV.* (Tetrad of Media Effects, 2009)

Our interest here is in the tetrad as an investigative framework for our students. Thus, we might focus on more modern digital technologies.

Here is my best guess about applying the tetrad to, for example, the cell phone:

- **Enhancement (figure).** The cell phone extends voice over distances, enhancing person-to-person communication.
- **Obsolescence (ground).** The cell phone reduces the importance of face-to-face communication and thus the importance of geographic context and some forms of meta-information.
- **Retrieval (figure).** The cell phone returns the importance of person-to-person (not face-to-face) communication in a world of broadcast media and group-oriented social media.
- **Reversal (ground).** The cell phone flips into video conferencing, returning much of the context that face-to-face communication used to provide. In a more extreme reversal, we can become saturated with virtual proximity in the Digital Age and revert to traditional travel, that is, actually moving our bodies in space in order to communicate with someone.

This is not an exact science. You can Google "McLuhan tetrad cell phone" and find other interpretations. What is important here is the perspective that students can gain by looking at technology in such a structured manner. Every technology in their lives can be explored via the tetrad, opening interesting avenues of research about how their gadgets impact them—and vice versa.

Part III

Character Education in the Digital Age

And the Case of the Ideal School Board

7 Imagining the Ideal School Board

PARTY-CIPATION: SETTING THE STAGE

When I began writing this book, I had no idea that my journey would ultimately bring to me the topic of character education. Yet in hindsight, it seems inevitable.

To provide some context for that journey, let me set the stage by using a metaphor to explain why issues of ethics, morality, personal safety, and the greater social good seem much more complex and confusing now than they did in previous eras.

Our metaphor is a party celebrating participation, the hallmark of Web 2.0. In fact, we call this party *Party-cipation*, pronounced *participation*. What follows is a description.

Party-cipation has millions of attendees, with more joining each day. It costs almost nothing to attend, and you can do so from just about anywhere. At Party-cipation you meet new people, make new friends, forge alliances, conduct business—whatever your encounters call for. While you are free to identify yourself, this party has a masquerade option, so that no one really has to know your true identity. Thus, you can be whoever you want and say basically whatever you want to whomever you want about whatever you want. This also means that you never really know whom you are talking to either, or whether what they say is remotely true.

At Party-cipation you can have multiple identities, allowing you to experiment with your persona as you encounter new social situations. At this gathering you also have access to an ever-expanding smorgasbord of resources that are dreamlike in scope and variety. You can literally think it, search for it, and find it—movies, old friends, animated children's books, augmented reality tattoos, ideas for vegan dinner parties, group conversations dedicated to effective poodle grooming. You name it. It's all there. You can take home a copy of much of what you see and hear, knowing that the owner will not lose his original. You can even modify whatever you find and give it back to Party-cipation as something borrowed but originalized. Whatever you contribute often becomes a matter of permanent public record.

All of this happens with only passing concerns about injury or repercussions—to oneself or others. And bonus, you don't need to dress up, and the only health issues are those associated with sitting too long. Given this much freedom, at this little cost, there were bound to be ethical issues at Party-cipation.

The foregoing is just one description of the social Internet. A competing metaphor is "the Wild West," but that image always conjured up too much gunslinging and too little civility for me. After all, many good things happen at Party-cipation as well.

Regardless of what metaphor you prefer, it is the fact that many of our children attend Party-cipation that drives much of our current interest in digital citizenship. In fact, there is one other aspect of Party-cipation not mentioned above that also drives this interest and weighs particularly heavily on the parental mind: Party-cipation can be used as a gateway to RL (real life)—and vice versa. The interplay between the two can be anything from complimentary to contradictory, from a direct way to reinforce an integrated view of identity to a way to circumvent public attention in order to pursue separate presentations of self. However it is used, we need to be concerned because "the job of adolescence is centered around experimentation—with ideas, with people, with notions of self" (Turkle, 2008, p. 125). Prior to the infosphere, adults could witness the identity play and development of emerging youth and intervene when necessary. As of the invisible world of personal networks, this becomes much more difficult.

However we may feel about Party-cipation, we shouldn't lose sight of how significant it is in the evolution of human endeavor. At Party-cipation, people basically reinvent society through their use of a number of options regarding how to identify themselves, interact with others, and develop and distribute information and creative content. What the Internet presents us with is, in many ways, the extreme freedom that the existentialists have been telling us has always been our natural state. We are free to create human nature as we see fit, and we do so by the choices we make. In the process, we establish norms, values, and a sense of personal and collective identity. The result is that the carte blanche of Party-cipation creates a window into the human condition and the nature of the human psyche that is historically unparalleled in terms of depth, scope, and intrigue.

Bottom line: While we might talk a good game about goals, ethics, and the greater good, Party-cipation reminds us that we are what we do. We can respond to the freedom we are presented by Party-cipation as seriously or lightly, as altruistically or selfishly, and as virtuously or nefariously as we wish. We can reinvent the world according to our better angels, or we can squander this opportunity by creating mountains of drivel and worlds of hurt. Connect-disconnect: It is up to us.

WHAT CONCERNS US: THE EXTREME EDGE OF FREEDOM

What concerns us is the misbehavior that occurs at the extreme edge of all this freedom, particularly when it comes to the safety of the children in our care. Some combination of disinhibition, an underdeveloped adolescent brain, the lack of a moral compass (which some would say indicates a lack of moral training), and, no doubt, grievous personal issues have led a number of people in digital community to behave rudely and injuriously.

The infosphere is filled with stories that illustrate this. As I write this in the spring of 2010, a national furor is erupting in the news about another teen suicide that has allegedly been caused by extreme cyberbullying. While the suicide is disturbing enough, equally so is the fact that cyberbullying is largely an underground activity. Given that it is largely out of public view until something horrendous like a suicide occurs, we are left to wonder what else happens in the largely invisible world of the infosphere.

But there is plenty to get our attention in public view as well, and not just in the United States. According to a recent AP report, an Italian court convicted three Google executives in absentia "for violating the privacy of an Italian boy with autism by letting a video of him being bullied be posted on the site in 2006" (D'Alessandro, 2010,

> **FYI**
>
> ### The Tragic Case of Megan Meier
>
> Particularly tragic was the case of Megan Meier, who hanged herself at age 13 after being taunted mercilessly on MySpace. The barrage began when she and a 16-year-old named Josh had an argument, and Josh began to bully her online. Josh was joined by others, and suddenly Megan was the victim of a cyberbullying frenzy. Six weeks after Megan's suicide, it was discovered that Josh was not a 16-year-old boy, but in fact was the mother of one of Megan's friends, with whom Megan had had a falling-out. The mother claimed she had intended her involvement to be a joke (Suicide of Megan Meier, 2010). Megan's mother, Tina, has created the Megan Meier Foundation to raise awareness about bullying and cyberbullying. You can read more at: meganmeierfoundation.org.

para. 1). Note that the boys who created and uploaded the video were not charged; Google was. Google executives, who plan to fight the ruling, claimed that Google did remove the video immediately after being asked to do so. In addition, they claim that they cooperated with Italian authorities to help identify the bullies and bring them to justice. However, the prosecutors accused Google of negligence, arguing that "the video remained online for two months even though some web users had already posted comments asking for it to be taken down" (para. 18).

Thus, part of digital citizenship is about addressing the issues that populate the outer edge of our new freedoms, including:

- **Cyberbullying.** Cyberbullying is being cruel to others by sending or posting harmful material or engaging in other forms of social cruelty using the Internet or other digital technologies (Willard, 2010a, p. 2).
- **Cyberthreats.** Cyberthreats are either direct threats or distressing material that raise concerns or provide clues that the person is emotionally upset and may be considering harming someone, harming him- or herself, or committing suicide (Willard, 2010a, p. 7).
- **Sexting.** Sexting combines the words *sex* and *texting* to produce a new verb that generally refers to using a cell phone to take and transmit pictures of a sexual nature of oneself or others.
- **Secording.** Secording combines the words *secretly* and *recording*. Secording arises in a number of ways; but in the K–12 world, it has been popularized through student recordings of teachers on a bad day. In fact, in some cases, students purposely aggravate teachers before turning on their recording devices in order to capture a public display of anger.
- **Accessing age-inappropriate materials.** This largely involves minors accessing sexual material and other resources intended for adults.
- **Using web materials that belong to others.** In a K–12 setting, this usually refers to kids using online materials without permission. Doing so falls into a murky area of the law, bounded by "fair use" and theft. However, using web materials should always cause some kind of reflection about the legality and ethics of doing so. Often, it doesn't.
- **Factition.** A factitioner "distorts fact and fiction for the betterment of their own personal agendas" (Factitioner, n.d.). There are many examples of urban legends circulating on the web that contain everything from half-truths to outright lies. Determining what is true has become extremely important as well as very difficult to do.

These are just a few of the many "new" kinds of behavior that now must be addressed by our concern with citizenship in digital community. I caution against the use of the word *new* in any comprehensive sense because some of them are onsite behaviors adapted to cyberspace. In fact, some work in concert. Cyberbullying is a good example, as it can often be an extension of behavior begun in a school hallway.

However, some of these behaviors are truly new, like sexting and secording, made possible by new technology that facilitates behavior that would be basically impossible without it—the medium in part forming the message. You can see a more complete listing of these kinds of cyber issues, as well as add your own, at my Digital Citizenship Resources Wiki (jasonOhler.com/dc).

> **FYI**
>
> **The Link Between Real Life and Cyberspace**
>
> Researcher David Finkelhor, reporting on a study conducted by Hinduja and Patchin, notes the following: "Most cyberbullying cases involve kids who know each other from the real world, typically from school. Finkelhor (2010) reports that in a 2008 study of middle schoolers conducted by Sameer Hinduja and Justin Patchin, 82 percent said that the person who bullied them is either from their school (26.5 percent), a friend (21.1 percent), an ex-friend (20 percent) or an ex-boyfriend or ex-girlfriend (14.1 percent)." (Finkelhor, 2010, para. 2)

FROM ISSUES TO PROGRAMS

Addressing these kinds of activities is under way in the form of new policies and laws that have either been passed or are under consideration by many school districts and state governments. I have no doubt that sooner or later school districts that have been affected directly or indirectly by cybersafety issues will address them in some kind of administrative or legal manner.

However, as well intentioned as our new policies and laws may be, I worry that they will not address many of the underlying issues associated with digital behavior for two reasons.

Reason 1: The mean world syndrome comes to the infosphere. The first reason is that issues like sexting and cyberbullying engender such understandable and palpable anxiety that we tend to overstate their actual prevalence (Willard, 2010b). Doing so may simply be an extension into the digital domain of what media researcher George Gerbner (1994) called the "Mean World Syndrome." Basically, the mean world syndrome says that, because of the media's attraction to reporting the worst in human nature, people think the world is much more violent and dangerous than it actually is. It is certainly more dangerous than how most of us experience it. Gerbner argued that this phenomenon prompts a desire for more protection than is warranted by any actual threat. Although Gerbner was writing during the 1990s and was concerned primarily with research about television, his theory seems particularly relevant today.

Let me be clear: One instance in which a child is at cyber risk is one too many. But overstating an issue only deflects from the truth and thus simply makes it more difficult to figure out what we should do to effectively address the situation.

An example of overreaction illustrates this point. In Connecticut, sexting is currently considered a felony for minors because it constitutes child pornography. As the *Daily Campus* (Daily Campus Editorial Board, 2010) online publication notes, "Children and young adults, if found guilty [of sexting], would be forced to register as a sex offender. This would haunt them for the rest of their lives, and they would have to live their future branded" (para. 2).

Now consider the very real case of a 14-year-old girl in Lacy, Washington, who sent a graphic picture of herself to her boyfriend. When their relationship ended badly, her boyfriend forwarded the picture to his friends, who in turn forwarded it to others. If she lived in Connecticut, she would need to register as a sex offender for the rest of her life. The same may be true for the boyfriend and everyone else involved in receiving or forwarding the picture (Rebik, 2010).

Obviously, everyone involved in this case needs to be held accountable, and there are many ways to do this. But arbitrarily branding 14-year-olds as sex offenders in situations like these does not seem our best option. Doing so will most certainly destroy their lives, and I doubt it will do much to deter other adolescents. Additionally, given our understanding of the cognitive vulnerabilities of the average 14-year-old brain, a topic discussed later, we need to ask whether such treatment aligns with a young teenager's abilities to apply adult judgment in a situation like this.

Currently, another very real result of overreaction can be seen in school districts' tendency to filter Internet access in their schools to such an extent that they block a good deal of legitimate Internet use. Not only does this limit important access to academic resources, but it also provides adults very little opportunity to guide students through hazardous online situations. The paradox here, whether we are talking about kids driving cars, dating, or using the Internet, is simply this: If students don't have a chance to fail, then they don't have a chance to learn from their experience and, ultimately, succeed. In other words, digital citizenship requires guided practice. Without reasonable access to the Internet, this is impossible.

To be clear, every school district that accepts eRate funding—which greatly reduces the cost of Internet access—has to employ some form of filtering as described by the Children's Internet Protection Act (CIPA). Filtering must prevent access to material that is "(a) obscene, (b) child pornography, or (c) harmful to minors (for computers that are accessed by minors)" (Federal Communications Commission, 2009, para. 2). In addition, CIPA requires that schools and libraries "adopt and implement an Internet safety policy" (para. 4) that addresses a number of issues with regard to minors, including security, hacking, and the dissemination of personal information. More information is available at the CIPA website (www.fcc.gov/cgb/consumerfacts/cipa.html).

What is important to understand is that CIPA provides a great deal of latitude in terms of how these issues are addressed. The result is that there is a great deal of variation from district to district. The norm seems to be to err on the side of caution by severely limiting access. However, I have spoken with a number of teachers from districts with more open policies who much prefer dealing with issues that arise due to increased access to those that arise due to heavy filtering. They claim that a balanced approach involves some combination of modest filtering, education, mentoring, and "trust but verify" approaches to Internet access. They also emphasize the involvement of parents as well as training kids to become their own filters. An adage circulating the Internet is, "The best filter kids can have is the one between their ears." This can happen only if students are actually schooled in positive Internet practice. And that can happen only if they have access to the Internet. Needless to say, a primary guideline in determining the appropriate balance between access and filtering is the age and developmental level of the students involved.

Reason 2: The disconnection of digital issues. The second reason I worry that our current response will not address the real issues associated with cybersafety is that we tend to respond to these issues individually, as though they were disconnected and resolvable only on a case by case basis. In reality, they are connected and need to be approached as such. We need a whole-school approach to behavior that sets the entirety of being digitally active within an overall ethical and behavioral context—character education for the Digital Age.

The new reality that character education must address is that we have entered an era of permanent innovative overdrive in which the development of new tools that facilitate new behaviors is an ongoing reality. The result is that invention goes from figure to ground so quickly that we barely notice it. If I told you 15 years ago that today you would be walking around with a pocket-size telephone that allowed you to watch TV and shoot movies that you could instantly share with friends a half a world away, you would have told me I was crazy. Remember how outrageous Second Life seemed when you first saw it? Or how amazing it seemed to use Facebook to reconnect with all those people you thought you would never hear from again? Now this all seems quite normal. Ground, as it were.

Now try to imagine the technology that will enter mainstream culture in the years ahead. Some of it is foreseeable, and then there is all the stuff we can't possibly predict because it defies current imagination. The future goes on for a long time. All we know for sure is that technology connects and disconnects, and that while the connections may be miraculous, the disconnections will be both powerful and troubling.

Bottom line: We will never keep pace with the issues of digital citizenship if we treat each issue as an isolated event. We need to use some form of character education to integrate and coordinate our hopes and concerns about living a digital lifestyle. Such an approach would allow us to establish expectations associated with student responsibility and safety in RL, cyberspace, and the world that bridges the two. Policies we create to address individual issues would then make much more sense.

LESSONS FROM THE PAST

How we are currently responding to cyber concerns reminds me of how we dealt with innovation in the arena of educational technology during the 1980s. Each new innovation (in those days that could mean adding a hard drive to a computer that used only floppy disks) was treated as an isolated, earth-shattering event. The response was often focused on just the particular innovation, as though all we had to do was make it through this particular storm of change, and we would be in the clear.

But as the innovations kept coming, our isolated responses to the challenges of change seemed doomed to fail. We needed to respond in a way that helped us see a bigger picture in order to provide context for the many individual challenges we finally accepted were never going to end.

Thus, we developed technology plans, codes of conduct, standards, frameworks, scope and sequence documents, and other instruments to guide us through changing and challenging times. The actual process of discussing and working through the details was just as important as the plans we produced. Everything was changing, and we needed to talk. Our documents were essentially static wikis that captured our evolving conversations about living during a time of unprecedented change. When we finally admitted that technological innovation was a permanent social process, we could finally begin to imagine our futures.

We need to approach digital citizenship in much the same way. In particular, we need plans based on the following assumptions:

- **Change is constant and often exponential.** It is largely driven by technology and how technology modifies and amplifies human behavior.
- **Humans are tool makers, explorers, and innovators by nature.** We will experiment with whatever new creative possibilities arise, sometimes reflectively and with a sense of purpose, sometimes not.
- **We have no idea what technological innovation awaits us.** Thus, we need approaches to living in community that are effective regardless of the nature of technological change.
- **We live in an era in which the new technologies and the behaviors they facilitate form a new, integrated foundation for how we live, think, imagine, and act.** We now live within a tEcosystem, a new ecosystem constituted of technology, connectivity, and the communication they facilitate. It provides a pervasive, invisible support system that massages everything we do. Unlike our natural ecosystem, it responds relatively quickly to human demands.
- **We simultaneously live in three ecosystems (natural, human, and technological) and three communities (local, global, and digital).** Any approach to citizenship needs to address all of these as well as the issue of integrating all of them in productive, meaningful ways. As always, children need training to understand the ethics and behavioral expectations involved in living in this new community.
- **The need for community remains constant.** What persists amidst all the change is our need to cultivate the social good and provide a context for effective, meaningful community. This need connects us to "the ancient human" (Dertouzos, 2001).
- **We cultivate the social good by clarifying our values and goals as a community.** We need to clarify the behaviors that will reflect these values and goals. From this, we can build an approach to character education for our school systems that is responsive to our needs.
- **We need practical processes and structures.** Our response needs to be pragmatic, identifying school processes and programs that promote general perspectives about being healthy, productive digital citizens. This includes the development of ways to address the individual behavioral issues associated with digital citizenship as they arise.
- **We need to understand that there is no turning back.** The future is endless and filled with life-changing technology that makes character

education eternally important. The need for character development has always been important. Our digital tools simply modify and amplify this.

- **The pursuit of character and academics are equally important**. Successful schools for the future will address both, integrate both, and do so with community support.

Currently, the educational world places only minimal emphasis on programs that help students understand digital behavior. Instead, it focuses on helping students use technology, and then it panics when it sees signs of misuse. This can lead to the kinds of misunderstandings and over-reactions that will derail any progress made in the development of digital citizenship. Ideally, a digital character education program would substantially help to prevent many of the cyber issues from happening in the first place as well as help to address them much more constructively when they do occur.

THE IDEAL SCHOOL BOARD

How do we approach all of this change?

Let's wax allegorical, and imagine that we belong to "digital community" in the broadest sense of the term, and that our community has a school board that is ideal, at least in terms of its intent. What makes our school board special is that it has adopted a mission to critically assess the opportunities, concerns, and social controversy surrounding kids, technology, and social media. As part of this mission, school board members publicly discuss the important issues of the day with the goal of helping students become caring, intelligent, responsible digital citizens. Inevitably, this leads to their interest in some kind of character education for their students.

Given this is pure fantasy, allow me to embellish. School board members freely admit that they did not grow up with the Internet or digital technology and therefore can't call upon their own experiences to guide them. Thus, they are open to advice from credible stakeholders who have insight to share. These include teachers, community members, students, and experts from many fields . . . anyone with a stake in building a better community by improving the school system. The school board has a healthy time budget (perhaps they are all retired university professors or outcasts from the recent economic downturn) and an unslakable curiosity to understand digital kids, Party-cipation, and life in the tEcosystem. In fact, board members are so committed to this goal that they have adopted the following mission points to guide them in their quest.

In order to help students become responsible, caring, creative, productive digital citizens, our school system will do the following:

- Help students combine their digital and nondigital lives into an integrated approach to identity;
- Help students use technology not just effectively but also creatively and wisely, so they can balance technology's opportunities and limitations in order to cultivate a life that involves critical thinking, creativity, hope, purpose, and a respect for themselves and their communities;
- Require that the use of technology, information resources, and media be considered not just as a means to employment, learning, and personal development but also as subjects of inquiry with regard to their impacts on ourselves, our society, and our environment; and
- Use test scores and academic achievement as only a partial gauge of the health of our school district. Equally important will be students' character development and their ability to contribute effectively and positively to the local, global, and digital communities in which they participate.

Pure fantasy? Perhaps. But unless we are going to ban selling technology to everyone under 18, this is exactly the direction we need to take.

BACKGROUND MATERIALS FOR CREATING AN AGENDA

Our school board's next step is to produce a school board agenda. But being as wise as they are, school board members know they need to conduct some research into perspectives about digital citizenship before proceeding. Here are resources to get them started that cover a wide spectrum of viewpoints. All of these have links on my Digital Citizenship Resources Wiki (jasonOhler.com/dc).

An Analysis of ISTE Standards

In 2005, I developed professional development materials that addressed ISTE Standard VI—the social, ethical, legal, and human issues related to the use of technology in education. Bear in mind that this was part of version 1.0 of the ISTE standards (2000), as the NETS refreshed standards were still a few years into the future. My approach was to first distill common themes from ISTE's many standard sets, including standards for students, teachers, and administrators. What emerged were the following themes:

- Social needs, cultural identity, and global community
- Equity, diversity, and equal access
- Legalities, ethics, and copyright
- Privacy and security
- Safety and health
- Media bias
- Responsibility and appropriate/inappropriate technology use

While the refreshed standards address many of these issues, they go much further by placing them within the purview of digital citizenship, giving these issues much-needed contextual focus. I admit to teasing "media bias" out of thin evidence. It is absolutely crucial as a survival skill for children, and it is addressed later as part of the digital literacy agenda item. My analysis is available as a PowerPoint presentation through my Digital Citizenship site (jasonOhler.com/dc) and has been updated to reflect the refreshed standards. It also includes material presented in Part II of this book.

Ribble and Bailey

Mike Ribble and Gerald Bailey's (2007) work, *Digital Citizenship in the School*, provides a comprehensive approach to understanding the issues of digital citizenship from a practical perspective. Their nine areas of digital citizenship are as follows:

1. Digital access
2. Digital commerce
3. Digital communication
4. Digital literacy
5. Digital etiquette

6. Digital law

7. Digital rights and responsibilities

8. Digital health and wellness

9. Digital security

Their work is accompanied by professional development materials that would be very helpful to anyone trying to establish or administer a digital citizenship program in a school district.

Carrie James: Young People, Ethics, and the New Media

James (2009) and her research team identify "ethical fault lines" rather than issues of digital citizenship. However, these verge on many of the issues commonly identified by those concerned about kids and social media. Her five areas of interest are

1. Identity;

2. Privacy;

3. Ownership and authorship;

4. Credibility; and

5. Participation.

James (2009) discusses these in terms of "good play," which she defines as "online conduct that is meaningful and engaging to the participant and is responsible to others in the community and society, in which it is carried out" (p. xiv). Her work describes many of the deeply personal issues that emerge as a result of Party-cipation.

Sherry Turkle: "Always–on/Always-on-you: The Tethered Self"

Dr. Turkle's wise and articulate research on the emerging nature of the digital self has been a key part of public and academic discussion of the nature of digital kids since personal computers first made their appearance in the 1980s. In this chapter from *Handbook of Mobile Communication Studies* (Katz, 2008), she connects the dots that confuse so many of us about the changing nature of self, identity, boundaries, and community in a wireless generation. Her focus on the wireless teen and its implications for maturity and socialization are essential to our understanding of creating schools that address the realities of the adolescent and teen experience.

The Center for Safe and Responsible Internet Use

Nancy Willard is director of the Center for Safe and Responsible Internet Use. She is also a lawyer, a social worker, and a prolific writer in the area of safety and the law with regard to kids and the Internet. I highly recommend her books, as well as the free materials she offers through her website, which address many of the issues we hear about in the media concerning kids and cyber behavior, including cyberbullying, sexting, copyright and plagiarism, and student privacy.

Her writing is clear and concise, including much bulleted information that provides quick but in-depth access to many of the issues faced in Party-cipa-tion. In addition, she maintains a listserv that features discussion involving a number of people experienced in this field. Much of my education about the specifics of cyber issues has come from her work and discussion group.

Character Education Materials

Like any substantial area of educational inquiry and practice, the area of character education has inspired a good deal of material, much of which I provide access to via my Digital Citizenship Wiki (jasonOhler.com/dc). However, here I will highlight two resources that were particularly important to me as I prepared this book:

1. *Educating Hearts and Minds: A Comprehensive Character Education Framework* by DeRoche and Williams (2001).

2. Materials found at the Character Education Partnership (www .character.org), in particular the work of Likona, and Berkowitz and Bier.

I reference these and other character education materials in greater detail later on.

These are just some of the many great resources that I have encountered while researching this book. I point them out because if you have a limited time budget, then these are a great place to start as you develop your own understanding of digital citizenship. Our ideal school board members agree to spend less time watching TV, so they can spend more time reading through as much of this material as possible. A month later, they convene to draft an agenda.

Also figuring into our school board's deliberations about a meeting agenda is the dialogue that is transpiring via a wiki that a brave AARP-age school board member set up to coordinate public communication about digital citizenship. Yes, kids and adults using wikis together, to process ideas, perspective, possibilities: It can happen.

Fortunately, in addition to reading all of these materials and being active on the wiki, our school board members attended a retreat that was funded by a local business consortium about how to facilitate effective change. This forward-looking consortium is happy to help because its members understand that the future of their workforce and their community relies on effective K–12 digital citizenship. Based on all these "inputs," school board members have come to a foundational decision: The school district needs an integrated approach to understanding and preparing kids for the personal, social, and ethical issues they will face as digital citizens. Thus, the school board accepts the concept of establishing a character education program for the Digital Age in broad terms. It then commits to working through the many details that this implies.

As a way of moving forward, they decide to address five issues related to this goal at each monthly meeting. The first five agenda items appear below and are addressed in this part of the book. Bear in mind that there are many important issues, but there are also many months ahead of them. If you don't see what is most important to you, rest assured that our ideal school board will get to it.

Childcare and free dinner are provided for everyone who physically attends the school board meetings, which is webcast as well as broadcast via a public service channel provided by the local cable TV company. Students will produce professional media based on the board meetings that synthesize the proceedings into a half-hour documentary. Teachers will use the documentary to discuss character education among themselves and with parents and students.

In addition, students are already contacting other school districts that are exploring digital citizenship to set up virtual meetings and discussions using social media to trade ideas. Collectively, they are building a set of resources devoted to character education in the Digital Age that the entire world of digital community can use. The school board is beginning to realize that one of the best resources they have is student experience. More than anyone, students are aware of the opportunities and pitfalls of life in the infosphere, and they are only too happy to share what they know.

THE IDEAL SCHOOL BOARD'S FIRST AGENDA

The board begins with the following five agenda items for its first meeting about developing a digital citizenship program:

1. **Agenda Item 1: Teachers and core ethics.** The front line of digital citizenship is the interactions that teachers have with students. Thus, the school board is committed to helping teachers understand

their own ethical framework, so they can more effectively teach issues associated with digital citizenship.

2. **Agenda Item 2: A crash course on kids.** Our school board needs short courses on three particular topics: (1) the specific characteristics of digital behavior to consider when developing a character education program, (2) how kids develop moral thinking, and (3) what brain research says about kids' abilities to think in moral terms.

3. **Agenda Item 3: Basics of character education.** Our board needs some basic orientation about developing a character education program and how to establish values based on public perspective in this area.

4. **Agenda Item 4: Digital literacy.** Our school board understands that citizenship is dependent upon literacy, and digital citizenship is dependent upon digital literacy. Board members seek an overview of the literacies necessary for students to be effective digital citizens.

5. **Agenda Item 5: What role for IT?** In response to numerous complaints by teachers, administrators, and students about not having access to many of the Internet resources needed to practice digital citizenship, school board members investigate how the school district's IT department can play a role in supporting their vision for character education in the Digital Age.

Each agenda item is addressed in the following chapters.

8 Agenda Item 1

Helping Teachers Understand Their Own Ethical Framework

W hile some may worry about the relevance of teachers in the Digital Age, I don't. More than ever, students need the inspiring, discerning voice of a teacher to help them sort among the options in an often exciting, distracting, and sometimes dangerous infosphere.

However, the role of the teacher is definitely changing. It is cliché at this point, but nonetheless significant, to note that the role of the teacher is shifting from being the primary source of information to being the team facilitator of a group of student researchers. Teachers have preeminence on the team because of their involvement in the content area and, hopefully, their ability to facilitate both group and differentiated learning. But they no longer expect all information to flow through them or to design every lesson without student input. Instead, their job is to help students focus their information-gathering efforts and deconstruct what they find with a sense of enlightened suspicion and hopeful application. In addition, teachers need to help students analyze their discoveries "creatically," blending creativity and critical thinking in the development of their own unique perspectives. Finally, it is their job to help students add their discoveries to the great wiki of the Internet by contributing what they learn via the many information-sharing venues that the Internet provides.

However, the shifts in teachers' responsibilities are not all academic in nature. A new role for teachers is emerging because of the complexities of the Digital Age: ethical coach. Given that much of what happens in the infosphere is ethically charged, this new role was unavoidable.

Our school board members support this new role wholeheartedly because they understand that part of helping students integrate technology into school and personal activities includes helping them place technology in

FYI

Everyone Takes Their Next Step

I had a serious aha moment many years ago when I was trying to show teachers how to use technology to shift from a teacher-centered to a student-centered approach to classroom management. This occurred during the early days of educational technology, and resistance was very great. As I witnessed the third meltdown of the day, it struck me. The teachers were not resistant to using technology. Instead, they were resistant to the assault on their core selves that their shifting role in a technology-rich classroom demanded. The presence of technology effectively required them to jettison a sense of identity as a teacher they had spent a lifetime developing. From then on, my motto became one foot on familiar ground, one on new territory, as we step slowly but ever forward into the world of new ideas. In a mantra: Everyone takes their next step.

a broader social context. Doing so includes helping students understand the connective and disconnective properties of technology so that they can better assess the moral decision making implied in technology use.

The public spars with school board members about their attempts to usurp the role of families with regard to moral education. But our ideal school board stays the course, citing that while they welcome parent participation, they also appreciate that parents typically don't understand the issues of living in the infosphere well enough to counsel their children effectively. Instead, the school board asks parents and community members to join in the board's exploration of important digital generation issues. To help facilitate this, the board offers free public presentations about the issues and ethics of life in the Digital Age so that adults are better prepared to have constructive conversations with kids. In addition, the board asks the public to join with them on the development of a character education program tailored to the Digital Age (more about this a bit later in the book).

To help teachers become better ethical coaches, the school board offers professional development aimed at helping teachers take the first step: understanding their own ethical cores. After all, teachers are no different than the rest of us in that they respond to life habitually and unconsciously, making many decisions every day that they don't have time to consciously consider. Many of these decisions have ethical implications, a reality that is exacerbated for teachers by the fact that they are responsible for children. Given how much the world is changing, they need the opportunity to disengage "ethical autopilot" and ask if they need to retune their ethical viewpoints in order to address the issues implicit in the Digital Age, many of which are new to them.

The purpose is not for others to judge their ethical core but to help them become aware of it and see it in action. Helping teachers understand their ethical cores will help them understand why they make the decisions they do, both inside and outside the classroom, and to modify their ethical perspectives if they feel a need to do so.

Teachers get the day off from work to attend a workshop based on the materials presented here. This is the first step of many, but the only one we have time to focus on in this book. This step is in many ways a brave one for teachers to take as it promises to reveal thinking patterns that might be difficult to look at. For their involvement, teachers receive merit pay, public commendation, and a free lunch. This is one enlightened school board.

WHAT IS YOUR ETHICAL CORE?

The problem with ethics—and the reason that reasonable, intelligent, caring people will often disagree about the ethics

---

FYI

The Interplay of Morality and Ethics

The terms ethics and morality are often used interchangeably, and in many cases that works. However, I distinguish them as follows: Morality deals more with how we act, while ethics deal with how we think about how we act. That is, ethical considerations inform moral actions. We can teach moral actions in that we can tell kids the right way to respond in a particular situation. But if we want them to understand why something is right or wrong, so they can transfer their understanding to other situations, then we need to engage them in ethical discussions.

The interplay between morality and ethics figures in Howard Gardner's (2006) book 5 Minds for the Future. In it, he identifies the following kinds of mind that each of us needs to cultivate in order to thrive in the eras to come: disciplined, synthesizing, creative, respectful, and ethical (p. 1). The respectful and ethical minds dovetail in the following way: Respect is a concrete representation of our moral interaction with others, while ethics compel us to consider moral action in broader, more abstract ways. Respect and ethics support and inform each other, and in some ways underpin the concept of thinking globally (ethically) and acting locally (respectfully and morally).

---

implied in the same issues and situations, now and forever—is that most ethical considerations are complex and consist of competing concerns that are rational and valued.

Yet when we come to an ethical fork in the road we can't, as Yogi Berra suggested, simply take it. We need to weigh and synthesize different points of view and ultimately make a decision about how to respond to a situation. For example, would you report a friend who stole something of relatively minimal consequence—A loaf of bread? A tank of gas? A pair of shoes? A photo from the web that specifically asked for compensation? Would you consider mitigating factors, like the fact that your friend was broke or hungry or too poor to own a camera, so he couldn't take his own picture? Would they cause you to react more directly and privately with your friend rather than more publicly by involving store owners or law enforcement officials? The competing interests—honoring the law and the viability of your community versus protecting a friend and maintaining your personal community—are both rational and valued. Ethically, situations like this are often a standoff. How you respond—that is, the moral action you take—reveals your ethical core.

CONSIDER AN INFOSPHERE ISSUE

Our ideal school board understands that ethical discussions are by nature abstract. To help make our discussion more concrete, the heart of our teacher training involves experts coaching teachers through understanding an issue that they might encounter. We then describe possible responses in terms of a set of ethical viewpoints. Finally, teachers are asked to align themselves with one of these viewpoints as the basis for considering their ethical cores. They are also asked to create a mantra about their ethical core as a way to review their core periodically.

Please bear in mind that there are professional ethicists who specialize in this area of inquiry for a living. I am certainly not one of them, and I make no claim to presenting a comprehensive treatment of this subject. But rather than let the perfect be the enemy of the good, I present the following viewpoints for your consideration as a beginning point if you are interested in this area.

The issue: From your perspective as a teacher, is it okay for a student to download a photograph from the Internet to be used in a school assignment, even though the assignment will be posted on a personal webpage on a commercial server rather than on a server the school provides? The student cannot use a service like Creative Commons (a free, legal source of media that I wholeheartedly recommend) because the picture she needs is of a specific sunset in a particular area of the country to illustrate a concept in a science project. The student has tried to obtain permission to use the picture, but the photographer has not responded. The student will cite the source of the picture and provide her teacher with a link to her project.

STIRRING THE MUDDY WATERS

A few points before continuing.

Part of the issue for a young mind grappling with this situation is that using someone else's photo doesn't *feel* like stealing. If it did, dealing with cyber issues like these would be much more straightforward. This perceptual confusion is understandable. In the predigital era, if I absconded with your photo, then I had your photo and you didn't. There was a clear physical cue to support the theft—your picture was gone! But in the digital era, if I take your photo, you still have your copy and plenty more for everyone else. It takes a leap of abstraction to understand the potential for harm in this situation.

I address copyright issues in a previous book (*Digital Storytelling in the Classroom*, 2008) as well as on my website (jasonOhler.com/copyright) and the wiki that accompanies this book (jasonOhler.com/dc). It is a complex area, and I don't want to open that can of worms here—at least not too wide. Suffice it to say that it would not be difficult to find experienced lawyers who would disagree about the legalities of this situation. I hope one brief anecdote will illuminate the legal ambiguity of situations like these.

Years ago, an information specialist came to my university to explain the Technology, Education, and Copyright Harmonization (TEACH) Act of 2002. Among other things, the TEACH Act updated fair use, the exception to copyright law that allows using material created by others for news reporting, research, educational, and other uses generally of a nonprofit nature within certain parameters. Ostensibly, the TEACH Act was created to address issues involved with distance education. However, it also updated copyright considerations for anyone wanting to use web material in education, onsite, and at a distance.

After a short presentation, the presenter fielded questions. Even though each question was very different, she prefaced nearly every answer with, "Well, that's sort of a gray area." In other words, "this would depend on the ability of the lawyers on either side of your question to present a compelling case."

> ## FYI
>
> ### Fair Use
>
> "Fair use is a doctrine in United States Copyright law that allows limited use of copyrighted material without requiring permission from the rights holders, such as for commentary, criticism, news reporting, research, teaching or scholarship. It provides for the legal, non-licensed citation or incorporation of copyrighted material in another author's work under a four-factor balancing test."
>
> From Wikipedia (Fair use, 2010, para. 1).

In fact, much of it is a gray area that has appeared rather recently. It used to be too difficult to use someone else's work. Now it is too easy. While some situations are very clear, many are born out of *competing concerns that are rational and valued.* Such would be the case here. A good deal of reading in this area has taught me that anything can be contested, and fair use is not so much law as it is a defense. Court is where matters of urgency are decided. But someone has to care enough to bring legal action.

Because copyright has a good deal of gray area to it, school policy doesn't enforce law as much as interpret it. It has to, in order to give school community members guidelines to follow. However, policy proceeds from dealing with new, often gray-area situations. When this happens, policy makers have no choice but to reason through the situation using a combination of law, ethics, and community sentiment on their way to creating acceptable-use guidelines.

Given that lawyers disagree about situations like these, what are the alternatives for the average teacher? And given that this area represents one of many digital citizenship issues—and that teachers already have a full day trying to prep for class, facilitate instruction, and make sure no child gets left behind—what can they do? In most cases, they can (1) fall back on legal precedent, which is hard for the nonlegal community to understand for reasons already explained; (2) fall back on school policy and hope that it is clear and supportive; or (3) approach this from an ethical perspective. There are benefits to the last approach:

- The conversation is no longer restricted to the legal community, which comprises a minute fraction of the overall population who speak a specialist language few of us understand.

- Even though law always trumps ethics, often the two align. In fact, a much easier way to approach the law is to ask people what they would do ethically and then show them how the law either supports or differs from ethics.

FYI

A Proposed Morality Research Project

One of the many research projects I would like to conduct is to ask teachers to respond to a series of questions about real digital citizenship issues, like the one described here, from the perspective of their own ethics. I would then compare their answers with prevailing legal opinion. My hypothesis? They wouldn't be far apart. My conclusion: Commonplace notions of what is decent, fair, and honest have a place in assessing digital citizenship concerns. Teaching how the law differs from these could be a much more efficient, effective way of actually teaching the law.

Thus, I purposely wanted to create an ambiguous situation so that ethics would play a more important role than legal interpretation. I also made the situation purposely ambiguous by intertwining the students' personal and school lives. I did so for the following reasons:

- Students live much of their digital lives outside school.
- As students grow increasingly frustrated with the limitations imposed on web services by school districts, we can expect them to move their work to personal and commercial venues where cyber life is much less restricted.
- Students' cyber lives are so connected that inevitably schoolwork and personal work become intermingled.

Please also note that I purposely did not choose an issue that involves student safety. While safety issues can also be complex, the goal is always clear: the safety of children. In the example I am using, not even the goal is clear, as can often be the case with cyber situations.

Bottom line: If we want to educate the whole student, then we need to address their cyber activity beyond school. We return to the question asked in the Preamble: Do we consider students to have two lives or one?

AN ETHICAL FRAMEWORK: CATEGORICAL VS. CONSEQUENTIALIST

A time-honored approach to framing ethical situations is in terms of categorical versus consequentialist thinking. For an in-depth, engaging video presentation about this, I recommend Harvard lecturer Michael Sandel's (2009) TV lecture series on justice (www.justiceharvard.org). In his series, Sandel presents a number of moral dilemmas to his audience to untangle and in the process provides a number of ways to view the ethical aspects of issues that occur in our personal and professional lives. In his first lecture, he pitches students a situation, fields their responses, and then deconstructs the conversation to produce two overarching ethical positions:

> **Consequentialist.** This position locates morality in the consequences of the act.

> **Categorical.** This position locates morality in certain duties and rights.

In other words, to a consequentialist, the morality of an action is a function of the consequences of the action. Sometimes called *utilitarianism*, consequentialism says basically that if the results are good, then the action must be right. Conversely, bad results indicate wrong action. On the other hand, a categorical thinker is concerned much more with whether the action is right or wrong in a theoretical sense, regardless of its impacts. Wrong is still wrong, regardless of the results.

Thus, our student who is using the photo might argue in consequentialist terms that there is no harm to the photographer, given she is not using the photo commercially, and the photographer gets wider exposure and a proper credit for a picture that the student would not use if she had to pay for it. The student's limited understanding of fair use might lead her to claim that she is using it as part of a research presentation, rather than simply to add flair to her project, and that doing so allows her to create a more accurate report for her class. She might even offer to make the website password protected, allowing only a very few people (teacher, classmates, and parents) to have access to it, thereby limiting the degree to which it is being published.

However, a categorical teacher (or student for that matter) would argue that using the picture without permission, regardless of impact, and despite the fact that permission was diligently pursued and that viewing it would be limited by password protection, is still wrong.

Bear in mind that a consequentialist can still argue against using the picture, perhaps by citing harm to the photographer. What is important here is the fact that there is no moral absolute that guides a consequentialist, only the impacts of the action. Conversely, a categorical thinker who firmly believes that "information is free no matter what" might argue in favor of the student using the photograph under any conditions. What is important is the fixed nature of this viewpoint.

> **FYI**
>
> **What You Say vs. What You Do**
>
> It is interesting to note that ethical researcher D. R. Forsythe (1980) discovered a significant disparity between ethical thought and moral action. He found that while people might align themselves with one ideology, their responses to actual situations aligned with different ideologies. Bottom line: Context often trumps ideology, and we never know what we are going to do until faced with an actual situation.

There are many gray-area issues like this one:

- Can a student include a link to a YouTube video in a homework assignment if YouTube is banned in the school? What if the assignment is posted on a commercial server, and the teacher evaluates the student's work from home? What is the reach of school policy?
- Does student behavior on social media sites fall under the purview of the school district if students access these sites only off campus using their own personal ID? How about if they are discussing school activities? How about if they access them off campus using a school ID?
- What if the situation of using the photograph described earlier involved your child making a website that had nothing to do with school—or any organization for that matter? What if your child were using it not so much for fun but rather to present a news report or political commentary?

Or just to make it really interesting, how about:

- Should students and staff correspond electronically, and if so, within what guidelines?

- Can students host a virtual beauty contest for avatars they create as a school activity? Can teachers act as judges?
- If students create an augmented reality cell phone app to document their community as part of a school assignment, and a business wants to buy it, who owns the app? Does the school district get a cut? Can the school provide an entrepreneurial opportunity for the students to develop and market it even though the school district is a publicly funded, nonprofit institution?

Keep in mind that there are what's legal, what's ethical, and what's appropriate. Sometimes they coincide. Sometimes they don't.

There are extensions to consequentialism versus categoricalism, notably Forsythe's (1980) taxonomy of personal moral philosophies, which identifies four ethical perspectives. Two of them, situationalism and absolutism, roughly correspond to consequentialism and categoricalism. However, he adds two more. The first is subjectivism, which bases moral judgments on personal feelings about the action and the setting, and exceptionism, which seeks to follow moral rules but values exceptions as permissible and even desirable under some circumstances.

> **FYI**
>
> #### Here Comes AR
>
> Augmented reality essentially annotates RL with a layer of VR. One example is the Wikitude AR Travel Guide. When it is fully functional, you will be able to point your cell phone camera at a geographical landmark, and an overlay of Wikipedia information about the landmark will appear on your screen. I suspect the ethical issues that arise with AR will make the issue of downloading a picture from the Internet seem like child's play.

Thus, in gray-area situations that do not involve issues of safety, a subjectivist teacher may turn it all over to the student, allowing her to decide what is right as long as she can defend her action, perhaps first to the teacher and then to the photographer should she receive a "cease and desist" order forcing her to stop using the photo. The teacher and student may agree to an arrangement that includes her removing the photograph should the photographer finally get back to her and ask her to do so.

An "exceptionist" teacher may see this situation as the exception that proves and strengthens the rule, honoring both the complexity of the situation and the student's efforts to obtain permission from the photographer. The teacher may require the student to use the kind of password protection described earlier that limits who may see her work and include a statement explaining the effort she has put into trying to contact the photographer, as well as the limited use of this particular work.

In all approaches, the work would be cited with an appropriate attribution.

Before you cry "situational ethics," keep in mind that each of us hovers among all the ethical viewpoints mentioned, weighing each situation on its merits. We do it as friends, citizens, parents, professionals, and jury members. If we use situational ethics as an excuse for doing something we know is wrong, then clearly it's wrong. But if we don't consider each situation on its merits, the way any judge or jury in a copyright case is compelled to do, then we are rightfully considered stubborn, uncompromising, and at risk of making an ill-informed decision.

Your Turn

Would your reaction to your student be more consequentialist or categorical? Subjectivist or exceptionist? Feel free to mix these as most people do. If you are considering conditional use, what are the conditions? Requiring password access to the site? Requiring that students include some kind of statement about their attempts to reach the photographer? What's important is to see as clearly as possible how you combine the natural and reflective inclinations of your ethical core.

Homework. Create a mantra—or perhaps a paragraph—that describes how you approach the ethics of using digital technology in your classroom. You may be able to use what you created for the technology mantra development exercise in Part II of this book. Then pick a week—any average week—and find some quiet time at the end of each day to recall the decisions you made regarding technology, kids, and moral issues. I find if I wait any longer than 24 hours, then my ability to consciously recollect my automatic decisions evaporates. (This could be an age thing.) Write out your decisions. Compare them with your conscious decisions about your ethical core. Do they align? Don't be surprised if they don't. We tend to pontificate about such things as ethics, but then react situationally. If they don't align, you are then left with two options:

1. "Reprogram" yourself, so your moral practice aligns with your ethics.

2. Reconstruct your ethical mantra so that it better reflects the true self you now discern in light of your moral practice.

It is interesting to note that brain research is now using MRI technology to decipher how the brain responds to moral situations. It appears as though our initial reaction to a moral situation emanates from the emotional part of the brain called the limbic system, and our secondary response originates in the frontal cortex, the seat of reason. More about this in the next agenda item.

DISCUSSING ETHICAL ISSUES WITH STUDENTS

While moral philosophy might be too abstract for some, there are other ways of understanding issues of character and ethics as they apply to digital citizenship that are a bit more down-to-earth. In the course of researching material for this book, I found many great resources for helping students think about, assess, and prevent risky and negative behavior. I provide links to them at my Digital Citizenship Wiki (jasonOhler.com/dc) and invite you to add yours. Here, I present two perspectives that seem to resonate with a wide audience: looking through the lens of safety and protection, which comes from Andrew Churches's (2010) *The Digital Citizen*, and the golden rule. These are especially helpful when dealing with students.

Looking Through the Lens of Safety and Protection

If approaching issues of digital citizenship from the perspective of "what's right or wrong" is too abstract for your students, try having them consider it more viscerally in terms of whether they feel respected and protected in cyber situations—and whether they think others might feel the same. Andrew Churches's (2010) approach to digital citizenship is instructive in this regard. It is made up of the following six tenets of citizenship.

1. Respect yourself.

2. Protect yourself.

3. Respect others.

4. Protect others.

5. Don't steal.

6. Honor intellectual property.

The first four collapse into a single mantra: Respect and protect yourself and others. In essence, such a mantra reflects a kind of transactional ethics, a win-win in what might otherwise be a murky cyber situation. If everyone involved feels respected and protected, then an activity passes muster.

Safety and respect describe a wide umbrella. Some of the spokes of this umbrella are described below and are based on my consideration of ethics in the infosphere for some time. Note that each of them refers not only to ourselves but also to others who might be involved in a particular situation:

- **Permanence (recordability).** Will you create a permanent event about yourself or someone else in the annals of digital community that could haunt you or them forever? After all, we are never around to explain ourselves. Even if we were, would anyone believe us?
- **Portability.** Can what you are doing be copied and reposted? Are you copying and reposting something of someone else's without their permission? After all, digital community is a fluid community. Things that appear in one place easily resurface in another.
- **Misrepresentation.** Could someone download, modify, originalize (known as "transformation" in the legal community), and misrepresent what you have created? Are you doing this? After all, no one will be around to explain the forgery, whether it is done in the name of art or retribution.

> **FYI**
>
> *Mottos of the digital citizen:* "I link therefore I am," and "Think before you link."

- **Identification.** Will you be indentified or be identifying anyone else? After all, doing so often crosses the line between RL and VR communication, introducing the possibility of a number of RL and VR ramifications.
- **Boundary crossing.** This was implied above, but more generally asks the questions, Will you be crossing the boundary between RL to VR or vice versa? And will you be causing someone else to do that? After all, doing so can reinforce negative behavior, such as bullying that can occur online and at school, or sexting, which may begin online but then set expectations for RL activity.
- **Reflection.** Is what you are initiating or responding to being done spontaneously or reflectively? Twitch speed does not breed reflection. Many of our online foibles can be thwarted with a little bit of thought and the waiting it requires.

None of these automatically imply a lack of safety or respect—only that safety and respect are issues to consider. Bottom line: Think before you link.

TRY THIS

IS THIS COOL?

Cool is one of those words that has survived many generations and continues to mean roughly the same thing: "The best way to say something is neat-o, awesome, or swell. The phrase "cool" is very relaxed, never goes out of style, and people will never laugh at you for using it, very convenient for people like me who don't care about what's 'in'" (Cool, 2010). Asking students, "Is that a cool thing to do?" usually elicits some kind of recognition on their part that they need to see things in a larger perspective. Downside: Adults don't feel comfortable using this word with kids.

The Golden Rule

The golden rule that our parents and grandparents taught us is still an effective place to begin conversations about digital citizenship. It is known to most of us as _Do unto others as you would have them do unto you,_ a pillar of Judeo-Christian ethics. It is known more secularly as the ethic of reciprocity, which states that "one has a right to just treatment, and a responsibility to ensure justice for others" (Golden Rule, 2010, para. 1).

Consider applying this to the example about the student who used a photo found on the Internet. The student would need to be able to claim that she would feel fine if someone used a photograph of hers in a similar manner.

However, there is an issue here, namely, that it is difficult to accurately compare the student and photographer in this situation. If the person who took the picture is a professional photographer supporting her family through her work, and the student is an amateur living at home with her parents, then their situations are hardly similar. If you are interested in pursuing this area of inquiry with students, try doing so by asking them the following question: "If you were a professional musician, and you were counting on Internet sales of your music to feed your family, how would you feel about people downloading your music for free?" While the answer to this might seem very straightforward to most adults, be prepared for unanticipated responses that make sense. One such response is, "That would be fine because it would be up to me to create a 'sticky' website that would compel advertisers to post links on my site, which they pay me for, and make visitors want to buy my products or attend concerts. Under those circumstances, they could have the music for free." If you have a hard time understanding this, you are not alone. However, it accurately reflects how commerce is often pursued on the Internet.

I close this chapter with some thoughts about the word *free*. In my day, free meant, well, *free*. A gift with no strings attached. Take this, and enjoy. Today, it has many new meanings. Almost all of these refer to the fact that free things are not really free but seem so, often because they are part of an entrée into other paid services, or are free to you because your consumption habits are being commodified and sold to others. Bottom line: In the infosphere, free is not free—it's only sort of free. This only helps to make issues of cyber theft harder to understand.

9

Agenda Item 2

A Crash Course About Kids

Before developing a digital character education program, our school board members do their homework and identify a few more inputs to inform their thinking. Specifically, they are looking for information and insight about the following:

- **Topic A: What's different about digital community?** Board members need bullet points about what makes activity in digital community different than activity in RL community, so they can adapt character education to a world that is pervasively digital.
- **Topic B: Moral development.** In the backs of their minds, board members remember that kids develop moral consciousness in stages, starting at "me" and ending at "we." A quick refresher would be helpful as they consider character education possibilities.
- **Topic C: Brain research and morality.** Parents involved with the school board's effort have been reading up on brain development in teenagers. One commented, "Finally, I understand why my children often make no sense! And why I often make no sense to them." An overview of the limitations or parameters associated with students' abilities to make moral judgments from a neurological perspective would be most helpful.

Because our school board is ideal, it establishes study groups to track these topics. Supported by students, they use social media to locate and aggregate information as it becomes available. A very cursory presentation of their initial findings in these areas follows.

AGENDA ITEM 2, TOPIC A: WHAT'S DIFFERENT ABOUT DIGITAL COMMUNITY

Any approach to character education that is adapted for digital kids would need to address characteristics of activity that did not exist prior to digital community. After all, our kids now live in three ecosystems simultaneously: natural, human, and digital. It is likely the adults in their lives, including the school board members, lived in only the first two. In addition, digital kids inhabit three levels of community: local, global, and digital. It is likely our school board members are used to focusing on only the first.

The time spent in these new environments gives rise to the following kinds of activities described below. I have alluded to many of these throughout this book. Here, for the benefit of our very busy school board, I have grouped them in terms of shifts in three areas (psychology, community, and identity) and provided them as bullet points that they can reference throughout their deliberations. Note that they are not mutually exclusive, and there is a good deal of overlap among them.

Shifts in Psychological Perspective

- **Disinhibited activity.** This was described earlier as the change in character that occurs when we communicate in the absence of the social cues that we typically rely on to guide our interactions. We have always been able to talk trash about someone when they aren't around. Now we can do it more pervasively, using e-mail, texting, avatars—whatever electronic communication channel is available. In some cases, we can even do it in real time. Addressing this quality of cyber communication is a key component of any Digital Age character education program.
- **Dissociated activity.** Dissociation happens in many ways, but here I am concerned with when it occurs due to the change in spatial and temporal relationships in the infosphere. Our sense of place contributes to how we behave; yet in cyberspace, place is often fully dissociated. Real time is the norm for RL communication, yet much online communication is asynchronous, or it happens in the "nearly now" (Heppell, 2008, para. 2). The result is that human interaction becomes blurry and disconnected due to temporal and spatial displacement. Thus, character education needs to address this kind of behavior as well as "normal" behavior.
- **Abstracted activity.** This is like dissociated activity but differs from it in the sense that even when we know something has concrete

elements, we elect to see it completely in abstract terms. Thus an email flame containing specific, insulting language becomes "honest communication" rather than "unnecessarily rude behavior exhibited toward Bob." While this can certainly happen in RL, VR facilitates it much more easily. Similarly, downloading and playing an entire song without permission becomes "free advertising for the musicians." Note that in both cases, the abstraction is not necessarily inaccurate. The issue is that each has morphed into a perspective that includes just enough distance to see the benefits and blur the potential injuries. Character education needs to address "keeping it real."

- **Generalized activity.** This is a special kind of dissociated action in which action is generalized rather than individualized because it is broadcast to a wide audience. Doing so makes it easier to avoid considering the impacts felt by actual individuals. An e-mail sent to a listserv and a movie posted on YouTube are good examples. Character education needs to address the fact that unlike previous generations, this one has an immediate, global audience whenever it wants one. This is a permanent addition to the communication landscape.

Shifts in Community Activity

- **Multicommunity activity.** As explained earlier, kids live in three communities (local, global, and digital) and within three ecosystems (natural, human, and technological). Thus, "character" plays out in all these situations. Our job is to help students understand how this happens so that they can effectively integrate all of their experiences into a unified approach to living.
- **"Transcommunity" activity.** Some of the impacts of dissociated, multicommunity activity span local and digital community (RL and VR) in very specific ways. As mentioned earlier, we see this in cyberbullying, in which RL and VR converge to support each other. Thus, character education needs to address issues of character that span both worlds.
- **Global activity.** This is implied above but is worth stating clearly on its own. The very real context of a distributed world is a global community. Thus, character education needs to address how students behave within a global context. This includes thinking globally and acting locally. It also includes considering global community in the more abstract senses described in Part I of this book, including "humanity" and "planet as a single natural environment." Thus, what we do not only impacts people but also humanity. And what we do locally also impacts the world ecosystem.

- **Distributed activity.** This follows from the point above. Prior to the Internet, distributed activity did not exist for the average person. Regularly projecting and sharing our work globally, and connecting with others who are doing the same, is an entirely new phenomenon. Thus, character education needs to address how to integrate and manage an expanded sense of place and self in ways that are positive and productive.
- **Leveraged activity.** Students use technology that gives them much more power than people had even a decade ago. The growth of "leveraged activity" is a permanent, exponential reality. As detailed in Part II of this book, we can't assume students understand how to handle technological power. Substantive character development will be needed to help them to understand it as well as manage it. This is an issue of community because leveraged power can upset a community's equilibrium. Thus, a balanced perspective of leverage activity is key.

Shifts in Identity

- **Managed identity activity.** Recall that part of Party-cipation is being able to re-create ourselves with many identities, each of which can have as much or as little to do with our RL selves as we like. It is ironic and at least a little strange that character education will have to address the characters we are as well as those we invent. In very real terms, this means that students need to know how to integrate their many selves into a coherent and productive vision of self.
- **Hidden activity.** This is related to managed identity in that it speaks to our ability to hide in plain sight by using multiple communities as well as multiple identities. Kids have always had secret hiding places—but not like they have today. They can gain entry to their secret space from just about anywhere, and they gather there quietly outside the view of parents, teachers, and peers they choose to exclude. Character education needs to help students balance public and private lives in their different communities.
- **Unaccountable activity.** Due to many of the preceding kinds of activity, fear of retribution is greatly reduced. As cyber researcher Willard notes:

> Negative consequences only work as a deterrent to misbehavior if there is a high enough risk of detection and punishment. On the Internet, there is a reduced likelihood of detection and punishment for activities that are illegal or

could lead to civil liability, much less actions that are merely unethical or rude. The internet is simply not a law and order paradigm. (Willard, 1997, p. 5)

Thus, character education is in many ways about accountability.

We will find, for the most part, that character development is timeless in concept. It just needs to be adapted to some of the specifics of the Digital Age mentioned above. In particular, we will need to develop activities for "seeing through the ether" in order to navigate the social dimensions of our digital lifestyle.

Cyber misbehavior may be an RL cry for help. Before leaving this section, I should mention something that I have come across many times in the course of developing this book: the belief that what appears to be simple misbehavior in cyberspace may actually be a cry for RL attention.

This is not unlike what happens in RL in that sometimes acting out becomes a way of telling others we need help. But when it happens in cyberspace, there are two issues that are quite unique: (1) It happens in a world in which the adults who need to hear the cry for help are often excluded, and (2) given adults' lack of involvement in cyberspace, they may not have the comfort level, perspective, or skills needed to be as helpful as they would like to be.

Thus, there are two components of having a character education program to consider in order to address this effectively. First, we must cultivate talents in both parents and school personnel to hear and help students who are asking for help in their own cyber way. As we do so, we should bear in mind that one of our best resources are the insights that can be provided by the citizens of cyberculture: the students themselves. Second, an important part of having a character education program in the Digital Age involves cultivating and coordinating the talents of guidance counselors, psychologists, and mental health officials where appropriate. We need to stop seeing cyber issues as purely technological issues and see them as manifestations of human problems. When we do, it becomes clear that professional counseling could play an important role in our efforts.

AGENDA ITEM 2, TOPIC B: MORAL DEVELOPMENT IN KIDS

No inquiry into character education would be complete without some consideration of the research conducted into the moral development of children. Within the education research community, this is concerned with how kids develop the abilities to evaluate moral situations and at what age we can expect certain kinds of moral abilities and ethical thinking to emerge. The essential question that drives our school board in this area of inquiry is simply this: Are there developmental limitations or parameters that impact the ability of students to engage in ethical thinking? This brief overview is intended as the first step in the school board's journey to learn more about this.

Modern moral education theory starts with Kohlberg, who based his work on Jean Piaget. It is impossible to graduate from a teacher education program without receiving a good dose of both researchers. While Piaget and Kohlberg were more concerned with cognitive and moral development, respectively, both came to similar conclusions: People generally develop cognitively and morally in stages that are cumulative, predictable, and irreversible (Nucci, 2008). This growth is characterized by the following particular qualities:

- We gradually decenter, gaining the ability to see things from someone else's point of view.
- We become less inclined to want to satisfy just our own needs and more interested in working things out with peers interpersonally.
- We gradually gain the ability to think more abstractly. This is particularly important given the often abstract nature of ethical and moral decision making. It is also particularly important for digital citizens because much of their activity in the infosphere is abstract in nature due to asynchronous and geographically dispersed communication, issues of identity management, and other factors.
- Cognitive and moral development are linked, with the latter preceding the former. In plain English, the smarter we become, the better able we are to puzzle through ethical decision making. In the process, we become more capable of autonomous moral reasoning. Thus, critical thinking is the solid foundation upon which moral development rests.
- Cognitive and moral development are best developed socially through interactions with peers in a constructivist environment. That is, an important part of moral development occurs when we work through situations with others and have to address *competing concerns that are rational and valued.*

Piaget ascribed age groups to developmental phases, citing abstract thinking as beginning around the age of 11 or 12. Kohlberg and others were less clear about when abstract thinking emerged. The insert suggests that Kohlberg felt that entering the upper domain of abstract ethical thinking becomes possible anywhere from age 12 . . . to never. That is, there are people who simply never get beyond Stage 4 in their moral development.

If we accept that kids have the ability to engage in moral discussions around age 12, then are we accepting that they are not capable of the kind of abstract thought needed for ethical reasons until this age? The jury is out on this. But if this is true, then we would have to accept that prior to around age 12, children would need to be told or at least nudged toward what is right and wrong, with the hopes that they can extrapolate to other situations without necessarily understanding the reasoning behind doing so. As they "decenter," they can engage in more abstract thinking about ethics on their own.

Predictably, Piaget and Kohlberg had their detractors. One was Carol Gilligan, who objected to the fact that Kohlberg interviewed only males in his work and thus produced a perspective that represented only half the population (Nucci, 2008). She also objected to the suggestion in Kohlberg's work that there was only one primary goal of moral development: developing a sense of personal and social justice. To Gilligan, the primary goal of moral development was nonviolence and caring. Her findings call into question a fundamental assumption about not only how we evolve but also the role of cognition in that evolution: Does cognitive

---

FYI

Kohlberg's Stages of Moral Development: A Summary

Author note: Kohlberg's theory says there are three levels of moral development, each of which has 2 stages, for a total of 6 stages. These are explained below.

- The first two stages, at level 1, preconventional morality, occur before the individual has even become aware of social conventions.
- At stage 1 (from about age 2 or 3 to about age 5 or 6), children seek mainly to avoid the punishment that authority figures such as their parents can mete out to them.
- At stage 2 (from age 5 to age 7, or up to age 9, in some cases), children learn that it is in their interest to behave well, because rewards are in store if they do.
- Level 2, conventional morality, is so named because at these stages (stages 3 and 4) it is no longer individuals such as parents, but rather social groups, such as family and friends, that children perceive as the source of authority."
- At stage 3 (from about age 7 to about age 12), children feel the need to satisfy the expectations of the other members of their group. In so doing, children seek to preserve rules that will lead to predictable behavior.
- At stage 4 (from age 10 to age 15, on average), the conventions that guide the individual's behavior expand to include those of the society in which he or she lives. In examining the justification for a given course of action, the individual considers whether it is consistent with the norms and laws of this society.
- Level 3, postconventional morality, is so named because in the last two stages, which it comprises, the individual's morality goes beyond the frame of reference of any one particular society.
- At stage 5 (starting as early as age 12, in some cases), individuals feel as if they have freely entered into a contractual commitment with every person around them. This commitment is

(Continued)

(Continued)

> based on a desire for consensus and a rational assessment of the benefits that everyone can derive from the existence of these rules.
> - At stage 6, individuals' judgments of good and bad become influenced by universal moral principles. People at stage 6 agree that laws and societal values have a certain validity, but if these laws conflict with their own principles of human dignity, they will follow these principles, which they regard as an internally imposed imperative.

Used with permission by Brain Top to Bottom Project, McGill University, www.thebrain.mcgill.ca.

FYI

Characterizations

"Character is doing the right thing when nobody's looking." —J. C. Watts

"Integrity—When you do the right thing even though no one is watching." —Anonymous

---

development precede developing the abilities associated with empathy?

The issue is addressed by psychologist H. L. Hoffman (Willard, 1997). In writing about the role of empathy and moral motivation, Hoffman viewed empathy as innate and dependent upon cognitive development. Empathy development seeks to internalize moral perspective so that we respond to some kind of norm or ethical standard, even when no one is watching.

An important takeaway from Hoffman's work is the following:

> . . . young people who have been disciplined in a manner that forces them to focus on the consequences of their actions and who have a well-developed sense of internalized empathy will be more likely to behave ethically in cyberspace, than those who have been raised in an authoritarian (rule and punishment) environment. (Willard, 1997, p. 7)

Eliot Turiel (in Nucci, 2008) added to the debate about moral education by introducing "domain theory," which suggests children are best served by being taught to distinguish between morality and convention because each constitutes a separate domain of concern. That is, some of the issues that we might consider to be moral in nature are actually issues of conventionality, in that they involve learning the accepted ways of doing things within a particular culture. Thus, hitting someone falls into the former while how to address an elder falls into the latter (Nucci, 2008). This is particularly interesting given the earlier discussion about interlational communication, in which students referred to their teachers by their first name in virtual reality but maintained a professional distance in RL. Separating these two domains helps us understand a good deal of the variation in how individuals develop morally. Willard's (1997) analysis of Turiel finds three key concepts that inform morality in cyberspace:

1. A key factor in distinguishing moral values from social convention is whether an action will result in harm to another.

2. Social conventions, versus moral values, are context dependent and variable.

3. Multifaceted issues often overlap social conventions, moral values, and personal choice.

The problem that emerges is that harming someone else is abstracted in cyberspace, and social conventions adapt to this abstraction. Thus, the moral implications of many of our activities in cyberspace at least appear to be context dependent and variable, muddying the moral waters.

From Gilligan, Hoffman, and Turiel we add the following to our understanding of moral development in kids:

- The pursuit of a higher state of moral consciousness is not limited to the pursuit of justice. It can involve the pursuit of caring, nonviolence, and empathy.
- Framing morality in terms of empathy and understanding the harm caused to others can be more effective than framing it in terms of rule and punishment.
- Sometimes, issues that may appear to be moral in nature actually have more to do with social convention.
- Sometimes, moral issues appear to be issues of convention because harm has been abstracted in cyberspace.

The bottom line is that we need new ways to help students "see through the ether" to be able to empathize with others and inform their actions.

AGENDA ITEM 2, TOPIC C: BRAIN DEVELOPMENT, KIDS, AND MORAL THINKING

Our school board's desire to have a rich picture of how students think and respond to situations of character inevitably leads them to ask how brain research can help them. The board's essential question in this area is simply this: What biological and neurological limitations or parameters influence how we should approach issues of digital citizenship with our students? What follows is a mere beginning of the school board's wiki on this topic.

The reality is that the brain is a vast, mysterious landscape that we are only beginning to understand. While there is a certain amount of pop philosophizing associated with brain inquiry, there is also a growing amount of very credible research that is beginning to illuminate this landscape and help us understand why humans develop the way they do. Interest in the teenage brain is relatively new. Most of the important discoveries about it have been made just in the last decade. As with all areas of specialized scientific endeavor, brain research is complex and uses a specialist language understood by a very few. Fortunately, some in the scientific community have created materials that can explain some of the major findings regarding the teenage brain in lay language.

Of particular interest to our text-weary school board members are the following excellent video presentations, most of which are free. Students worked with board members to identify these and make them available through the school board's wiki. In most cases, the video descriptions are direct quotations from the sites on which they appear. Links to these also appear on my Digital Citizenship Resources Wiki.

The Teenage Brain—In 3 Parts (2008)

www.youtube.com/watch?v=RpMG7vS9pfw

Frances E. Jensen, MD, Senior Assistant in Neurology at Children's Hospital Boston and a professor at Harvard Medical School, is translating the most up-to-date research on the teen brain, which she shares with parents, teachers, and teens during her presentation, "Teen Brain 101." (Jensen, 2008, para. 1)

Adolescent Brains (2008)

www.youtube.com/watch?v=cLkV8isrGNA

Silvia Bunge, Assistant Professor of Psychology, tells about her research team's work, showing that adolescent minds haven't yet developed the same reasoning abilities as adults, and her hopes that this research can improve education methods, as well as the legal system. (Bunge, 2008, para. 1)

Frontline: Inside the Teenage Brain (2002)

www.pbs.org/wgbh/pages/frontline/shows/teenbrain/view/

In "Inside the Teenage Brain," *Frontline* chronicles how scientists are exploring the recesses of the brain and finding some new explanations for why adolescents behave the way they do. These discoveries could change the way we parent, teach, or perhaps even understand our teenagers. (Spinks, 2002, para. 2)

Growing Up: The Teenage Brain (2009)

www.youtube.com/watch?v=EnJ-2eWF55w

Dr. Greg Berns talks about a new study using brain imaging to study teen behavior. It turns out that adolescents who engage in dangerous activities have frontal white matter tracts that are more adult in form than their more conservative peers. (Berns, 2009, para. 1)

My note: What is important about Berns's (2009) work is that his findings seem to contradict current theory that teens do not engage their more rational functions when considering risk.

EQ and the Emotional Curriculum (2004)

Films for the Humanities and Sciences, www.films.com

This comes in DVD form only and can be purchased from Films for the Humanities and Sciences. It is an engaging overview about how brain research can help students use EQ, Daniel Goleman's term for emotional intelligence. This video shows how EQ is actually being employed in school curricula to help improve intelligence related to self-understanding and interpersonal communication.

While you are looking for time to watch these videos, here is a thumbnail sketch of some of their more salient points. In a nutshell, part of the reason that teenagers can sometimes seem petulant, disrespectful, and overly anxious to engage in negative, risky behavior is because the average teen's prefrontal lobe—the seat of reason and better judgment in the brain—is in flux on its way to becoming fully formed. While this is going on, the fluid prefrontal lobe (also referred to, somewhat erroneously, as the frontal lobe or frontal cortex) is doing battle with the limbic system, the brain's emotional center. Often, the prefrontal lobe loses. The result is that developing the qualities of a good citizen at a young age, neurologically speaking, is a bit of an uphill battle.

Teen Brain Factoids

Here is a quick summary of some teen brain facts distilled from the video material:

- **Teenagers only appear to be adults.** While teens stop growing physically between 13 and 17, and thus appear to us to be fully grown while in high school, their brains do not fully mature until in their early 20s. This is a fairly recent discovery, overturning the long-held belief that brains were fully developed by around the age of 12.

- **The brain grows, thickens, and prunes itself.** The brain grows much like a tree, sprouting branches and roots. Some take hold, and others are pruned through the process of use and disuse (Spinks, 2002). Which neural pathways are pruned is largely determined by the activities in which teens engage. Playing sports, reading, watching TV, playing video games, interacting with others—every activity encourages different neural pathways to form. Entering maturation, the brain is largely hardwired, though theories of neuroplasticity now challenge that. Given what we know about neuroplasticity—which is not much as of this writing—it may be more accurate to say that once matured, the brain is set on a particular trajectory, with the capability to adjust should experience warrant it. For example, accident recovery (Phillips, 2006) as well as Internet use (Carr, 2010) can cause significant kinds of brain rewiring. Current belief in the possibility of brain rewiring is great enough that scientists are deliberately experimenting with it (Kluger, 2007). Clearly, we should be vigilant as the brain yields more of its mysteries to the probing of science. New neurological discovery will help us with our work.
- **The teenage brain is at a crossroads, between child and adult brainhood.** In particular, two aspects of the teen brain are experiencing rapid change: prefrontal lobe development and myelination, which is the process of wiring all the parts of the brain together. The last part of the brain to be connected during myelination is the prefrontal lobe (Jensen, 2008).
- **The prefrontal lobe controls many brain functions associated with adulthood.** These include insight, judgment, planning, and moral maturity. The tendency of the prefrontal lobe is to invoke caution and block risk taking.
- **At odds with the frontal lobe is the limbic system, which controls many brain functions associated with survival and the emotions.** The limbic system is concerned with our emotional states, needs, and motivations. It controls our instinct of fight or flight. It drives us to find food when we are hungry and water when we are thirsty. The powerhouse of the limbic system is the amygdala, which controls the extreme edges of our passions, including anger and aggression, as well as love and affection. When we are stressed or threatened, it kicks in. It is the oldest part of the brain and has helped us survive for thousands of years (Films for the Humanities and Sciences, 2004).
- **The amygdala can "hijack" the frontal lobe.** This can be entirely appropriate. After all, doing so could save our lives or the lives of others. But the amygdala also hijacks the frontal lobe in inappropriate or destructive ways. Our amygdala compels us to spontaneously strike out at someone or send a flaming e-mail, while our frontal lobe regrets it (Films for the Humanities and Sciences, 2004).

- **We need to help teens make better use of their frontal lobe.** Recall that the frontal lobe is, evolutionarily speaking, rather new. Asking it to hijack the ancient amygdala and take over its role of coordinating a response to a stressful or threatening situation is a fairly recent development. Yet that is our task as humans living in community. It is our socioneurological calling as citizens.

What Are the Risks?

The teen brain is incredibly facile and capable of learning, a quality that diminishes after maturation. However, its robustness is also its Achilles heel. Because neither myelination nor frontal lobe formation is complete during adolescence, the teen brain is very vulnerable. This vulnerability can result in poor judgment and bad risk assessment as well as what might appear to be a lack of intelligence, empathy, and the interpersonal capabilities associated with EQ.

In the worst cases, this vulnerability can lead to substance abuse. In fact, it appears as though addiction and learning utilize similar kinds of neural processes, and that the former is an extreme form of the latter (Jensen, 2008). Because the teen brain is so adaptable to learning, it is much more receptive to addiction than a fully mature adult brain. As brain researcher Dr. Jeidd points out, it is a cruel irony of nature that teens have the most temptations for negative behavior when they are most neurologically vulnerable (Spinks, 2002). It is also a compelling irony that they need to engage their reflective, cautionary abilities at a time when it may be most neurologically difficult to do so.

> **FYI**
>
> ### Kids Need Sleep!
>
> Neurology is just part of what challenges teens. Many experts think they are sleep deprived and out of synch with natural sleep patterns. Teens need over nine hours of sleep each night, and they rarely get it, largely because they have so many electronic ways to stay awake, including being on the Internet, texting with friends, and watching TV (Spinks, 2002). And let's not forget diet. If you have had kids, you know how bad their eating habits can be. Keep in mind that these habits are fully supported by the advertising industry, which has daily access to their attention.

> **FYI**
>
> ### Brain Rules
>
> Aside from issues of moral reasoning, there are other things to know about the brain that can help us teach kids. Addressing these is simply beyond the scope of this book. However, a good place to start is Medina's (2010) Brain Rules. From it, we conclude at least the following: Brains need sleep, exercise, multisensory environments, and opportunities to explore in order to learn. Make a mental note to keep up on brain research. It holds one of the keys to restructuring education.

THE FUTURE OF NEURO-MORALITY RESEARCH

Before leaving the topic of brain research and morality, let's take a peek into the immediate future.

The application of MRI technology to moral research has given birth to a new area of inquiry: neurophilosophy. In her article, Ada Brunstein (2007) reviews the groundbreaking work of moral researcher Joshua Greene, who studies brain activity as people make moral decisions. This has yielded a number of interesting results.

First, some history, illuminated by recent discovery, that will help set the stage for Greene's discoveries. According to social psychologist Jonathan Haidt (2007), there is evidence to suggest that moral reasoning is a recent evolutionary luxury, perhaps evolving as the neocortex evolved. So what did we do before we had the neurological equipment to weigh moral issues?

One view is that the ancient human handled moral judgment affectively, as instantaneous intuitive judgments in response to survival situations. These were cognitive in nature, but not deliberative. As we fast-forward to modern times, we carry this with us, but we now engage in two kinds of moral judgment: the ancient, intuitive response and the more modern, cortex-driven, reasoned response (Haidt, 2007). Greene came to a similar conclusion:

> The overall lesson is that moral judgment is not a single kind of process . . . at least in my view not a single moral faculty or moral sense, rather it's different systems in the brain in some cases competing with each other. (Brunstein, 2007, para. 15)

However, it seems that our ancient selves tend to speak first. That is, typically our initial moral responses come automatically. We might call this an expression of our intuitive or impulsive ethical core. We then step back and engage in a second round of evaluation, moving from our emotional to our rational brain, a fact that shows up in MRI scans. We reflect on the situation in terms of, for example, its legal ramifications or how our decision might make us look to others. Greene also looked at the length of the delay between the two responses, which he interpreted as indicative of the difficulty faced in overcoming a primary emotional response (ScienceDaily, 2001).

The result is that our moral judgment is a combination of what we initially wanted to do, tempered by what we thought we ought to do, and that these considerations play out in different parts of the brain. Our second thoughts may reflect a more considered moral position or simply a more socially acceptable position. Whatever it represents, it forms the crux of the modern moral decision.

Bottom line: Moral decision making involves a number of mental processes in addition to a reasoned process associated with the frontal lobe. Emotional responses influence moral decision making and are not simply coincidental side effects. The emotional responses are part of the actual moral judgment itself (ScienceDaily, 2001). One day, neurophilosophy may well reveal who we truly are versus who want to be. Do we want to know?

HELPING STUDENTS DEVELOP CHARACTER

While the deck may seem to be stacked against teens and good decision making, there is a good deal of optimism among experts. First of all, each of us knows plenty of "good kids" who evaluate situations fairly well in their teens. Whether their abilities are due to nature, nurture, or some combination of the two, "good kids" remind us of the fact that what moral theorists and brain researchers tell us are guidelines, rather than hard-and-fast rules. Parenting, positive rewards for good behavior, and constructivist opportunities to build peer relationships and test-drive evolving moral awareness under guided conditions are key to helping kids develop in this area.

Second, there is another school of thought on this matter that says that kids are more reflective about the risks they take than we might think. For example, researcher Dr. Valerie Reyna (2007) concluded that often "teens overestimate the risk of risky behaviors" (para. 18). Research by Lindberg, Boggess, Porter, and Williams (2000), conducted for The Office of the Assistant Secretary for Planning and Evaluation of the U.S. Department of Health and Human Services, showed that "almost all risk-takers also engage in positive behaviors; they participate in desirable family, school, and community activities. These positive connections offer untapped opportunities to help teens lead healthier lives" (p. 2). In one of the video resources referenced earlier, brain researcher Dr. Greg Berns (2009) suggests that teens may actually engage in risk much more deliberately than previously thought from a neurological perspective. The bottom line here is that all of this is good news. It suggests that teens have more ability than we might think to assess, avoid, and prevent risky behavior.

Third, there are many approaches to helping students develop moral judgment and good decision making skills. I will highlight just a few of them, most of which appeared in the video materials referenced earlier. Consult the Digital Citizenship Wiki (jasonOhler.com/dc) for resources. As always, feel free to add your own.

Teach EQ

Featured in the EQ and Emotional Curricula DVD (Films for the Humanities and Sciences, 2000) is the story of Dave Edwards, headmaster of a primary school in the United Kingdom, who has incorporated EQ into the school's curriculum. His work reflects two of Howard Gardner's multiple intelligences that rarely receive focus in school: interpersonal and intrapersonal. It also reflects the work of Daniel Goleman, who founded the EQ movement and appears several times on the DVD. Goleman points out that IQ is associated with the cortex, while EQ is associated with the limbic system. The process of putting your IQ in charge of your EQ is used for two of the most important skills in the adult world: anger management and impulse control. Goleman distinguishes between IQ and EQ in the following way: IQ can help determine what field you can get into. But once you are in your field, you discover that everyone is equally as smart as you. Therefore, it is your EQ that will distinguish you.

Headmaster Edwards's (Films for the Humanities and Sciences, 2000) program begins with brain study. Children pass around a bag of sand that is roughly equivalent to the weight of a brain while he explains the brain's different parts using models and charts. His focus is on explaining the relationship between the cortex and limbic system and what that means in terms of behavior. Children then focus on what makes them angry and setting goals for themselves in terms of improving their interpersonal and anger management skills. He uses a number of strategies to teach EQ, including games, student diaries, and group EQ debriefing meetings. Parents, teachers, and children report an improvement in the students' skills that are necessary to work in teams and deal with conflict constructively.

Give Them Information

Frances E. Jensen (2008), MD, senior assistant in Neurology at Children's Hospital Boston, a professor at Harvard Medical School, and the presenter in the Teen Brain 101 video series, puts it this simply: Our kids are part of the information age, so let's give them information. The reality is that teenagers have always had at least some of the issues that we see today; they just occurred within a more restrictive social context. Besides changes in permissible behavior, what has also changed is our understanding about the neurology of their behavior. Everyone benefits from having a better understanding of how teen thinking works. Teens have more to think about as they weigh options, parents gain perspective about their teenagers' behavior that may have eluded them, and our ideal school board can move forward in a more informed manner.

Help Students Build Better Relationships With Adults

Experts often comment on the importance of helping kids build better relationships with adults as a way to cultivate responsibility in young people. This speaks directly to the heart of community: youth learning from and forming positive relationships with elders (and vice versa), giving rise to the relationships that sustain communities over time. One study revealed that teens were much more keen for adult interaction than they cared to admit (Spinks, 2002). After all, part of the teen's job is to develop an independent identity. Admitting to a desire for adult interaction would seem to contradict that. Yet teens seem to know its value and are looking for ways to connect with adults. It is up to us to find ways to provide these opportunities in ways that work.

Engage Students in Responsible Roles

An effective way to help students build better relationships with adults within the context of a digital citizenship is to involve them in taking responsibility for how technology is used and maintained in their schools. It is almost cliché to point out that young people have an ease with technology that adults often don't. Using their talents to work with adults as well as their peers to not only solve technical problems but also develop the perspectives for their own peers in terms of digital citizenship is a win-win for everyone, particularly our ideal school board. Gen-Yes is an excellent example of this (see genyes.com).

There are many effective perspectives and strategies to use to help cultivate a sense of community and responsibility among our digitally oriented youth. I have been able to mention only a few of them in this chapter. To read about others, visit the Digital Citizenship Resource Wiki (jasonOhler.com/dc). As always, your additions are welcome.

10 Agenda Item 3

*Character Education for the
Digital Age*

With a good deal of background work completed, our school board now turns to the issue of what a character education program would look like for digital citizens. Developing such a program will take time, experimentation, and a good deal of public involvement. What follows is our ideal school board's initial pass at fleshing out some of the details.

CONNECTING DIGITAL CITIZENSHIP AND CHARACTER EDUCATION

When I raise the topic of digital citizenship with friends and colleagues, many respond by asking, "What's that?"

Explaining digital citizenship and its implications for education can be difficult, especially for those who do not have much experience with social media. When I attempt an explanation, I find myself waving my hands a good deal and using too many metaphors.

But I can make the topic much more accessible if I refer to digital citizenship as "character education for the Digital Age." Character education has been around long enough that many have heard of it. Those who haven't can easily surmise what it is about. Even though it began long before the Internet was a permanent, invisible fixture in our lives, character education still offers a perspective that is very useful for us today. Thus, it provides a good point of departure for our school board. It is up to them to blend its timeless qualities with new considerations that have emerged in the Digital Age.

THE ESSENCE OF CHARACTER EDUCATION

Googling "character education" uncovers a vast area of educational thought and activity. However, there are some foundational framing points that appear to be widely adopted. These are drawn primarily from the work of DeRoche and Williams (2001), Likona (1991), and the Character Education Partnership (2008):

- There are two major purposes of schooling: cognitive development and character formation. Unfortunately, the latter often receives far less attention than the former. The reality is that in order to educate the whole person, we need to address thinking, feeling, and behavior, as well as academics.
- Character education embraces both personal values and civic competencies. Thus, it serves as training for moral behavior in our personal and public lives.
- Character education is about developing virtues—rather than particular views. Thus, it deals with values that are generally acceptable to the local citizenry.
- Character education is best approached from a "whole school" perspective rather than as a set of individual issues.
- Character education happens whether we intend it to or not. Therefore, it needs to be deliberately planned and developed. Otherwise, it will not produce the results that a school community wants.

The last point is key. In the words of Dr. Marvin Berkowitz (Berkowitz & Bier, 2006),

> The inescapable fact is this: as adults involved intimately with children, educators cannot avoid "doing" character education. Either intentionally or unintentionally, teachers shape the formation of character in students—simply by association—through positive or negative example. Character education is thus not optional in the school—it is inevitable, and therefore merits intentional focus and priority status in the school. (p. iii)

Therefore, it makes much more sense to pursue character education in a thoughtful, deliberate fashion than it does to simply let it happen randomly with no sense of purpose or direction.

A SHORT HISTORY OF CHARACTER EDUCATION

The role of the teacher in teaching character education has changed dramatically over the years. The following brief historical overview of this topic identifies four phases of teacher involvement. It is presented here so the reader can place our current Digital Age interests in some historical context.

Teacher Involvement in Teaching Values

Phase 1. From Plato to Eisenhower

For centuries, character and academics were taught together in a very deliberate fashion, with moral instruction receiving as much emphasis as content instruction. This approach to teaching "the whole student" has been part of the Western tradition at least since Plato. Similar sentiments drove colonial education: "Our Founding Fathers were profoundly aware that the health of the new democracy would rest on the virtues of its people" (Tatman, Edmonson, & Slate, 2009, p. 3). Content and virtue were seen as intertwined and thus taught together.

There was little change during the 1800s:

> Not just the land grant colleges, but nearly every higher educational institution founded in the 18th and 19th centuries—religious as well as secular, private no less than public—counted among its leading founding principles a dedication to training competent and responsible citizens (Tatman et al., 2009, p. 4).

In fact, we see deliberate character education generally supported in some form well into the 1950s. Public education supported school prayer, patriotic assemblies, and the direct inculcation of moral values as a matter of course. Teachers were expected by the public to teach moral education, draw upon biblical literature for stories, and to lecture about the morality of the day.

Phase 2. The Socially Recalibrating 1960s

Character education responds to social mood, stresses, and influences. In the 1960s, there was a significant shift in the teacher's role in values instruction due to a number of social pressures, including the civil rights movement, personalism, secularism, and the pressure to separate church and state (DeRoche & Williams, 2001). There was also another factor that changed how America saw itself forever: television. During the 1960s, we were watching the war in Vietnam in our living rooms and experiencing the realities of a pluralistic, multicultural society on a daily basis. As a result, the idea that we could entrust mainstream society to prescribe moral values for everyone became suspect.

Around this time, Kohlberg's work stressing moral evolution rather than moral values began to gain influence. Also popular was Louis Rath's book, *Values and Teaching,* which promoted the idea of "teacher as value-neutral facilitator, helping students clarify their own values, and admonished any direct teaching of a prescribed set of values" (DeRoche & Williams, 2001, p. 19). Also during this time, we began to experiment with different approaches to education. We heard terms like *open classroom, alternative education,* and *programmed learning,* which seemed foreign to a culture used to teaching values directly.

The combined effect of all these changes was to cause the public to ask teachers to take a huge step back from teaching values and ask them to become "moral clarifiers." "Many public schools abandoned systematic, formal attention to character education beginning in the late 1960s" (Huffman in Tatman et al., 2009, p. 6). Tatman and colleagues (2009) note the inevitable results of this: "The roles of classroom teachers became more restrictive as moral reasoning entailed teachers serving as facilitators in the moral development enterprise" (p. 6). In other words, there were no right values, just those that each of us determined were right for us. It was the teacher's job to help us discover what those were.

Phase 3. Mood Swings: 1970 to Almost Now

Our interest in character education during this period seems to be a generalized response to any number of significant social stressors, including the presence of drugs, gangs, sexual promiscuity, and AIDS, as well as a persistent lack of respect for government or authority in traditional terms (Likona, 1991). Society interpreted these stressors as assaults on its survival, as well as its identity as a community of values, and identified a lack of common values as part of the root cause for what seemed to many to be our collective moral decay. When this happened, character education in some form moved to the forefront.

An overview of this period would show character education undergoing various revivals in terms of specific programs, like Service Learning, Social and Emotional Learning, Smart and Good High Schools, as well as a number of localized efforts without program association (Tatman et al., 2009). While these programs were important, their impact was limited to the institutions that adopted them.

Around the year 2000, the No Child Left Behind (NCLB) era began, which was characterized by a focus on an aspect of education that politicians thought would be relatively values-neutral: literacy. The NCLB era was and still is primarily a commitment to high-stakes standardized testing in areas of basic literacy. School districts were often threatened with a loss of funding if they didn't show "continuous improvement" in the areas associated with literacy and thus focused on preparing students for a future of successful test taking.

There have been numerous criticisms of NCLB, including its use of ineffective approaches to literacy development and its employment of flawed methodology in determining student progress and continuous improvement for districts. However, there is another criticism that interests us here, namely, that as it forced districts to obsess about standardized, high stakes testing it deprived students of a much more meaningful, well rounded education. The NCLB approach to schooling stands in stark contrast to other movements in education at the time, such as 21st Century Learning Skills, which emphasized innovation, creativity, citizenship, and learning in a social context. One can't help but wonder what our school systems would be like today had we spent the last decade focusing on digital citizenship, character education, and 21st Century Learning Skills with the same zeal that we have applied to NCLB and test scores.

Phase 4. The Digital Era and the Rebirth of Public Values

As the Digital Age dawned, and society realized the exponential change it represented in terms of innovative thinking, personal behavior, and social reorganization, concern for values and character education entered overdrive.

In my 53 years as a member of the broader educational community, including 30 years as an educator, I have not seen values pursued this openly, though haphazardly, since I attended elementary school. Like many previous attempts to rally character education, this one is in response to a social stressor: the extreme freedoms, pervasiveness, and invisibility that characterize digital community. Add to this the very real concerns of safety and invasiveness, as well as hot-button issues like sexting and cyberbullying, and suddenly dealing with issues of digital citizenship becomes unavoidable.

It is important to note that unlike many past social stressors that were negative in nature, the Digital Age has many upsides that compel us to accept what it offers in broad terms, despite whatever stressors, limitations, and negative aspects are associated with it. Also, unlike past social stressors that varied in intensity from community to community, the digital experience is broadly based, inspiring what could turn out to be a very broad-based commitment to addressing values, character, and citizenship.

The result is that character education has already emerged in a somewhat camouflaged and disjointed manner in the Digital Age. It is documented in the form of acceptable use policies, student Internet use contracts, parental permission agreements, and scope and sequence documents detailing how to approach digital education within a K–12 environment. While these might appear to be straightforward informational documents or contractual arrangements, they specify moral, ethical, and behavioral parameters for using technology in a K–12 environment. That is, they set expectations about character related to digital citizenship. Some go so far as to ask students and parents to sign a moral code with regard to using the Internet. Given this, it might make more sense to deal with issues of values and character more directly, with more forethought and public input. Our ideal school board certainly thinks so.

CHARACTER EDUCATION BEGINS WITH VALUES

The first step in creating a viable character education program is to involve the public in drafting a set of values to use as the program's foundation (Character Education Partnership, 2008; DeRoche & Williams, 2001). Value inventories have been part of the educational landscape for centuries. Let's consider some examples to help put our efforts in context.

Tatman, Edmonson, and Slate (2009) note that from the *Constitution of the Commonwealth of Massachusetts* (1780), the oldest written constitution still in effect in the world today, comes the following, written by John Adams, Samuel Adams, and James Bowdoin. It called for public institutions to

> countenance and inculcate the principles of humanity and general benevolence, public and private charity, industry and frugality, honesty and punctuality in their dealings; sincerity, good humor, and all social affections, and generous sentiments among the people. (*Constitution of the Commonwealth of Massachusetts*, Chapter V, Section II, para. 1)

In his Report of the Commissioners for the University of Virginia in 1818, Tatman and colleagues (2009) note that Thomas Jefferson cited that the "objects of primary education" included such qualities as "morals, understanding of duties to neighbors and country, knowledge of rights, and intelligence and faithfulness in social relations (Noddings, 2005)" (Tatman et al., 2009, p. 4).

More recent examples of educational value inventories are abundant. In 1988, a panel on moral education sponsored by the Association for

Supervision and Curriculum Development (ASCD) produced the following list of values under the heading, "The Morally Mature Person":

1. Respects human dignity, which includes

   o showing regard for the worth and rights of all persons,
   o avoiding deception and dishonesty,
   o promoting human equality,
   o respecting freedom of conscience,
   o working with people of different views, and
   o refraining from prejudiced actions.

2. Cares about the welfare of others, which includes

   o recognizing interdependence among people,
   o caring for one's country,
   o seeking social justice,
   o taking pleasure in helping others, and
   o working to help others reach moral maturity.

3. Integrates individual interests and social responsibilities, which includes

   o becoming involved in community life,
   o doing a fair share of community work,
   o displaying self-regarding and other-regarding moral virtues—self-control, diligence, fairness, kindness, honesty, civility—in everyday life,
   o fulfilling commitments, and
   o developing self-esteem through relationships with others.

4. Demonstrates integrity, which includes

   o practicing diligence,
   o taking stands for moral principles,
   o displaying moral courage,
   o knowing when to compromise and when to confront, and
   o accepting responsibility for one's choices.

5. Reflects on moral choices, which includes

   o recognizing the moral issues involved in a situation,
   o applying moral principles (such as the golden rule) when making moral judgments,
   o thinking about the consequences of decisions, and
   o seeking to be informed about important moral issues in society and the world.

6. Seeks peaceful resolution of conflict, which includes

o striving for the fair resolution of personal and social conflicts,
o avoiding physical and verbal aggression,
o listening carefully to others,
o encouraging others to communicate, and
o working for peace.

From ASCD Panel on Moral Education. "Moral Education in the Life of School." (1988, May). *Educational Leadership, 45*(8), 5. © 1988 by ASCD. Reprinted with permission. Learn more about ASCD at www.ascd.org.

In 2005, the International Center for Leadership in Education identified the following 12 guiding principles upon which to base a character education program. Collectively, they are referred to as the Twelve Guiding Principles of Exceptional Character:

1. **Adaptability**—The ability and willingness to change. To put oneself in harmony with changed circumstances. To be ready and willing to adjust as necessary to the changes in people and circumstances that arise in daily life.

2. **Compassion**—Kindness. The desire to help others in distress. To show kindness and concern for others in distress by offering help whenever possible.

3. **Contemplation**—Giving serious consideration to something. To think things through with proper care before taking action.

4. **Courage**—Bravery. The willingness to put one's beliefs into practice, the capacity to meet danger without giving way to fear. To face difficulty or danger and express your beliefs even if you are afraid.

5. **Honesty**—Truthfulness, sincerity. The act or condition of never deceiving, stealing, or taking advantage of the trust of others. To be truthful in all that you do and never deceive, steal, or take advantage of the trust of others.

6. **Initiative**—Eagerness to do something. To take responsible action on your own, without prompting from others.

7. **Loyalty**—Faithfulness, dependability. The quality of being faithful to another person in the performance of duty; adhering to a contract with another person. To show others that you are dependable when you have a commitment to them.

8. **Optimism**—Positive beliefs. The inclination to take a hopeful view or think that all will work out for the best. To strive to be positive in your beliefs about yourself, others, and the future.

9. **Perseverance**—Hard work. The quality of trying hard and continuously in spite of obstacles and difficulties.

10. **Respect**—Regard, value, admire, appreciate. Special esteem or consideration in which one holds another person or thing. To show regard for yourself, others, and the world around you.

11. **Responsibility**—Accountability. To consider oneself answerable for something. To demonstrate that you consider yourself to be accountable for your actions and that you follow through on your commitments.

12. **Trustworthiness**—Reliability. Dependable, deserving of trust and confidence.

From *Character-Centered Teaching—A Guide to Creating Teachable Moments for Character Education.* Used with permission from the International Center for Leadership in Education (2001–2006).

The inventories presented here skim the surface of what is available. Many states have created educational values inventories, as have many educational and professional organizations. You are probably guided by a number of values inventories by virtue of your professional associations and may not even know it.

FYI

What Values Inventories Guide Your Professional Life?

For homework, find out whether your school district or state government has created a values inventory for character education. Also, find out what guiding principles have been adopted by any organizations you belong to. If you are not in education, find out what values the professional associations in your field have adopted. Then ask yourself the following questions: Do they reflect your personal values? Would you suggest changes if you could do so?

Heartwood Ethics Curriculum

Before leaving this area of inquiry, let's look at one more values inventory that I find particularly enlightening: The Heartwood Ethics Ethical Framework (2010).

Go to the Heartwood Ethics Curriculum (www.heartwoodethics .org/). Under *Attributes in the classroom* under Teaching Heartwood, you will see their seven core values: courage, loyalty, justice, respect, hope, honesty, and love. But under the same tab, there are also two other links, named *Other ethical attributes* and *Other ethical frameworks*. Clicking on the first reveals a list of over 100 other values, most of which may not be considered mainstream, but all of which are reasonable and important. Here are just a few of them that could inform a digital character education program: balance, discretion, empathy, manners, and thoughtfulness. While these do not typically appear in a values inventory, they seem particularly appropriate given our conversations about Party-cipation and life in the infosphere.

Clicking on *Other ethical frameworks* is equally enlightening. Doing so reveals values inventories associated with Benjamin Franklin, Kwanzaa, and Confucius, to name just a few. All of them make sense and inform our inquiry into building a solid foundation of values for pursuing character education.

We draw the following conclusions from our review of values inventories:

1. Some qualities of character appear to be universal, like respect and responsibility.

2. Some are more unique, like balance, optimism, and empathy.

3. We can assume that each inventory is an expression of the particular perspectives and needs of the community that created it.

4. We can assume that our values inventory will reflect universal as well as unique perspectives and needs.

5. We can assume that our concern with digital citizenship will inform our choices and lead either to identifying values not normally considered or defining traditional values in new ways.

6. There is a practical limitation to the number of values we can identify before an inventory becomes unwieldy. Therefore, we shouldn't assume that the values that organizations identify are the only ones that are important but rather are those that they find most important.

Our school board has 10 minutes before taking a break and chooses to take a first pass at developing a values inventory. They assume that some ethical stalwarts will make the short list, like responsibility and integrity. But for now, the board is more interested in brainstorming values and characteristics of behavior that address the unique aspects of digital community. Board members use the bullet points from Agenda Item 2, Topic A: What's Different About Digital Community to frame their work. Some values are drawn from the inventories presented in this chapter; others are new.

1. **Shifts in psychological perspective** (disinhibition, dissociation, abstraction)

Possible values. Contemplation, "think twice, type once," empathy, humanization (as the antidote to abstraction), ethereal empathy (trying to project the impacts of what we say and do through the ether of the infosphere), seeking input, prudence, netiquette

2. **Shifts in community** (activity that is multicommunity, transcommunity, global activity, distributed, and leveraged)

Possible values. Focus, centeredness, "ethereal empathy," connectedness, appreciating and respecting multiculturalism, finding commonalities, consensus building, working in diverse teams, honoring what is unique and universal

3. **Shifts in identity** (managed and hidden identity, unaccountability)

Possible values. Knowing yourself, identity clarification, balance, safety for yourself and others, gentleness, accountability (this is like responsibility but more focused), knowing when to unplug

There is a good deal to consider here. The fact is we may not even have words yet to clearly describe all of the values needed to be a good digital citizen. Ideas like empathizing with someone at a distance who may be using an obscured identity is at least different, if not substantially new. But our direction is clear: Some of our values need to focus on the unique character of digital community in order for them to speak to our students and their future as digital citizens.

Further Thoughts About Values: Let Students Create Their Own Values Inventory

While our ideal school board has been careful to include students in this brainstorming session about values, one board member has an epiphany, shouting, "Eureka," and spilling his coffee in the process: Most values inventories (including those featured in this chapter) are created by adults for youth. What would happen if the school board asked students to create their own inventory, specifically tailored to being a digital citizen and their experiences in the infosphere? One result might be that lofty, more abstract goals like "respect" would become something more concrete, like "not hurting anyone" or "leaving people alone who ask to be left alone."

In the end, we will probably opt for adopting both lofty values and more specific mission values that speak directly to the experience of being a student in the Digital Age. Doing so would help adults understand the student viewpoint while helping students transition into the adult world of value assessment.

The school board member who came up with the idea of kids creating their own digital citizenship values inventory agrees to chair a subcommittee about this topic. His report will be Agenda Item 1 at the next school board meeting.

CHARACTER EDUCATION STANDARDS AND EVALUATION

DeRoche and Williams (2001) and others provide very detailed approaches about how to proceed with creating a character education program. Steps include building frameworks, developing community partnerships, training, infusion throughout the school community, and assessment. Detailing this process is not feasible here. I simply recommend you consult the resources cited in this book and adapt them to the needs of your situation.

Instead, I am going to skip forward to evaluation, and specifically to the *Eleven Principles of Effective Character Education* developed by the Character Education Partnership (Likona, Schaps, & Lewis, 2007). Any character education program, regardless of the process used to create it, should be able to show evidence of all 11 standards. What is particularly helpful about CEP's work is that it includes a self-assessment tool for determining the health

---

FYI

Involve Everyone

Buy-in by the entire school community is particularly important so that digital citizenship becomes as normal a topic across the curriculum as value teaching used to be during earlier times. In practical terms, we need classroom teachers who embrace digital citizenship as a subject that potentially touches any lesson or unit, whether through issues of appropriate Internet use, honoring copyright considerations, effective social media application . . . whatever their classroom activities connect to. We also need specialists, like counselors, psychologists, and health teachers, who understand the specifics of more complex and damaging situations that fall under the purview on digital citizenship. We need parents and community members who are willing to carry on the conversation at home as well as in appropriate public venues. And we need librarians now more than ever. They are our information specialists in an information age. Teachers should be able to turn to them routinely for clarification on issues of digital citizenship.

of each standard in your school district. Their *Eleven Principles of Character Education* are as follows:

1. Promotes core ethical values and supportive performance values as the foundation of good character.

2. Defines "character" comprehensively to include thinking, feeling, and behavior.

3. Uses a comprehensive, intentional, and proactive approach to character development.

4. Creates a caring school community.

5. Provides students with opportunities for moral action.

6. Includes a meaningful and challenging academic curriculum that respects all learners, develops their character, and helps them to succeed.

7. Strives to foster students' self-motivation.

8. Engages the school staff as a learning and moral community that shares responsibility for character education and attempts to adhere to the same core values that guide the education of students.

9. Fosters shared moral leadership and long-range support of the character education initiative.

10. Engages families and community members as partners in the character-building effort.

11. Assesses the character of the school, the school staff's functioning as character educators, and the extent to which students manifest good character.

From Likona, T., Schaps, E., & Lewis, C. (2007). Used with permission from the Character Education Partnership.

Our school board asks whether there is anything missing from this list of principles that is needed to address digital citizenship. Most principles seem very adaptable, regardless of social or technological era. However, a quick brainstorm produces the following suggested modifications, which appear in italics:

1. Promotes core ethical values and supportive performance values as the foundation of good character *in all communities, local, global, and digital.*

2. Defines "character" comprehensively to include thinking, feeling, and behavior *with regard to both onsite and online activities.*

3. Uses a comprehensive, intentional, and proactive approach to character development, *including training for online etiquette and behavior.*

4. Creates a caring school community, *including social media communities that are a part of school activities.*

5. Provides students with opportunities for moral action, *including providing guided access to the Internet so that students can practice digital citizenship.*

6. Engages the school staff as a learning and moral community that shares responsibility for character education and attempts to adhere to the same core values that guide the education of students. *These core values should be expressed both onsite within local community as well as online within global and digital communities.*

7. Strives to foster students' self-motivation, *with regard to all facets of their lives, including virtual activities.*

8. Engages the school staff as a learning and moral community that shares responsibility for character education and attempts to adhere to the same core values that guide the education of students. *This should happen regardless of whether the community is actual or virtual in nature.*

9. Fosters shared moral leadership and long-range support of the character education initiative *in all aspects of school life, whether onsite or online.*

10. Engages families and community members as partners in the character-building effort, *including efforts that extend into the digital domain. This includes the development of policies to guide technology use at school and at home.*

11. Assesses the character of the school, the school staff's functioning as character educators, and the extent to which students manifest good character *within local, global, and digital communities.*

The board considers an alternate approach that is, simply, adding a 12th principle that deals directly with digital citizenship. Perhaps something like, *All of the preceding principles apply to both onsite and online venues and refer to behaviors both in physical and virtual community. Policies that are developed to guide the fair, acceptable, and safe use of technology and the Internet should be grounded in a school's approach to character and citizenship.* We might also add a standard that reflects the leadership mantra we mentioned earlier in the book: *Students will study the personal, social, and environmental impacts of every technology and media application they use in school in order to develop character with regard to living in highly technical times."*

However, the board opts for yet another option: Simply leave the 11 principles as they are, and add digital citizenship criteria to CEP's self-assessment tool: Character Education Quality Standards. CEP has crafted an evaluation instrument that helps schools determine the degree to which each of the 11 principles of character education are present. Let's consider one of CEP's principles to see how this happens. For this exercise, we will look at Principle 5, which states, "Provides students with opportunities for moral action." The principle and its assessment criteria appear on pages 201–202.

5.1 The school sets clear expectations for students to engage in moral action in terms of civility, personal responsibility, good sportsmanship, helping others, and service to school and community.	*0*	*1*	*2*	*3*	*4*

- Staff model, endorse, teach, and expect good sportsmanship, civility, compassion, and personal responsibility.
- There are clear guidelines and expectations regarding community service, service learning, and/or other more programmatic opportunities for moral action.
- These guidelines and expectations

    a) Are clearly articulated and relevant to students.

    b) Are frequently communicated to and known by relevant stakeholders (students, teachers, and parents).

    c) Serve as obligations for the students when appropriate (e.g., mandatory recycling, required community service hours, cross-age mentoring activities implemented on a classroom level).

- (For districts): The district encourages and sets clear guidelines and expectations for community service and/or service learning and other programmatic opportunities for moral action.

5.2 The school provides students with repeated and varied opportunities for engaging in moral *action within the school*, and students engage in these opportunities and are positively affected by them.	*0*	*1*	*2*	*3*	*4*

- The school effectively provides students with opportunities for moral actions within the school by

  a) Endorsing and encouraging participation in activities like cooperative learning, peer or cross-age tutoring, classroom or student body governance, and service projects or work such as planting and tending a garden, beautifying the school, and helping keep the school clean.

  b) Providing opportunities that are valued and initiated/directed by students.

  c) Setting aside school time for supporting, engaging in, and individually and collectively reflecting on moral action.

  d) Explicitly acknowledging student moral action.

- The majority of students take advantage of these opportunities and benefit from them.

5.3 The school provides students with repeated and varied opportunities for engaging in moral *action in the larger community,* and students engage in these opportunities and are positively affected by them.	0	1	2	3	4

- The school effectively provides students with opportunities for moral actions by

  a) Endorsing and encouraging participation in community service work (e.g., working with the elderly, the homeless, or on environmental projects).

  b) Providing opportunities that are valued and initiated/directed by students.

  c) Setting aside school time for supporting, engaging in, and individually and collectively reflecting on moral action.

  d) Explicitly acknowledging the positive consequences of community service and other moral actions in the larger community.

- The majority of students take advantage of these opportunities and benefit from them.

From Character Education Quality Standards (2008). Used with permission by the Character Education Partnership.

As we scrutinize Principle 5, we see ample opportunity to add a digital citizen dimension to the criteria. The modifications are in italics:

5.1 The school sets clear expectations for students to engage in moral action in terms of civility, personal responsibility, good sportsmanship, helping others, and service to school and community, *within local, global, and digital communities.*

- Staff model, endorse, teach, and expect good sportsmanship, civility, compassion, and personal responsibility. *This includes any communication that occurs in cyberspace.*
- There are clear guidelines and expectations regarding community service, service learning, and/or other more programmatic opportunities for moral action. *This includes helping to teach others digital skills and to find ways to bridge the digital divide within the school district.*
- These guidelines and expectations

  o Are clearly articulated and relevant to students, *especially in terms of their activities in cyberspace.*
  o Are frequently communicated to and known by relevant stakeholders (students, teachers, and parents), *using both conventional and online media.*
  o Serve as obligations for the students when appropriate (e.g., mandatory recycling, required community service hours, cross-age mentoring activities implemented on a classroom level, [*digital skill-building programs, cyber etiquette classes, etc.]).*

- (For districts): The district encourages and sets clear guidelines and expectations for community service and/or service learning and other programmatic opportunities for moral action.

5.2 The school provides students with repeated and varied opportunities for engaging in moral action *within the school and associated online venues,* and students engage in these opportunities and are positively affected by them.

- The school effectively provides students with opportunities for moral actions within the school by:

  o Endorsing and encouraging participation in activities like cooperative learning, peer or cross-age tutoring, classroom or student body governance, and service projects or work such as planting and tending a garden, beautifying the school, *managing online venues,* and helping keep the school clean.
  o Providing opportunities that are valued and initiated/directed by students.
  o *Providing opportunities to use the Internet in minimally filtered situations as part of a program to encourage and determine student responsibility in this area.*

o Setting aside school time for supporting, engaging in, and individually and collectively reflecting on moral action, *including activity that happens in cyberspace.*

o Explicitly acknowledging student moral action.

o *Explicitly asking students to develop value inventories, as well as rules and training procedures for students in terms of acceptable online behavior and appropriate technology use in general.*

- The majority of students take advantage of these opportunities and benefit from them.

5.3 The school provides students with repeated and varied opportunities for engaging in moral action, and students engage in these opportunities and are positively affected by them. *These opportunities are provided at the school level and within the community that the school serves, as well as within the global and digital communities in which the students are involved.*

- The school effectively provides students with opportunities for moral actions by:

o Endorsing and encouraging participation in community service work (e.g., working with the elderly, the homeless, *those with limited access to technology or online resources,* or on environmental projects).

o Providing opportunities that are valued and initiated/directed by students, *including providing leadership for issues that occur in cyberspace, that are related to cybersafety and virtual behavior.*

o Setting aside school time for supporting, engaging in, and individually and collectively reflecting on moral action, *including the appropriate use of technology, as well as issues that occur in cyberspace, like cyberbullying, sexting, and new issues of digital citizenship as they arise.*

o Explicitly acknowledging the positive consequences of community service and other moral actions in the larger community, *including issues in cyberspace and global community as part of any "think globally, act locally" initiatives.*

- The majority of students take advantage of these opportunities and benefit from them.

This is a first pass by the study group. No doubt it will undergo many rewrites before the first draft is completed. However, this much is clear: It is not a difficult stretch to expand existing character education policies to embrace issues of technology use and cyber behavior. All it takes is a lot of work!

11 Agenda Item 4

Literacy in the Digital Age

(Chapter adapted from Ohler, 2009.)

Our ideal school board is wise enough to understand that effective citizenship within any community relies on the literacy of its citizens. In addition, board members understand that the nature of literacy has changed dramatically since their pen and paper days. This chapter addresses the issue of literacy in the Digital Age and how to best prepare students—as well as teachers, administrators, and the public—for the shifts in literacy that are upon us.

Some historians object to the use of the word *literacy* to denote anything other than literacy with one medium: letters. They have an historical basis for their objection. After all, the word *literacy* arose centuries ago in reference to those very few who were considered educated precisely because they "knew the letters" (Harper, 2001–2010). Generally speaking, a literate person is still considered to be someone who has the ability to read, write, and understand words.

Yet there is another way to view literacy that works for both the world of Gutenberg and Google: being able to both read and write narrative in the media forms of the day, whatever they may be. For many years, this has meant consuming and producing words, primarily through reading and writing, though to some extent through listening and speaking. But the age of digital expression challenges this for three reasons:

1. **New media demand new literacies.** The proliferation of inexpensive, easy-to-use, new media tools has generated new literacy demands in terms of being able read and write using new media forms, including sound, graphics, and moving images, as well as text.

2. **New media coalesce into a collage.** Literacy also requires being able to use multiple media simultaneously, integrating them into a single narrative or "media collage," such as a digital story, movie, gaming scenario, webpage, or blog.

3. **New media are largely participatory, social media.** The world of Web 2.0 demands that digital literacy occur within the context of the social web. This occurs in many ways, including collaborative narrative construction and publication through wikis, blogs, document-sharing services like Google Docs, video posting sites like YouTube, and social sites like Facebook.

Understanding the nature of literacy has been challenging in recent times because the word *literacy* is in such wide use. We find references to research literacy, responsibility literacy, math literacy, health literacy . . . you name it. In most of these cases, the word *literacy* roughly means "a skill area that is fundamental to successful citizenship as well as the abilities associated with that skill area." Thus, we need to keep an eye on what the public defines as *literacy*, so we can understand how *illiteracy* is being defined as well.

However, if there is one umbrella literacy that seems to subsume many of the others, or at least plays a major role within all of them, it can rightfully be called *digital literacy*. My interest in digital literacy is in the skills associated with "consuming and producing the media forms of the day." In addition, I am interested in the mind shifts that need to occur in order to make implementation of new approaches to literacy possible. What follows are major guidelines for considering digital literacy within a school system and beyond.

SHIFT FROM TEXT-CENTRISM TO MEDIA COLLAGE

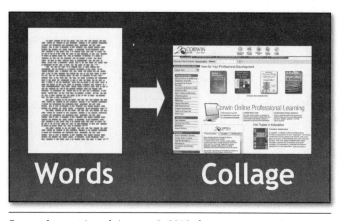

Screenshot retrieved August 8, 2010, from www.corwin.com

If literacy means being able to read and write the media forms of the day, then today this translates into being able to construct or at least manage an articulate, meaningful, navigable media collage. Media collages abound in many forms, including webpages, digital stories, mashups, virtual environments, and social media sites. Keep in mind that the *essay media form* on the left in this picture represents what we test for in school, while the *collage media form* on the right represents what we hope and pray kids will be able to produce before they enter the workforce. The cognitive dissonance this produces fractures kids' lives in two, a nondigital one at school and digital one out of school. This brings us back to the question posed in the Preamble of this book: Should we help ours kids live two lives or one?

While mediasts may claim to understand the pedagogical implications of media, the reality is that much of what we know about media and learning was developed before Web 2.0 exploded and created the plethora of new media that are now widely available. Thus, while everyone may have an opinion about how to approach Web 2.0 learning, expert advice is in short supply.

What should our school board do? Encourage teachers to experiment fearlessly with their own work and the work they ask students to create. Movies can show scientific processes or document history concepts; social media can be used to create lively, informed discussions about a poem, piece of art, or item in the news; and so on. Experiment, trust your instincts, become an action researcher in your classroom, ask your students for guidance in the use of media, and troll the web for what other educators are doing. We are all relearning our sense of literacy together.

VALUE WRITING, NOW MORE THAN EVER

Amidst the explosion of new media, writing has become more important than ever. There are new reasons for this that might not be immediately apparent.

First, while the essay form of writing is still very important, long narrative pieces don't read well on the web, where they appear as walls of text to everyone except the few who are truly committed to their content. In contrast, a new kind of presentation is in wide use for effective blog or web writing that I call "visually differentiated text" (VDT), a kind of visual rhetoric that employs a number of writing conventions that are used to visually sculpt text. Paying more

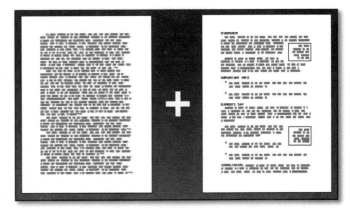

attention to the visual presentation of text has become important because reading words onscreen is more difficult than reading them on paper. In addition, information overwhelment has produced a need for information that is more concise so that it can be scanned and referenced more easily. Typically, sculpting text requires using the 7 Bs (breaks, bullets, boldface, boxes, beyond black and white, beginning, and banners). More about the 7 Bs on my Digital Citizenship website (jasonOhler.com/dc).

Rest assured that essay writing is still important. But students need to be able to command multiple approaches to writing. While essays, such as the one you are reading right now, focus on detailed argument presentation, VDT is used to present text concisely—a combination of narrative and factoids. Bear in mind that while essays are generally written for an audience of instructors, web material is read by the general public. Thus, the pressure is on for web writers to write clearly and precisely for a wide audience. After all, while our eyes may skip paragraphs, readers tend to focus on bullets surrounded by white space.

The second reason writing is so important is because it still serves as the foundation of much of the new media that we see onscreen. Digital stories, movies, documentaries, and many new media narrative forms are built upon clear, well-researched, creative writing. The old theater saying "If it ain't on the page then it ain't on the stage" is particularly true today in a world in which it is easy to create personalized media. I have helped students and teachers create many hundreds of pieces of media over the years and have discovered the following: If there is one element of student media production that separates the good projects from the not-so-good projects, it is that the former are built on solid written foundations.

What should our school board do? It should honor multiple forms of writing, including essay, report, story, scripts, and VDT. It should expect to find examples of each in student portfolios, and in the web writing that students develop for student projects.

ADOPT ART AS THE NEXT R

Clearly, in the world of the media collage, our students need new foundational literacies that will help them "consume and produce the media forms of the day." I am not referring simply to the ability to use the media effectively but also to the ability to craft media that is clear, creative, and expresses a sense of vision and personal statement. Given the current structure of schooling, this is best addressed as a specialty area within the art curriculum, which deals with narrative that combines form, color, design, and collage as part of everyday communication. I am also referring more generally to "the arts" as well, including music, drama, and other art forms, which also play a major role in the forms of media collage that populate infosphere.

Yet the reality is that art is largely viewed as expendable in K–12 education, particularly when budgets get tight and high-stakes testing brings pressure to bear on the other three Rs. At those times, art is often seen as fluff with no ties to the real world of work. Given that the world of work is now built upon visual presentation and the media collage, a dumber thought was never had.

What should our school board do? Solidify art's place in standard K–12 learning fare by treating it as a literacy rather than just a content area. After all, while content areas may come and go, literacies are forever. Art needs that kind of permanence in our curriculum. In addition, our school board should infuse art across the curriculum the way reading and math have been infused over the years. This will ensure that the media forms of the day are being pursued broadly throughout academic pursuits.

BLEND TRADITIONAL AND EMERGING LITERACIES: PRACTICE THE DAOW

The ancient human (Dertouzos, 2001) would find much that is familiar in the major literacies that support the Digital Age. Art and oracy, which have been with us for many millennia, underlie many of the media collage forms in wide use, including storytelling, narrated documentaries, movies, PowerPoint presentations, and even games and virtual realities. Writing, while not ancient, has been around for centuries in Western civilization, and often forms the foundation for much of what we see on the screen. Thus, implied in the move to the new media collage is that a well-rounded approach

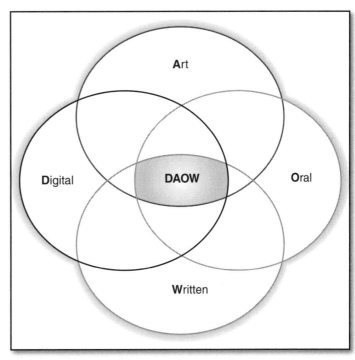

to education requires blending a number of literacies, both traditional and emerging, into a cohesive narrative. I call this the DAOW of literacy.

It is important to note that oracy—the ancient literacy of speaking and listening—is central to many of the media collage forms currently in wide use. Yet it receives very little attention in a standard school curriculum. It is also a key component of leadership. After all, we often find evidence of leadership in the way that people speak with and listen to others.

What should our ideal school board do? First, it should require that student portfolios include projects that blend the best of the ancient, recent, and emerging literacies into coherent narrative and that do so with a sense of research and "creatical" thinking. Second, it should provide the professional development necessary to help teachers assist their students in doing so. The DAOW of literacy is now the way of life.

HARNESS BOTH REPORT AND STORY

If we don't present information within the context of some kind of container or metaform, then we risk reducing that information to nothing more than disconnected data points. Traditionally in school, that metaform has been a report, list, or essay. As new media emerge that must be incorporated into the media collage, the need for effective metaforms to bind them together becomes more important. One kind of metaform that offers a good deal of help in this regard is the story form.

Story is much more than a feel-good experience. It is an ancient information container that connects data points very well, helping us to remember individual facts as well as overall perspectives.

An important book in the development of my understanding of storytelling and learning is Kieran Egan's (1986) *Teaching as Story Telling*. Egan notes that students come to school well versed in the story form, which involves tension, resolution, opposing forces, and character transformation. However, the information they are required to deal with is often presented in list form, which is devoid of the characteristics of story. The result is cognitive dissonance. Thus, when students tell us they are bored or that material is too difficult, we need to consider that what they may be really saying is, "Where's the story?" It is their way of telling us that the structure and nature of the information container itself has caused them to disengage with what they are studying.

Where did they learn the story form? From movies, TV, and the endless flow of stories they hear from their friends and family. The net effect of the presence of the dramatic elements of story for all of us is to cause us to emotionally engage in the presentation of information. This increases our interest in the presentation and the likelihood that we will remember it.

Reports and stories are both important, but differ in a number of ways. Reports are typically linear, less creative, and inspire little emotional engagement, focusing instead on objective research and critical thinking. Stories, on the other hand, can certainly be the result of research and critical thinking, but they present information within a more creative, engaging construct, making use of the narrative elements of tension, transformation, and resolution. The result is that stories engages us emotionally and communicate with us in ways that reports do not and vice versa.

What should our school board do? Require students to present their understanding of schoolwork in multiple formats, including essay, report, and story. In fact, one of the truly fertile pedagogical frontiers that awaits us is learning how to combine report and story, blending critical thinking and emotional engagement in new, interesting ways. Digital stories, gaming, and virtual immersions may well be where we find examples of this.

PRACTICE PRIVATE AND PARTICIPATORY SOCIAL LITERACY

McLuhan (1964) explained that conventional literacy caused us to trade an ear for an eye, forcing us to trade the social context of the oral tradition for the private point of view of reading and writing. To counteract this impact of literacy, television facilitated our first step in what he called "retribalization" by providing a common social experience that could serve as the basis for community dialogue in the global village.

But television was a mass medium in the classic sense of the term. That is, a very few producers used it to deliver a very limited amount of content to vast audiences of consumers. In this scenario, the mass mediasts told their stories, not ours. With the advent of Web 2.0, however, consumers could join the ranks of producers. Much of the emerging nature of literacy is a result of Web 2.0 tools that are often free, easy to use, and eminently available. The result is that literally anyone with standard gear and modest Internet access can play a part in reinventing literacy.

One of the results of this development is that literacy is no longer a purely private pursuit. The new media collage depends upon individual and collective thinking and creative endeavors. We work together, responding to each other's blogs, editing each other's work, and annotating each other's wikis. Our new approach to literacy requires that we balance our contributions as individuals with those we make as team members.

What should our ideal school board do? Require students to maintain social media that facilitate team research and expression. Bear in mind that many schools currently block social media for fear it will be misused. However, there is another approach to addressing this fear: Model how to use social media in ways that are productive, articulate, and representative of their best uses, particularly as we see them employed in the world beyond K–12 education. Again, we return to the question in the Preamble— should we help our students live two lives or one?

DEVELOP LITERACY NOT JUST WITH DIGITAL TOOLS, BUT ALSO ABOUT DIGITAL TOOLS

I won't belabor this point because much of this book is devoted to developing literacy about digital tools. Doing so forms a large part of digital citizenship training. However, there are two areas of literacy in this regard that deserve special attention.

Media Literacy

While media literacy may be a core component of digital literacy, its roots make it a bit of a special case. It emerged forcefully in the 1960s—I refer to this as Media Literacy 1.0—due to concern about how mass media was being used to persuade and convince its audience to think in particular ways, buy certain products, and otherwise influence their behavior. Because Web 2.0 and the inexpensive tools of media development were decades into the future, we only consumed media in those days. Our only possible media literacy responses were to either ignore the media or develop the critical thinking skills necessary to understand how media influence worked.

The basic premise of Media Literacy 1.0 is still intact. Professional mediasts are very adroit at bypassing our discriminating minds in order to influence our behavior. In brain research terms, they dodge the frontal cortex and head straight for the limbic system. Providing students with the critical thinking tools to become discriminating consumers of media will always be important. There are a number of effective programs that help students do very practical "minds-on, hands-on" kinds of activities, like deconstructing advertisements and media programming in order to understand both the mechanics and biases of media persuasion. These are identified on my Digital Citizenship Wiki (jasonOhler.com/dc). I invite you to add resources you use to the wiki as well.

However, in the era of Web 2.0 and the media collage, we have graduated to Media Literacy 2.0. The primary difference between versions 1 and 2 is that media literacy has been expanded to encompass production. I define Media Literacy 2.0 as "understanding how to identify, evaluate, and apply the techniques of media persuasion." Production is important for one simple reason: There is no better way to understand the persuasion of media than to reflectively create media. When you do, you come face-to-face with the techniques of persuasion as you choose particular images or background music to achieve particular effects. This is not much different than how we approach writing in school. Students are required to write persuasive essays, harnessing the medium of words in order to convince readers of a particular perspective. Ideally, writing helps them deconstruct the persuasive writing of others, making them more discriminating readers and consumers of information.

Bear in mind that if you want students to be cognizant and reflective about the media development decisions they make, then you will need to require they do so as part of the project you assign. This kind of reflection does not come naturally in the flurry of media creation.

Information Literacy

Information literacy is a particular kind of media literacy that emerged in response to some of the "fears about technology" articulated earlier in Section II, namely, that information was ubiquitous, ephemeral, and biased. The reality is that we are caught in between two uncomfortable realities: (1) It is unthinkable not to use the web these days as the basis for most of our decision making, and (2) we have nowhere near the time we need to deconstruct the web's rapidly changing information in order to detect its bias and determine its veracity. Thus, addressing the credibility of the information we use is paramount but highly problematic.

There are two basic approaches to evaluating the credibility and value of information: informal and formal. Informal involves understanding the overall grammar of a website, including what URLs mean, who owns the site, what they link to, and so on. It also includes looking for basic clues in the content that might reveal bias, weak reasoning, or an absence of research. This seat-of-the-pants kind of determination is often all we have as we whiz through our information searches in an average day.

But now and again, the validity of a particular information source becomes especially important, perhaps because we are using the information in a formal report or study. When this happens, there are other tools we can use that take more time but yield better results.

One of my favorite informal approaches to information evaluation is Shermer's (2009) *Baloney Detection Kit*. He has produced a video about it that is easily accessible on the web. It asks the following 10 questions:

1. How reliable is the source of the claim?

2. Does the source make similar claims?

3. Have the claims been verified by somebody else?

4. Does this fit with the way the world works?

5. Has anyone tried to disprove the claim?

6. Where does the preponderance of evidence point?

7. Is the claimant playing by the rules of science?

8. Is the claimant providing positive evidence?

9. Does the new theory account for as many phenomena as the old theory?

10. Are personal beliefs driving the claim?

If you go to his website (michealshirmer.com), read the comments about his *Baloney Detection Kit*. Not everyone agrees with him, but many support his efforts and offer ways to augment and improve his list of questions.

In the mood for something more formal? I use this checklist from John Hopkins University (Kirk, 1996, accessible at www.library.jhu.edu/researchhelp/general/evaluating). It is reasonably complete and well thought out.

More informal and formal resources can be found on my Digital Citizenship Wiki (jasonOhler.com/dc). As always, I invite you to contribute your own.

What should our school board do? Require that media and information literacy become a part of a general approach to studying any content area. To facilitate this, value librarians and information specialists as sacred resources in any school community. On average, they know more about finding solid information on the web than the rest of us. In fact, in 1989 the American Library Association became one of the first groups to develop a solid working definition of information literacy as the abilities to "recognize when information is needed and have the ability to locate, evaluate, and use effectively the needed information" (American Library Association, 1989, para. 1).

While all content-area teachers need to assume responsibility for the information they use, we need information specialists to help them. We need information literacy across the curriculum. We need librarians.

PURSUE FLUENCY RATHER THAN JUST LITERACY

Literacy has become the hallmark of a civilized society. There is a very practical reason for this: It solidifies language, thereby facilitating the development of laws to serve a common citizenry. Through literacy, we can communicate with each other, form social cohesion, and hold each other accountable.

The next step for the communities that have harnessed literacy is fluency, not so much in terms of using language in a traditional sense, but in terms of using new media to innovate, problem solve, and lead others.

Note that digital fluency has very little to do with being the biggest geek in the room. In an era in which literally anyone with a laptop and an Internet connection can be a well-educated entrepreneur, technical literacy may become a second tier skill-set. Instead, leaders will need the ability to practice literacy at the advanced levels required for sophisticated communication within the workplace and other social environments, both onsite and online. They will need to be able to facilitate the language of leadership and innovation that allows the merely literate to translate their ideas into compelling professional practice. This is the emerging nature of digital fluency.

What should our ideal school board do? The first step is to develop standards for fluencies that build on the literacies they already consider essential. They also need to look beyond content and skill areas to broader concerns, like communication, problem solving, and "creatical" thinking. From these will emerge the leadership skills that our students will find most helpful in the real world beyond school. The next step of course is tackling how to infuse these throughout the curriculum and school community. An early attempt at defining fluency can be found on the Infosavvy Fluency website (www.21stcenturyfluency.com) (2010). Key fluencies are defined in the following areas: solution development, information use, creativity, media use, collaboration, and digital citizenship. Together, they make up a promising fluency toolbox for aspiring leaders.

No doubt other approaches to fluency will be developed as the idea that literacy is not enough spreads. In fact, keep your eye on the evolution of *fluency* as it surfaces within academic as well as public discussion. It is destined to evolve and become one of the next hotly debated topics as we struggle to build schools for the future. All we really know at this point is that the fluent will lead, the literate will follow, and everyone else may get left behind.

12 Agenda Item 5

What Role for IT?

RETUNING YOUR IT DEPARTMENT

Why, you might ask, do I have a chapter in this book about the IT department? Because the IT departments at our educational institutions constitute the most formidable gatekeepers of our day. Without their consent, new ideas about using our new digital tools simply cannot happen. More important, any consideration of revamping our schools to embrace digital citizenship will falter without IT's full support. The reality is that the IT community is a part of everything we do as digital citizens and thus needs to be involved more deliberately as we move forward with character education in the Digital Age.

First, let me give the IT world its due. From an interpersonal communication standpoint, the job of the average IT employee can't be too much fun. IT folks usually hear from us only when a printer is broken, an Internet site is blocked, or a web service is down. They listen to us whine about how our dependence on technology is their fault, and how we need something fixed right now, or an entire day's activities are going to be ruined. And when they do make the hardware and software upgrades that we asked them to make, we show zero tolerance for bugs and other inevitable setbacks that come with change.

If that weren't enough, it is their job to keep their small corner of the infosphere humming along without allowing viruses and other enemies of community to pass through our gates. And they must do so while translating their school district's interpretation of the Children's Internet Protection Act (CIPA) into technical terms. The truth is, we take them for granted and rarely stop in at network central just to thank them for what they do.

But the complaints I hear about teachers being denied the tools they need in order to teach and practice 21st-century digital citizenship skills are strident and unending. In a nutshell, teachers summarize their frustrations with the following statement: "The IT people won't let me do that."

This is not just the view from teachers but from administrators as well. A short anecdote should suffice to illustrate this.

I was having dinner recently with five superintendents, each of whom voiced the same complaint: They wanted their teachers to use technology more innovatively, but their IT department wouldn't let them! In each case, they said something like, "I go to IT with a request, they say something in technobabble that ultimately means 'no, you can't do that,' and I have to go back to the schools and give them the bad news without really understanding why."

Then I told the superintendents something that I hope changed their lives: *Your IT department works for you!*

Thus, our ideal school board needs to remind itself that the school district's IT department ultimately works for them, and that board members need to engage IT in meaningful, productive conversations about their vision for digital citizenship.

I also told the five superintendents about a unique experience I had that forever changed my perspective about how techies and teachies—that is, IT departments and instructors—could get along, help each other, and prosper. I was speaking at a conference and had brought up this issue to the audience. Afterwards, a group of teachers introduced me to their IT director, whom they clearly loved. When I asked the director what he did that engendered so much affection, he responded by offering the following three pieces of advice for other IT professionals:

1. **Attend any curriculum meeting to which you are invited.** He made it his mission to go to as many curriculum meetings as he could and even to ask for invitations where appropriate. When he worked directly with teachers at the department level, he could immediately help them work through technical issues related to curriculum ideas. This approach allowed teachers to understand his limitations so that everyone could negotiate a middle ground. The result was that the wait time between ideas and implementation was greatly reduced, and everyone could keep moving forward. In the end, he assured me, there were usually ways to do the things that teachers wanted to do, he just had to think a bit out of the box. The key to his success was brainstorming with teachers—rather than just with other IT workers.

2. **Require everyone in the IT department to spend a half hour a week in a classroom.** This was a requirement in his department— no exceptions. While his IT employees were free to talk to teachers and kids, all they were required to do was observe. Their directive from him was to look for ways for IT to help teachers do their job and for students to make better use of IT resources. The IT director told me that having his staff visit classrooms was his way of reminding them who the client was.

3. **Fight for a place at the vision table.** As he explained it to me, in most districts every major player in a school community has a place at the vision table except IT. This included academics, financial services, administration, and even physical plant. Why wasn't IT there? He wanted to provide the same kind of input about the future of the school district as everyone else. Given that he was the gatekeeper for much of the district's resources and communication, it only made sense. He claimed that when he was involved with the visioning process, he made it much easier for others to imagine their options.

Since talking to him, one of the primary challenges that has emerged to define an IT department's job in K–12 is administering software blocking and other restrictions required of The Children's Internet Protection Act (CIPA). Fortunately, there are enlightened IT directors who assure me of the following: (1) CIPA comes with a good deal of latitude; (2) Internet filtering should be used as a way to meet a district's interpretation of CIPA and not as a way to manage activity that seems too bothersome to deal with; and (3) IT's goal should be to give the teachers as much latitude as they want and are allowed to have, so kids' use of the Internet becomes a teachable event rather than a blocked event. Without a reasonable approach to balancing restricted access with trust and innovation, teaching and practicing digital citizenship becomes very difficult.

Thus, as our school board moves forward with unblocking Internet sites, it needs to balance the risk it takes with the fact that it is providing more opportunities for students and teachers to actually practice real digital citizenship skills. Blocking is a particularly poignant issue with regard to younger children. In the end, our school board will need to employ a sliding scale of access that considers the age and developmental level of the students involved.

Equally important, our school board will need to determine what process to use to address requests from administrators, teachers, and students to selectively override Internet blocking. Any approach to these issues will work best within the context of a character education program in which everyone involved understands the school district's overall digital citizenship mission and has the training needed to pursue that mission effectively.

TAKING THE NEXT STEP

Our ideal school board has decided to ask IT and administrators to work together to begin opening up Internet resources as a way to begin encouraging more active development of the district's digital citizenship program. They are going to approach unblocking Internet access selectively but proactively as they begin encouraging the use of technology in innovative ways. They want this shift in policy to gain momentum quickly. Here is some advice for them as they move forward:

- **Find innovators.** Actively seek out teachers who could make use of 21st-century tools, and ask them to pilot a project using an otherwise blocked Internet resource, like YouTube, Facebook, games, or virtual environments. In addition, consider how they might use cell phones and other personal technology. Then work with IT to make it happen.
- **Encourage challenging the status quo.** In addition to seeking out innovative teachers, make it easier for them to find you. That is, make it much easier for teachers with good ideas to propose new uses for technology and Internet resources to their administrators or others in charge. Examples of successful projects using selective unblocking abound. For example, I know a teacher who went directly to her school board to obtain permission to use blogging resources, which were blocked in her school district. The board granted her permission, and she is now modeling an effective and innovative use of a web service with her students that is critical to navigating the infosphere.

    There should have been an easier process for this teacher to use to pursue her ideas. School boards are busy, and teachers rarely want to attract a school board's attention. Our ideal school board needs to make sure that there are approval processes for innovative teachers to use for new projects at the building level that are accessible and rational. IT will play an important role in this.
- **Support risk taking.** This follows directly from the points above but is worth restating on its own. When I ask teachers what they want from administrators in terms of educational technology support,

they are clear: They want administrators to support them when they want to take risks and run innovative pilot programs. Things like new equipment, extra prep time, and more training are also important, but they are meaningless if teachers can't explore new ideas. Teacher can't go out on an innovative teaching limb alone. They need administrative support.

- **Require students to use social media and to create media.** One way to counter the material we don't like on YouTube and in the blogosphere is to shut it down in our schools. Another is to require our students to create the kind of material we would like to see. Making media—whether social media, media collages, or video— is one antidote to our displeasure with bad content. Every time I help students create good media, I help them become more discriminating media consumers. I am hearing more stories these days about districts that actually require students to do things like maintain blogs and use them for homework and projects. They have the right idea.

- **Block sites, not genres.** For example, YouTube is not the only video venue on the Internet; there are others that are more K–12-friendly. However, districts often block "video streaming" rather than particular services. The result is that a good deal gets blocked that doesn't need to be. Our ideal school board can ask the IT department to block just the sites that fall outside the board's CIPA interpretation of what is appropriate for K–12 and allow others within the same genre that do meet its criteria.

- **Build on successes.** The natural tendency might be to support risk takers quietly, for fear that others will want the same consideration. But in this case, quiet is not good. Anyone who can show a good use for using technology should be encouraged as publicly as possible. In addition, they should be publicly recognized for their efforts. Recognition is inexpensive—a mention on the school website or a shout-out at an assembly is always appreciated. As you build on your district's successes, you simply make it easier for other innovators to come forward. Having too many teachers who want to engage in digital citizenship activities is a great problem to have.

- **Use cyberspace for home-school connections.** Parents and the public want to know what is going on at school. After all, the better part of their local taxes pays for education, and their kids spend the better part of their day there. That makes it important to provide easy, clear access to school events and general information via your school's website. Also, provide parents password-protected access to see their children's work, homework assignments, and other pertinent information. Doing so will help make them friends of the school board.

- **Empower educational technology committees.** In my experience, I have found that the schools that thrive in the educational technology arena are often those with vibrant ed tech committees. Teachers need to talk, swap ideas, and pursue grants. This should happen onsite as well as online. Educational technology committees are also excellent meeting grounds for techies and teachies to sort through possibilities and issues.

   Administrators shouldn't wait for teachers to create the educational technology committees at their schools; they should do this for them and then actively solicit involvement. They should invite teachers, students, and administrators, as well as members of the public, to join. The best tool a school district has in creating an effective digital citizenship program is the collective intelligence of the school community. Educational technology committees are an effective way to help that intelligence coalesce. Our ideal school board can lead the way on this by empowering educational technology committees at the school district and building levels.

- **Provide whole-community training.** I have seen this happen particularly with regard to one-to-one programs, in which kids are given laptops to use at home and school. Parents step forward wanting to know more about what their children are doing so that they can engage with them in meaningful ways about their digital lifestyle. The result for parents is threefold: (1) They learn how to become more digitally literate themselves, (2) they can engage in more informed conversations with their kids about the dangers and opportunities related to what they do online, and (3) they become an active part of the digital citizenship effort. Our ideal school board sees the obvious benefits in this and begins actively looking for ways to involve parents in their digital citizenship efforts by providing training and open dialogue with parents and the community through both face-to-face meetings and online resources.

As I write this in the spring of 2010, I am watching our federal government ask teachers to bear the brunt of whatever failures exist in our school systems, while giving them almost no authority to fix what they don't like. Responsibility without authority never works. The result is that we miss the fact that success and failure are results of the combined efforts of teachers, parents, the school board, the public, the IT department—everyone.

What teachers need to be successful is a school board that makes the following clear in terms of pursuing a digital citizenship program:

- Their expectations, in terms of outcomes for students, teachers, and even the public
- Their willingness to support the kind of risk taking that a digital citizenship program will need
- Their understanding that teachers need help negotiating with the IT department so that they can honor the school board's intentions concerning the development of a digital citizenship program
- Their desire to retune their IT department as necessary, redefining it as an academic support unit as well as a technical support structure
- Their understanding that IT can take only as much risk as the school board will support

Our ideal school board vows to make it so.

ISTE STANDARDS FOR IT PERSONNEL?

I close this chapter by asking you to consider this fact: While ISTE has created several sets of standards for teachers, students, and administrators, they have not created standards for IT personnel. In fact, one of my favorite workshops to conduct with technology leaders asks participants to address this question: If ISTE created standards for IT management and technical support people, what should those standards look like? Participants often rate hard skills (technical skills) as secondary to soft skills (emotional intelligence and interpersonal communication abilities). I call this workshop "Teachies are from Venus, Techies are from Mars." Among the most enthusiastic participants are IT professionals. As you might imagine, the workshops are always engaging, informative, a good deal of fun—and perhaps a bit emotional at times.

Epilogue

Advice? Of Course!

Of course, I have advice for our school board. After all, they might be ideal, but they aren't perfect. But I am also sensitive to the fact that they have been bombarded with information and probably need a break at this point. So I will limit what I have to say to one piece of advice: *Turn concerns into goals.* Allow me to explain.

We have all experienced having our good ideas trampled by insecure co-workers. Here is how this typically happens in the world of educational technology.

You are at a committee meeting, sitting around a table, discussing some great idea about using technology in education. It might involve posting students' new media narrative on an international student video site as part of a language arts project, or opening up some Internet resources that the school district has blocked so that students can pursue a line of historical inquiry, or web posting student-created animations explaining science processes to serve as contributions to a common online educational library, or using virtual reality to build geometric forms in math class . . . whatever the great idea might be. Everyone thinks the idea is great, except for Bob, who has "concerns." We all know what happens. The meeting grinds to a halt because no one wants to step on Bob's toes. To do so would be insensitive. Thus, we walk away from the meeting hoping Bob has some kind of epiphany and that in the meantime none of the other committee members develop concerns of their own.

Concerns are just negatively stated goals. So it is your job to turn Bob's concern into a productive, measurable goal. Doing so is not at all difficult. If Bob has a concern, for example, that too much social media will keep kids from developing face-to-face team-building skills, then add the development of these skills to the list of objectives for the assignment. If he thinks that student media production reduces the amount of writing that teachers can assess to an unacceptable level, then make sure that students submit not only their finished media for evaluation but also their scripts, research, and any other written work they may have generated in the process of developing their projects.

That is, turn Bob's concerns into goals. Then vote! Bob may still vote against the great idea on the table, but at least you and your students will move forward. And whether he knows it or not, Bob gets to take his next step in understanding how to blend traditional and emerging tools in the pursuit of teaching and learning.

Turning concerns into goals is particularly important with regard to your digital citizenship efforts. Should, one day, our educational systems actually take on the task of integrating our students' digital reality into the content and perspectives they pursue at school, then no doubt many around you will have concerns about helping kids *live one life instead of two*. These concerns will surface in real ways, as apprehension about such things as exploring selective Internet unblocking, forming student-based think tanks charged with figuring out what to do about cyberbullying, or including "netiquette" as part of a character education values inventory. As with Bob, you will need to flesh out the real fears that lie behind people's concerns in order to move forward.

Sometimes, these concerns are very subterranean, in which case understanding them can be very difficult. In my novel about the future of technology and learning, *Then What? Everyone's Guide to Living, Learning and Having Fun in the Digital Age* (Ohler, 2002), I created a new technology called a subtextometer to help determine the true cause for the resistance to change. The subtextometer looks like a reversed megaphone and plugs into any garden-variety computer. It works as follows: You speak into the large opening, and out the small opening comes what you really meant. For example, an anxious school board member might say something into the subtextometer like, "I am very concerned about kids using blogs," and out the other end might come something like, "As a child, all I ever wanted was a dog, but my mom and dad wouldn't get me one."

There's not much you can do about issues like these. But fortunately, many of the concerns about digital citizenship are closer to the surface and have a practical focus. One of the most prevalent, legitimate concerns I hear from teachers is their lack of time in the school day. I continually hear about their overcrowded days that are filled with testing and other well-intentioned mandates that keep them from doing the real teaching they know their students need.

What we don't realize is that their concern with time is due to our lack of vision, mission, and focus as a society. Teachers don't fill their days with standardized testing; we do.

What our students desperately need is to learn how to blend creatical thinking, emerging literacies, prodigious information synthesis, and moral perspective in order to thrive as they are tested by new technologies and evolving ethical situations we can't even imagine. Yet as I write this, standardized testing is on the rise, promising to squeeze out whatever time might have been available for addressing 21st-century digital citizenship skills training. Schools, afraid they will face being defunded if their students' test scores are low, will revert to the factory model of schooling that does little to prepare students to be lifelong learners. Teachers are often left in the middle to fend for themselves, often without the digital citizenship training that might help them at least try to integrate many of the issues addressed in this book into their already overcrowded days. The bottom line is that we need to come to grips with our concerns about digital citizenship, so we can turn them into goals for ourselves, our schools, and our children.

The question I asked in the Preamble, which has driven so much of the inquiry in this book, is not just a question for educators. Rather, it is a question for taxpayers, parents, politicians, citizens, the business community—all of us. After all, the reality is that we will inherit whatever the school system produces. Thus, I end the book where I began, asking this question, and hoping that enough vision and common sense will converge on our collective approach to education to produce digital citizens capable of meeting the needs of the new world that awaits us all:

When it comes to educating our children, shall we consider them to have two lives or one?

It is up to us.

References

Adhocracy. (2010, February 18). In *Wikipedia: The free encyclopedia*. Retrieved June 24, 2010, from http://en.wikipedia.org/wiki/Adhocracy

Adkins, L., & Adkins, A. (1998). *Handbook to life in ancient Rome*. Oxford, UK: Oxford University Press.

American Library Association. (1989). *Presidential committee on information literacy. Final report*. Chicago: Author. Retrieved April 18, 2010, from http://www.ala.org/ala/mgrps/divs/acrl/standards/informationliteracycompetency.cfm#f1

Apple® is a registered trademark of Apple Inc.

Apple® IIe is a registered trademark of Apple Inc.

AppleWorks® is a registered trademark of Apple Inc.

Berkowitz, M., & Bier, M. (2006). *What works in character education*. St. Louis, MO: Center for Character & Leadership.

Berns, G. (2009). *Growing up: The teenage brain* [Video]. Retrieved April 18, 2010, from http://www.youtube.com/watch?v=EnJ-2eWF55w

Brooks, M. (Producer/Director). (1981). *History of the world: Part I* [Motion picture]. USA: Twentieth Century Fox.

Brunstein, A. (2007). Tracking down the seat of moral reasoning—Joshua Greene pushes into a new field. *Harvard Science Culture and Society*. Retrieved April 18, 2010, from http://www.harvardscience.harvard.edu/culture-society/articles/tracking-down-seat-moral-reasoning

Bunge, S. (2008). *Adolescent brains, 10/16/2008* [Video]. Retrieved June 24, 2010, from http://www.youtube.com/watch?v=cLkV8isrGNA

Burke, J. (Writer). (1978). The trigger effect [Television series episode]. In M. Jackson (Producer/Director), *Connections*. UK: BBC.

Cadiff, A. (Director). (1957–1963). *Leave It to Beaver* [Television series]. New York: CBS, ABC.

Carr, N. (2010, May 24). The Web shatters focus, rewires brain. *Wired*. Retrieved July 4, 2010, from http://www.wired.com/magazine/2010/05/ff_nicholas_carr/all/1

Character Education Partnership. (2008). *Character education quality standards*. Retrieved June 24, 2010, from http://www.character.org/uploads/PDFs/Pub_Quality_Standards_.pdf

Churches, A. (2010). *The digital citizen*. Retrieved June 24, 2010, from http://edorigami.wikispaces.com/The+Digital+Citizen

Community. (2010, June 20). In *Wikipedia: The free encyclopedia*. Retrieved June 24, 2010, from http://en.wikipedia.org/wiki/Community

Constitution of the Commonwealth of Massachusetts. (1780). Chapter V, Section II. Retrieved June 24, 2010, from http://www.mass.gov/legis/const.htm

Cool. (2010). In *Urban dictionary.* Retrieved June 24, 2010, from http://www .urbandictionary.com/define.php?term=cool

Cosmopolitanism. (2010, June 24). In *Wikipedia: The free encyclopedia.* Retrieved June 24, 2010, from http://en.wikipedia.org/wiki/Cosmopolitanism

Creamer, M. (2009, September 21). French lawmakers want warnings on airbrushed photos. *Advertising Age.* Retrieved June 24, 2010, from http://adage .com/globalnews/article?article_id=139162

Cronin, V. (1972). *The Florentine renaissance.* London: Collins/Fontana.

Daily Campus Editorial Board. (2010, February 23). Editorial: Sexting' bill would bring positive changes. *The Daily Campus.* Retrieved June 24, 2010, from http://www.dailycampus.com/commentary/editorial-sexting-bill-would-bring-positive-changes-1.1171286

D'Alessandro, M. (2010, February 24). Google executives convicted for Italy autism video. *Reuters.* Retrieved July 4, 2010, from http://www.reuters.com/article/idUSTRE61N2G520100224

Declaration of the Rights of Man and of the Citizen. (2010, April 15). In *Wikipedia: The free encyclopedia.* Retrieved June 24, 2010, from http://en.wikipedia.org/w/index.php?title=Declaration_of_the_Rights_of_Man_and_of_the_Citizen&oldid=356231600

DeRoche, E., & Williams, M. (2001). *Educating hearts and minds: A comprehensive character education framework* (2nd ed.). Thousand Oaks, CA: Sage.

Dertouzos, M. (2001). *The unfinished revolution: Human-centered computers and what they can do for us.* New York: HarperCollins.

Dill, K. (2009). *How fantasy becomes reality: Seeing through media influence.* New York: Oxford Press.

Edwards, B. (1999). *The new drawing on the right side of the brain.* New York: Penguin Putnam.

Egan, K. (1986). *Teaching as story telling.* Chicago: University of Chicago Press.

Facebook® is a registered trademark of Facebook, Inc.

Factitioner. (n.d.). In *Urban dictionary.* Retrieved June 24, 2010, from http://www .urbandictionary.com/define.php?term=factition

Fair use. (2010, March 11). In *Wikipedia: The free encyclopedia.* Retrieved June 24, 2010, from http://en.wikipedia.org/w/index.php?title=Fair_use&oldid=349297841

Faulks, K. (2000). *Citizenship.* London: Routledge.

Federal Communications Commission. (2009, September 21). *Children's Internet protection act.* Retrieved June 24, 2010, from http://www.fcc.gov/cgb/consumer facts/cipa.html

Films for the Humanities and Sciences. (2000). *EQ and the emotional curriculum* [DVD]. Available from http://ffh.films.com/search.aspx?q=EQ+and+the+Emotional+Curriculum+

Finkelhor, D. (2010, March 5). Study identifies strategies for dealing with bullying. *Safekids.Com.* Retrieved June 24, 2010, from http://www.safekids.com/2010/03/05/study-identifies-strategies-for-dealing-with-bullying

Flash® is a registered trademark of Adobe Systems Incorporated.

Forsythe, D. (1980). A taxonomy of ethical ideologies. *Journal of Personality and Social Psychology, 39*(1), 175–184.

Frost, R. (1946). *The poems of Robert Frost: With an introductory essay "The constant symbol" by the author.* New York: Modern Library.

Gardner, H. (2006). *5 minds for the future.* Boston: Harvard Business Press.

Gerbner, G. (1994, Spring). Reclaiming our cultural mythology: Television's global marketing strategy creates a damaging and alienated window on the world. *In Context.* Retrieved June 24, 2010, from http://www.context.org/ICLIB/IC38/Gerbner.htm

Golden Rule. (2010, March 12). In *Wikipedia: The free encyclopedia.* Retrieved March 15, 2010, from http://en.wikipedia.org/w/index.php?title=The_Golden_Rule&oldid=349500671

Haidt, J. (2007, May). The new synthesis in moral psychology. (Review). *Science.* Retrieved June 24, 2010, from http://www.sciencemag.org/cgi/content/abstract/316/5827/998

Hall, E. T. (1966). *The hidden dimension.* New York: Anchor Books.

Hansen, M. H. (2006). *Polis: An introduction to the ancient Greek city-state.* Oxford, UK: Oxford University Press.

Harper, D. (2001–2010). *Literate.* Retrieved June 24, 2010, from http://www.etymonline.com/index.php?term=literate

Heartwood. (2010). *The seven attributes.* Retrieved June 24, 2010, from http://heartwoodethics.org/1-approach/framework.asp

Heater, D. (1999). *What is citizenship?* Cambridge, UK: Polity Press.

Heater, D. (2004). *A brief history of citizenship.* New York: New York University Press.

Heppell, S. (2008, March 18). Back and forth. *The Guardian.* Retrieved June 24, 2010, from http://www.guardian.co.uk/education/2008/mar/18/link.link27

Herbert, F. (1965). *Dune.* New York: Penguin.

Hiltz, S., & Turoff, M. (1978). *The network nation.* New York: Addison-Wesley.

Hunter, B. (1983). *My students use computers: Learning activities for computer literacy.* Reston, VA: Reston Publishing Company.

IBM PC® is a registered trademark of International Business Machines Corporation.

iLearn Technology. (2010). *Track my T.* Retrieved June 26, 2010, from http://ilearntechnology.com/?tag=track-my-t

Infosavvy. (2010). *21st century fluency project.* Retrieved June 28, 2010, from http://www.21stcenturyfluency.com/

International Center for Leadership in Education. (2001–2006). *The 12 guiding principles of exceptional character.* Retrieved April 16, 2010, from http://www.leadered.com/guiding_princ.html

International Society for Technology in Education. (2000). *National educational technology standards for teachers.* Retrieved June 24, 2010, from http://www.iste.org/Content/NavigationMenu/NETS/ForTeachers/2000Standards/NETS_for_Teachers_2000.htm

International Society for Technology in Education. (2007). *Refreshed national educational technology standards for students.* Retrieved June 24, 2010, from http://www.iste.org/Content/NavigationMenu/NETS/ForStudents/2007Standards/NETS_for_Students_2007.htm

International Society for Technology in Education. (2008). *Refreshed national educational technology standards for teachers.* Retrieved June 24, 2010, from http://www.iste.org/Content/NavigationMenu/NETS/ForTeachers/2008Standards/NETS_for_Teachers_2008.htm

Isbouts, J.-P. (2010). *Young Jesus: Restoring the lost years of a social activist and religious dissident.* New York: Sterling.

iTablet® is a registered trademark of Amtek System Co., Ltd.

James, C. (with Davis, K., Flores, A., Francis, J. M., Pettingill, L., Rundle, M., & Gardner, H.). (2009). *Young people, ethics and the new media: A Synthesis from the Good Play Project (John D. and Catherine T. MacArthur Foundation reports on digital media and learning)*. Cambridge: MIT Press.

Jefferson, T. (1818). Letter to Joseph C. Cabell. *Monticello research department*. Retrieved June 24, 2010, from www.monticello.org/reports/quotes/education .html

Jensen, J. E. (2008). *The teenage brain* [Video]. Retrieved June 24, 2010, from http://www.youtube.com/watch?v=RpMG7vS9pfw

Johnson, S. (2006). *Everything bad is good for you*. New York: Riverhead Books.

Kantor, A. (2006, August 17). AOL search data release reveals a great deal. *USA Today*. Retrieved April 18, 2010, from http://www.usatoday.com/tech/columnist/ andrewkantor/2006–08–17-aol-data_x.htm

Katz, J. E. (Ed.). (2008). *Handbook of mobile communication studies*. Cambridge: MIT Press.

Kawasaki, G. (2007). *Don't write a mission statement, write a mantra*. Retrieved June 24, 2010, from http://www.youtube.com/watch?v=jT7xlFTinIw

Kirk, E. (1996). *Evaluating information found on the Internet*. John Hopkins Sheridan Libraries. Retrieved June 24, 2010, from http://www.library.jhu.edu/ researchhelp/general/evaluating

Kluger, J. (2007, August 30). Rewiring the brain. *Time*. Retrieved July 4, 2010, from http://www.time.com/time/magazine/article/0,9171,1657822,00.html

Lawrence, D. H. (1957). *Lady Chatterley's lover*. New York: Grove Press.

Likona, T. (1991). *Educating for character*. New York: Bantam Books.

Likona, T., Schaps, E., & Lewis, C. (2007). *CEP's eleven principles of effective character education*. Washington, DC: Character Education Partnership. Retrieved May 2, 2010, from http://www.character.org/elevenprinciples

Lindberg, L., Boggess, S., Porter, L., & Williams, S. (2000, June). *Teen-risk taking: A statistical portrait*. Retrieved June 24, 2010, from http://aspe.hhs.gov/health/ Reports/TeenRisk/TeenRiskTaking.html

Macintosh® is a registered trademark of Apple Inc.

McLuhan, E. (1998). *Electric language: Understanding the present*. Toronto, Ontario, Canada: Stoddardt.

McLuhan, M. (1964). *Understanding media: The extensions of man*. New York: McGraw-Hill.

McLuhan, M. (1967). *The medium is the massage*. Corte Madera, CA: Ginko Press.

McLuhan, M. (1974). *How to study media*. Retrieved June 24, 2010, from http://www.media-ecology.org/mcluhan/mc_38.txt

McLuhan, M., & McLuhan, E. (1988). *Laws of media: The new science*. Toronto, Ontario, Canada: University of Toronto Press.

McLuhan, M., & Powers, B. (1989). *The global village: Transformations in world life and media in the 21st century*. Oxford, UK: Oxford University Press.

Medina, J. (2010). *Brain rules*. Seattle, WA: Pear Press.

Meyrowitz, J. (1985). *No sense of place*. New York: Oxford University Press.

Microsoft Office® is a registered trademark of Microsoft Corporation.

Moral Education in the Life of School. (1988, May). *Educational Leadership, 45*(8), 4–8.

Mossberger, K., Tolbert, C. J., & McNeal, R. S. (2008). *Digital citizenship: The Internet, society, and participation*. Cambridge: MIT Press.

Nucci, L. (2008). *Moral development and moral education: An overview*. Retrieved June 24, 2010, from http://tigger.uic.edu/~lnucci/MoralEd/overview.html

Ohler, J. (2002). *Then what? Everyone's guide to living, learning and having fun in the digital age*. Juneau, AK: Brinton Books.

Ohler, J. (2008). *Digital storytelling in the classroom: New media pathways to literacy, learning, and creativity.* Thousand Oaks, CA: Corwin.

Ohler, J. (2009). Orchestrating the media collage. *Educational Leadership, 66*(6), 8–13.

Orwell, G. (1946). *Animal farm.* New York: Random House.

Phillips, H. (2006, July 3). Rewired brain revives patient after 19 years. *New Scientist.* Retrieved July 4, 2010, from http://www.newscientist.com/article/dn9474-rewired-brain-revives-patient-after-19-years.html

Picciano, A. (2009). K–12 online learning. A 2008 follow-up of the survey of U.S. school district administrators. *Sloan-C.* Retrieved June 24, 2010, from http://www.sloan-c.org/publications/survey/k-12online2008

Postman, N. (1982). *The disappearance of childhood.* New York: Random House.

Postman, N. (1993). *Technopoly: The surrender of culture to technology.* New York: Vintage.

Prensky, M. (2001). Digital natives, digital immigrants. *On the Horizon, 9*(5). Retrieved May 2, 2010 from: http://ow.ly/27iDT

Rebik, D. (2010, February 17). Three middle school students facing criminal "sexting" charges. *KTLA.Com.* Retrieved June 24, 2010, from http://www.ktla.com/news/landing/ktla-sexting-charges,0,7789810.story

Reyna, V. (2007, March 3). Why do teens take risks? *Youth Communication.* Retrieved April 18, 2010, from http://www.youthcomm.org/NYC%20Features/March2007/NYC-2007-03-08a.htm

Ribble, M., & Bailey, G. (2007). *Digital citizenship in the school.* Eugene, OR: International Society for Technology in Education.

Sandel, M. (2009). *Harvard University's justice, with Michael Sandel* [Video series]. Retrieved June 24, 2010, from http://www.justiceharvard.org

ScienceDaily. (2001, September 14). Brain imaging study sheds light on moral decision-making. *ScienceDaily.* Retrieved June 24, 2010, from http://www.sciencedaily.com/releases/2001/09/010914074303.htm

Sen, A. (2009). *The idea of justice.* Cambridge, MA: Harvard University Press.

Shakespeare, W. (1975a). Macbeth. In *The complete works of William Shakespeare* (pp. 1045–1070). New York: Gramercy. (Original work published 1606)

Shakespeare, W. (1975b). Romeo and Juliet. In *The complete works of William Shakespeare* (pp. 1011–1044). New York: Gramercy. (Original work published 1599)

Shermer, M. (2009, June). *Baloney detection kit.* Retrieved July 5, 2010, from http://www.michaelshermer.com/2009/06/baloney-detection-kit

Shirky, C. (2008). *Here comes everybody.* London: Penguin Books.

Solidary. (2010). In *Dictionary.com unabridged.* Retrieved June 24, 2010, from http://dictionary.reference.com/browse/solidary

Solove, D. (2007). *The future of reputation: Gossip, rumor and privacy on the Internet.* New London, CT: Yale University Press.

Sourcemap. (n.d.). *Sourcemap: Open supply chains.* Retrieved June 26, 2010, from http://stage.sourcemap.org/index.php

Spinks, S. (Producer/Writer/Director). (2002). Inside the teenage brain [Television series/webcast episode]. In *Frontline.* Boston: WGBA and Spinfree Productions. Retrieved June 24, 2010, from http://www.pbs.org/wgbh/pages/frontline/shows/teenbrain/view

Stone, B. (2010, January 9). The children of cyberspace: Old fogies by their 20s. *New York Times.* Retrieved July 1, 2010, from http://www.nytimes.com/2010/01/10/weekinreview/10stone.html

Stone, L. (2009, November 30). *Beyond simple multi-tasking: Continuous partial attention.* Retrieved June 24, 2010, from http://lindastone.net/2009/11/30/beyond-simple-multi-tasking-continuous-partial-attention

Strathern, P. (2005). *The Medici: Godfathers of the Renaissance.* London: Pimlico.

Suicide of Megan Meier. (2010, June 7). In *Wikipedia: The free encyclopedia.* Retrieved July 4, 2010, from http://en.wikipedia.org/wiki/Suicide_of_Megan_Meier

Tatman, R., Edmonson, S., & Slate, J. (2009, March 27). Character education: An historical overview. *Connexions.* Retrieved June 24, 2010, from http://cnx.org/content/m20338/1.2

Tetrad of Media Effects. (2009, January 28). In *Wikipedia: The free encyclopedia.* Retrieved May 2, 2010, from http://en.wikipedia.org/w/index.php?title=Tetrad_of_media_effects&oldid=266867250

Thornburg, D. (1992). *Edutrends 2010: Restructuring, technology and the future of education.* Torquay, UK: Starsong.

TiVo® is a registered trademark of TiVo Brands, LLC.

Tonnies, F. (1988). *Community and society.* New Brunswick, NJ: Transaction Books. (Original work published 1957)

Turkle, S. (2008). Always-on/always-on-you: The tethered self. In J. E. Katz (Ed.), *Handbook of mobile communication studies* (pp. 121–138). Cambridge: MIT Press.

21st Century Fluency Project. (2010). *The fluencies.* Retrieved July 5, 2010, from http://www.21stcenturyfluency.com/fluencies.cfm

Venter, C. (2010, May 21). Craig Venter unveils "synthetic life." *YouTube.* Retrieved July 3, 2010, from http://www.youtube.com/watch?v=QHIocNOHd7A

Weizenbaum, J. (1976). *Computer power and human reason: From judgment to calculation.* San Francisco: W. H. Freeman.

Wellman, B. (1988). Structural analysis: From method and metaphor to theory and substance. In B. Wellman & S. D. Berkowitz (Eds.), *Social structures: A network approach* (pp. 19–61). Cambridge, UK: Cambridge University Press.

Wellman, B., & Leighton, B. (1979, March). Networks, neighborhoods and communities. *Urban Affairs Quarterly, 14,* 363–390.

Wiggins, G., & McTighe, W. (2005). *Understanding by design.* Alexandria, VA: ASCD.

Wikiquote. (2010a, May 21). *Isaac Newton.* Retrieved July 4, 2010, from http://en.wikiquote.org/wiki/Isaac_Newton

Willard, N. (1997). *Moral development in the information age.* Eugene, OR: Center for Safe and Responsible Internet Use.

Willard, N. (2004). *I can't see you—you can't see me: How the use of information and communication technologies can impact responsible behavior.* Eugene, OR: Center for Safe and Responsible Internet Use. Retrieved June 24, 2010, from www.cyberbully.org/cyberbully/docs/disinhibition.pdf

Willard, N. (2007). *Cyberbullying and cyberthreats: Effectively managing Internet use risks in schools.* Retrieved July 3, 2010, from http://new.csriu.org/cyberbully/docs/cbctpresentation.pdf

Willard, N. (2010a). *Cyberbullying, cyberthreats & sexting: Responding to the challenge.* Eugene, OR: Center for Safe and Responsible Internet Use. Retrieved June 24, 2010, from csriu.org/documents/sextinginvestigationandintervention_000.pdf

Willard, N. (2010b). *Technopanic.* Eugene, OR: Center for Safe and Responsible Internet Use.

Index